"Judy Gaman writes from the heart, with honesty, humility, and tenderness. This story offers a profound and invaluable lesson but it also grabs you from the first chapter and keeps you reading. What a treat! A wise page-turner. Wish there were more out there like it."

—WILLIAM KENOWER, author of *Fearless Writing*, and Editor-in-Chief of *Author magazine*

"Lucille captured the lives of so many in the Dallas area and around the country. This is a behind-the-scenes look at how Lucille and Judy forged an inseparable bond. A story that had to be told!"

—JANE MCGARRY, host of *Good Morning Texas*

"Our book club laughed and cried through *Love, Life, and Lucille*. This book demonstrated how we can learn from each other at any age and opened up many discussion topics, including respect for your fellow man, true friendship, and finding care through the end-of-life process. The author was genuine and vulnerable and we learned that it is never too late to find a friend who can truly change our life! We highly recommend *Love, Life and Lucille* for book clubs of all sizes."

—NINFA FLEWITT, member of the Mineral Wells Book Club

"I've traveled the globe studying people who live past their 100th birthday. What an amazing and emotional story about how friendship really knows no age. We can all learn something from this book. Prepare to laugh, cry, and laugh again—sometimes all in the same chapter!"

—NICK BUETTNER, program director
of Blue Zones Project

"Riveting, heartwarming, emotionally moving, and beautifully written in a folksy manner, Judy Gaman's latest book, *Love, Life, and Lucille*, is an easy read and must-read for ALL!!"

—FRAN WALFISH, Beverly Hills family
and relationship psychotherapist, author of
The Self-Aware Parent, and costar of WE tv's *Sex Box*

Love, Life, & Lucille

Love, Life, & Lucille

Lessons Learned from a Centenarian

Foreword by
Suzanne Somers

Judy Gaman

She Writes Press, a BookSparks imprint
A Division of SparkPointStudio, LLC.

Published 2020
Printed in the United States of America

ISBN: 978-1-63152-882-8
ISBN: 978-1-63152-883-5
Library of Congress Control Number: 2019912669

For information, address:
She Writes Press
1569 Solano Ave #546
Berkeley, CA 94707

She Writes Press is a division of SparkPoint Studio, LLC. All company and/or product names may be trade names, logos, trademarks, and/or registered trademarks and are the property of their respective owners.

Names and identifying characteristics have been changed to protect the privacy of certain individuals.

This book is dedicated to the most extraordinary best friend a girl could have. Lucille, you made me laugh, you made me cry, but above all you made me feel loved. You enriched my life in so many ways. I always said that the whole world needs a Lucille in their life. Now, I can give that to them. May all who read these pages be filled with your spirit, your spunk, and your wisdom.

Contents

Foreword

I only met Lucille once, yet it was unforgettable. There she was, all dressed in red with a bow in her hair. I remember there were feathers somewhere, lovely jewelry, high-heeled shoes on her feet, and in that moment, my general overall impression was, *what an adorable woman*. The second thing I noticed right away was her energy; she was old (chronologically) but she wasn't "old." There was a light about her and she possessed sparkling, twinkling eyes that looked right at you with a "knowing." She had humor, savvy, a quickness, and a spirit that was disarming.

In life, if you are lucky, people will appear before you when you are ready to "hear and see"; these are our opportunities to learn and grow, to evolve. And at the moment, the planet is wobbly and sadly lacking wisdom. Gone are the matriarchs and patriarchs, replaced by older persons, shells of themselves, often lost in a sea of pills and more pills.

Immediately upon meeting Lucille, I could feel her one hundred years of perspective that didn't connect in any way with her remarkably youthful appearance. What did she know having lived all these decades? In these brief moments together, I longed for her to infuse her knowledge into me; she had answers about the universe, I was sure.

Is life, as we all know it, "difficult" as M. Scott Peck states at the beginning of his book, *The Road Less Traveled*? Or in the end, does life actually reveal itself as simple? Have we merely complicated the process by overthinking it?

As I watched Lucille, I noticed that she laughed a lot, she smiled (a lot), she clearly cared about her appearance, and there was nothing withdrawn or shy about her, which is so often the case with the elderly. As I watched her, I wondered, was attitude the key to longevity? Was acceptance in fact crucial to the aging process? She didn't seem lonely or sad, or cast aside. In fact, she was the center of attention! I take a lot of "light" in a room due to my celebrity, but Lucille was the STAR. People were drawn to her. What was it? I wondered curiously. How did she get this way?

I met her at the dinner before I gave a lecture and then at a chance meeting and photo-op afterwards in the hallway, and that was all it took to know intuitively that she held within her secrets that only those who lived long and well could teach us.

Wisdom and perspective are the gifts of aging. But in today's world aging has a negative connotation. The picture we all have in our mind is of the present paradigm, our final years rendering us frail, decrepit and sickly, usually with one of the big three: cancer, heart disease, or Alzheimer's. And then the awful final destination, the nursing home where we corral our aging souls and drug them up until they no longer know who they are or who they were. Such a terrible way to end this beautiful thing called life. So, it's people like Lucille who hold the secrets to successful aging within them who can teach us a new way forward.

Why not her? How did she escape the terrible present paradigm? Why was she so upbeat, so energetic, so full of fun and energy? I wanted to know what she knows. And now with this book, I can. Author Judy Gaman has uncovered Lucille's secret, and you will find it here within these pages. This book is a peek inside a life well lived. As you will see, Lucille is a prophet, a philosopher, and a storyteller. She is aspirational, inspirational. We all want what she has.

We learn by example. Lucille enjoyed her life to the fullest, taking each day and focusing on what she had, rather than what she didn't.

Aging, for so many people is a long, drawn-out, lonely, sickly experience. Through Lucille and her example, you will realize, life is what you make it. Life is what you choose. She chose to be fun, upbeat, and happy, and she dressed the part, too. When you met her, you smiled, you felt warm, you wanted to know her, and you wanted to be like her. You wanted her to be here forever.

She is gone now, but her spirit and example live on. Rest in peace, dear Lucille. And thank you from all of us.

—Suzanne Somers

Chapter One

The Day that Changed My Life

The day I met Lucille, I had a number of preconceived notions of what a centenarian might be like. As I climbed out of the car and walked across the parking lot to the assisted living center where she lived, the hot Texas sun beating down on the top of my head in spite of the cooler temperatures of the fall season, I wondered if she'd be able to hear me okay, or how her memory was. Would she be one of those little old ladies that I had to reintroduce myself to every few minutes? *Gosh, I hope not*, I thought to myself as my writing assistant and I approached the set of crisply painted white doors at the front entrance, decorated with a pair of matching autumn wreaths. I opened the doors and we made our way to the elevators, then down a long hallway, the dark, sensible heels I wore each day for work at the office and radio station now soundless on the brown and white rug underfoot.

Of course, the usual stereotypes of a very old person crossed my mind: *Is she going to smell?* I wondered. Many people I had met in nursing homes had a particular cloying smell, and I was never sure if it was the smell of urine or the scent of their own impending death. But as we stopped outside Lucille's door, the only thing I could smell was the delicious aroma of bacon wafting up from the dining hall, mixed with the delicate, floral scent of freshly cut flowers.

Emily, my assistant, and I exchanged a glance and smiled in anticipation, feeling uncertain about what we would find on the other side of the door. I had barely even finished knocking when it flew open. "Hello. I'm Lucille Fleming!" she energetically proclaimed as she threw her arms up with joy, her face alight with one of the biggest smiles I'd ever seen.

Without even thinking about it, I responded with equal volume and enthusiasm, "And I'm Judy Gaman!"

Nothing I had ever known about older people, and I thought I knew a lot, prepared me for the woman standing before me. She was dressed to the nines in red high heels and a colorful red and white flowing skirt, a red silk blouse, and a string of pearls and had perfect hair and red lipstick to match. She even had a wide red belt to show off her figure. But all that red was carefully offset by the large white flower pinned to her left shoulder. Standing next to her, I felt completely underdressed in my navy pants and patterned blouse in shades of bright blue and black. Had I known that Lucille was so stylish, I certainly would have worn a dress. At least I was able to wear a matching smile of my own.

Yet despite her stunning appearance, her looks were secondary compared to her contagious energy. Her smile was ear to ear and totally genuine. Her voice was full of inflection, something I wasn't expecting at her age, as I'd anticipated her to sound old and frail. She even stood up straight, minus a little curve in her spine, but at her age, that was to be expected.

Lucille invited us into her perfect little apartment. Nothing was out of place, and it was decorated with incredible style and sense of purpose, right down to the arrangement of the crystal goblets and china tea cups in the hutch. The china had dainty floral patterns, the kind of china most people collect but never use, and each chair had its place across from the soft white couch. The throw pillows on the couch matched the muted shades of coral and sea blue found elsewhere in the room, and the art was hung at perfect height and the framed pictures on the side tables were evenly spaced, not crowded at all. There was even a very tall green glass candle with a wick that had never been lit.

After some small talk, I explained the purpose behind our visit and told her about the book I intended to write, about aging gracefully. "At some point, it dawned on me that all the studies in the world can't teach me more than what I could learn by meeting people like you," I finished.

She nodded in agreement. "Yes, that's true."

"So, would you mind sharing? Can I get your top ten tips for how to live to one hundred?" I held my pen to my notepad, ready and willing to jot down anything and everything she was going to say.

In response, she gave me a beautiful smile. Her lips were perfectly painted to match her outfit, the crimson color drawn on precisely. I couldn't help but wonder if those were all her own teeth. I found myself wanting to search for a wizard behind the curtain, thinking, *Is she for real?*

"I'm going to have to think about that a minute," she said. "In the meantime, I have to show you the dress I just wore to my hundredth birthday party." She climbed out of her brightly colored blue-and-green chair and made her way over to the closet, which wasn't far. I glanced over the partition that separated the bedroom area from the living room of her studio apartment. Her bed was meticulously decorated with a cream silk bedspread, a few large, soft bed pillows covered with ruffled shams, and a few throw pillows in shades of jade and turquoise, which complemented the cream-colored silk drapes that flowed down each side of the nearby window.

A moment later, she returned with a multi-tiered, golden full-length gown that sparkled in the sunlight, throwing rainbows across the room. "Here it is! What do you think?" She held the gown up against her body, moving this way and that in order to model it for us. I was amazed that someone her age could wear something so formfitting, but she definitely had the figure for it.

"It's beautiful," I said sincerely.

"Just gorgeous," added Emily, pushing her sheaf of dark brown hair from her eyes, and then reaching out and lightly stroking the material with one finger.

"It was a wonderful party," Lucille said with a smile, as she seemed to reflect upon the event, her eyes glazing over for a few moments. She hugged the dress to herself and danced back over to the closet. "I picked it out myself, if you can believe that," she hollered to us as she hung the dress back up.

Emily looked at me, her mouth open, and we shook our heads in tandem. At that point, we were having a hard time believing any of it.

"Look on the bright side and be happy," she said firmly, returning to her seat, her mind clearly having processed what she wanted to say. "That is definitely one of the things that has kept me going. Oh, and eat a good diet. I always eat three times a day—plenty of fresh fruits and vegetables, especially blueberries. I eat blueberries all the time, though; if you eat them, you need to be sure to take care of your teeth. I brush three times a day. Never been one for flossing, though," she added with a wave of her hand.

Oh my gosh—those are her real teeth! I thought. I leaned in to get a better look, trying not to make it obvious.

"Walk every day," she continued. "I used to do six miles a day, but now I'm at about one to one-and-a-half. I walk down to the dining room for all my meals. It's important to be social and have friends, you know. Friends keep you young." She went on, listing a few more tips that seemed like fairly standard answers. Then she leaned back in her recliner and crossed her legs, which were wrapped in tan pantyhose. "Keep yourself looking nice. I always lay my clothes out the night before. I always do my makeup, keep my hair fixed, wear a flower on my lapel, and tie a ribbon around my neck just to finish it all off," she said, pointing a pink, manicured nail at the crimson ribbon around her neck.

Emily and I enjoyed our visit so much that before we knew it, our one-hour appointment had turned into more than three, and I found myself wracking my brain for more questions to ask her, not wanting to leave. I hadn't looked at my watch or phone once, which was quite a rarity. Lucille and I talked easily, the words flowing back and forth between us like a river, and we seemed to have an almost instant connection with one another. It didn't feel like I was meeting her for the first time; instead, it felt like I had known her my whole life.

As we were leaving, I embraced her and was surprised at how strong she was and how tightly she returned my hug, her strong hands patting my back. And as she wrapped her arms around me, the scent of Chanel No. 5 that enveloped me put to rest all of my previous worries about what a typical older person might smell like. Clearly, Lucille was anything but typical.

"Now, if you think of anything else you want to tell me, here's my number," I said with a big smile, secretly hoping to return and spend more time with her. She represented everything I wanted to be someday. Even at over one hundred years old, an age that frankly terrified most people, myself included, she was happy, beautiful and full of life. The fact that her apartment was so impeccably organized didn't hurt either, my inner neat freak pointed out . . .

As Emily and I walked down the long hallway toward the elevator, we were silent. It wasn't until we reached the car that the silence broke, like an emotional bomb had gone off. We began to laugh like two cackling hens. "I told you," Emily managed to get out between giggles, nudging me in the side with her pointy elbow while hoisting her heavy, black messenger bag higher up onto one shoulder. "I told you she was amazing. Aren't you glad we came over as soon as we could?"

The next day, I received a voicemail from a number I didn't recognize. "Judy, please call me. It's urgent." It was Lucille, and she sounded very serious, so I immediately called her back.

"Hey, Lucille, it's Judy. Did you think of something else?"

"Yes. Yes, I did." She said quickly. "I'm so glad that you called me back. I was up all night when I realized that I had left out the most important thing. The most important thing to living long, or even just living in general, is . . ." She paused for a moment and then, with great conviction, told me the single most important ingredient to living a long and happy life. Little did I know that those words she spoke into the phone would be so prophetic, profound, and so very necessary for what lay ahead.

Chapter Two

Morning Tea

A few weeks before, somewhere around my fortieth birthday, I was sitting at the dining room table with my husband, Walter, who is twenty years my senior. Together we have ten children, his, mine and ours. Some women marry men with baggage, but I have jokingly stated many times over the years that I married Mr. Samsonite himself. While most of our children had left the nest at this point in our life, we still continued our morning ritual of reading the paper together long before anyone else in the house was awake.

This was our time, just Walter and me, alone in our dining room, sitting at the long wooden table that seated ten. It wasn't like in the movies, where stuffy married folks always sit at either end of the table, rarely conversing. Nope, Walter always sat at the head of the table and me directly to his left. The dark wooden table with its leather padded seats was almost camouflaged among the faux-finished brown walls of the room. Even the wooden chandelier blended right in. However, our love for each other and the great conversations we'd shared over the years always colored the room beautifully.

When I was a child, especially a teenager, I'd always imagined marrying a particular type of man. I even made a list once: over six feet tall, full head of hair, extremely well built, and very handy with cars and household repairs. I also had the expected two kids and a family pet on there, but that list turned out to be a lesson in futility. Been there, done that, and to make a long story short, it didn't work out. As it turns out, my husband is five-foot-six on a good day and has beautiful brown hair with a bald spot that reminds me of my dad's. As far as handyman work, it's never been his strong suit. He prefers that repairs be made by the professionals who were meant to make them. While Walter has always been an attractive man, I must admit, his heart and his intellect have always been irresistible—attributes that made his profession as a family physician quite fitting.

I have consistently felt that I was the lucky one in the relationship because Walter didn't mind that I'd lied on my driver's license, stretching my height to five feet tall, or that I tend to be a little obsessive compulsive over somewhat trivial matters. He also never complained about the money I spent to keep my hair colored a light blonde.

This particular morning, there we were at the table, me in my usual position, hunched over the obituaries. I was hanging on every word I read when I came across two side-by-side obituaries for two men named John. The first one, John #1, described the time his family had spent with him, inside jokes they had shared, and the marks he had left upon their hearts. The accompanying photo was of an older man, whose smile told the story of a life well lived. There may have been a brief mention of what he did for a living, but that wasn't at all the point of his obituary. On the contrary, John #2 had a column just a few paragraphs longer and a photo that looked like it had been taken thirty years before. In it, he looked serious and very professional. Each paragraph of John

#2's obituary boasted of the important positions he'd held, boards he had sat on, and professional accolades he'd earned throughout the years. While these were all impressive, the obituary lacked any mention of love from family members or the inclusion of any special moments or anecdotes.

I read these two obituaries closely, my pointer finger following the words, a technique I used to keep my dyslexic brain from losing my place so that I didn't have to start over again and again. The finger drag inevitably resulted in a black finger, and black fingerprints all over my pajamas, the wooden table . . . and my white teacup. This morning my finger was even blacker than usual, as it nearly pressed through the paper in my eager attention to every sentence. I didn't know these two men, but I knew their stories, especially that of John #2. As I read, my heart hurt, and an unexpected tear fell, hitting the paper and spreading out into a dark splotch.

"What's wrong?" Walter asked, noticing my distress.

"Two Johns in a row," I said through the sudden lump in my throat. I pointed to their pictures. "It makes me think of Dad and Grandpa, that's all." John being a family name, it seemed like a rational excuse for my emotional response, but in reality, my tears were caused by something much deeper.

As I read John #2's obituary, I suddenly realized that I would someday have to write my parent's obituaries, and that my children would eventually have to write mine. I imagined all of our obituaries lined up side by side. The thought of everyone scrambling to remember useless facts, dates, and meaningless accolades made me feel suddenly nauseous, the toast and tea I'd consumed a few moments earlier rolling wildly in my stomach.

The dining room, which was always a little chilly in the morning, suddenly felt warm and stuffy. I was thinking back to when I would accompany my mother to work as a child—she was always so busy scrambling around as the head nurse, or director of nursing. She always wore a white lab coat that came down to just above her knees, the pockets filled with pens, papers, a few dollars, and coins that would jingle as she strutted through the halls as the boss lady. Her white duty shoes were always perfectly polished. I would watch her dab on the bright white polish to the leather every weekend, as if she were applying a fresh coat of paint. This usually took place right after she'd starched her freshly washed lab coat. When Monday would roll around, she'd be back out the door again to start a new week. Work seemed to be her life.

Ironically, my life seemed to revolve around my work as well. I had so many hats to wear, so many things to juggle. As the director of business development for one of Walter's practices, I obsessed over every detail. Since it was a high-end practice that serviced busy executives and high-profile individuals, my obsession seemed to be warranted, at least in my own mind. Nonetheless, leaving work behind and enjoying the evenings and weekends was something I struggled with, much like my own mother had. Being married to my job didn't help either.

My body felt flushed with heat, and regret seemed to boil within my veins as I suddenly realized I was just like my parents. Their emphasis on work was all I'd ever really known about them. Now, I too had fallen into the trap of defining my own worth through my job. What if I couldn't get to know my parents on a deeper level before I had to write one of those dreadful columns for the both of them? Plus, not really knowing them meant that perhaps I didn't know myself. And what about my children? Would they know me? What would they say about me after I was gone? Would they look back at their childhood and associate my parenting with my job? Would they be sad that I didn't pack their lunch and have freshly baked cookies waiting for them when they got home? I wondered if they would respect my decision to have a career, or if they'd resent it? And if they resented it, could I really blame them? When I was young, it was hard to really know my parents as I really had no frame of reference—I could only imagine who they were and what they did all day. Was I fooling myself to think that my own kids knew me any better?

As our children had left the nest, some off working corporate jobs, some in college, with only the two youngest still at home, I thought about all of the lost opportunities. I didn't have their undivided attention anymore. How could I impart wisdom, share stories, or just enjoy living in the moment when so many moments had simply passed us by?

I sat there wondering how and why my priorities had gotten so mixed up. I knew that at that moment, I'd give anything to go back and pick them up from school, just to hear about their day while it was still fresh on their mind. I remember being at a school play once, and halfway through I realized that I'd missed my daughter's line completely. Her moment to shine was occluded by the work problem I was trying to solve in my head. And there was that time that I was at work past ten in the evening and looked down at the date, realizing I'd missed my daughter's birthday—and not just any birthday, her thirteenth birthday.

When I was growing up, certain birthdays were sacred, a rite of passage. I still remember my thirteenth and sixteenth birthdays quite well, although, my mother managed to forget my sixteenth birthday, and I spent it at the country club driving the golf cart of my high school boyfriend while he teed off. I was teed off too, but in a different way. I had looked forward to that day so much, and it wasn't anything I had imagined. And without even realizing it at the time, I had made my own daughter feel the same way.

My parents had always worked long hours, creating lots of content for their obituaries, no doubt, but it also taught me the importance of a strong work ethic. Dad, a journeyman pipefitter, was always working, sometimes even traveling to a project. Wherever work took him, he went. I guess for him, he belonged wherever his current job happened to be. Mom, who was always a nurse, changed jobs a lot over the years. When I was little, she taught nursing students, then she was a labor and delivery nurse, then a charge nurse. That was all before she gained the title of Director of Nursing (DON), which she only gave up for a short time to own her own consulting firm.

When I was about eleven, I remember telling my friend's parents that my mom delivered babies. One parent asked if my mother was an obstetrician. I was too young at the time to understand the question. I did, however, notice how impressed they were when I simply replied, "Yes." I like that she delivered babies, but I didn't like that she was on-call and often left us home alone in the middle of the night. The DON jobs weren't bad though. I enjoyed going to the nursing homes and meeting all the old people, well, most of them anyway. Once a sweet old lady with long, flowing silver hair was sitting in her purple nightie singing to a baby doll that she was holding tightly. The doll was so cute with her pink frilly dress and brown spiraling ringlets that peeked out from each side of her bonnet. I leaned over and asked very nicely if I could play with her doll. Instead of a sweet old lady response, she screamed bloody murder at me, accused me of kidnapping her child and chased me down the hall as fast as her wheel chair could carry her, my shoes leaving black streaks on the linoleum floor as I skidded around the corner to safety. It was at least a year before I ventured over to the Alzheimer's side of that facility again.

Mom was always happy to chase a promotion or climb the ladder to higher pay or a more impressive title. Both of my parents liked being the boss; it's what they seemed to live for. After all, titles and salary are the makings of a successful person, right? At least, that's what I used to think. I remember before my parents divorced, Dad was talking about taking a supervisory position in another state. That job would take him away from us for weeks, even months at a time. Both my parents seemed to think this was a great idea. In hindsight, the long hours and little to no family time didn't fare so well. The job paid well, and I remember a new car in the driveway of our two-story brick home, but it wasn't even a year or so later that the family fell apart. I don't think it was that particular job that led to the divorce, but as a result, I also have never believed that distance makes the heart grow fonder.

As I sat there at the dining room table, my ink-stained finger still pressing down on the paper below the last sentence of John #2's obituary, I longed deep within my heart to become John #1. What if I had heard my children's school stories, would that have sparked longer conversations between us? Maybe I should have obsessed more about their needs and less about my job. Even spending more time for myself, perhaps going to the spa more or taking up yoga would have made me a calmer person, more centered. But, staying on the treadmill of life with a packed calendar of meetings and a long list of to-dos seemed to be the safest place, the only one I had ever known.

"Hey, you best get moving," Walter said as he straightened up in his chair and gathered the paper into a neat stack. He then placed his cold hand over my warm forearm, shaking me slightly to bring me out of my trance. I looked up at his beautiful blue eyes as he continued, "You've got a full day's work ahead of you, and it's already six twenty."

Chapter Three

The Treadmill

Over the next few days, I had been thinking that there's something to be said for a five-minute commute. I liked the short drive through my suburban neighborhood, where tall trees flanked each side of the street. I had almost memorized which households would have lights on, bustling with activity, and which ones sat still and dark in the wee hours of the morning. The office was only a few stoplights down the main drag of my small town, past the dry cleaners and across from the town square. Working so close to home would be a blessing for most, but for me it was often a curse. Since the house was only minutes away, there was always one more detail I could cover before leaving work for the day.

This was one of the rare days when I actually drove to work with the sun beaming through my front windshield. "Good afternoon," the receptionist at the front desk said sarcastically. She was thirty-something, petite, with dirty blonde hair. She hadn't been there very long, and I always had trouble remembering her name. Nonetheless, she was giving me a taste of my own medicine: I couldn't even count the number of times I'd said that to someone who was late, even if it was only by a few minutes.

"Very funny," I replied. It wasn't afternoon at all, though nine o'clock on a Monday morning was very late for me indeed. "Hey, there's a light burned out in the chandelier above the nurse's station. I think it went out a few days ago. Did you call maintenance yet?"

She turned from the copier and said, "Not yet. I'll email him right now, but do you want to take a look around first? Without fail, you always find five other things wrong the moment he leaves."

I often felt the need to control every aspect of the patient's experience. That strong work ethic that was instilled in me from an early age was so relentless, that at times it gave me tunnel vision. Each day was always full steam ahead, and over the years, more than one employee has referred to me as the "Inspector General." I couldn't seem to make it to my desk without finding something out of place. Some called it picky, but I called it ownership.

As I continued down the hall, I straightened the diplomas on the wall as part of my usual morning ritual. "I could understand if this were California and we had earthquakes all the time," I mumbled under my breath. I often had to control the urge to walk over and rearrange things on other people's desks. What can I say? I have always liked things a certain way, even if that way seems a bit impractical to others.

"Morning," I said to my officemates. My private office had been hijacked the previous year when we needed more space. Back then, I only shared my office with the doctors, Walter or Dr. Anderson, when they needed a quiet spot to write up patient notes. It was perfect, as both of them only worked at my location on specific days, and they were half days at that. Dr. Anderson liked to talk between patients, and I always knew when he was about to go on a tangent about something because he would sit back in the chair, cross his long, lanky legs and bring one elbow up on the arm of the chair. He was opinionated, but his rants didn't last long since he was on a tight schedule. His off-color remarks and redneck attitude were in stark contrast to his expensive suit and nicely polished shoes.

Walter was so different at work. He wasn't a real talker, just highly focused on each case and on keeping with his schedule. He absolutely hated to keep people waiting. He was the only doctor I'd ever known who would schedule people twelve minutes apart instead of an even ten. Over his almost forty years in practice, he had appointment times down to a science. As for his outfits and shoes, his suits were always tailored made, but mostly because of his oddly-sized thick neck and short arms and legs. His shoes could do with more polish and he often broke his shoelaces because he was in such a hurry getting out the door.

Now, I had to share my office with two more people, Andrew and Kasey, who were there full-time. We all agreed that it wasn't ideal, but the fact that the business was growing meant we were doing something right, so I couldn't really complain. Kasey was a rather large girl, tall and strong. She always dressed professionally and always came to work in classic work attire, in either a dress or slacks and a blouse with large, open, flowing sleeves that fluttered in the air as she walked around the office. The prints were large and sprawling, never small. Her mannerisms were big and boisterous, generally happy and enthusiastic, much like the prints she wore. She loved to talk and smile quite a bit, regardless of how early or late it was.

"Good morning," said Kasey, who, as always was far too bubbly for a Monday morning. Her teeth gleamed as if she had just completed a whitening treatment. "Wait until I tell you about my weekend," she said excitedly, her eyes sparkling. "You will not believe it. First . . ."

I honestly don't remember what followed; I had already

moved on to my seemingly impossible to-do list. Kasey loved to fill me in and play catch up on Mondays. I did, too, and I enjoyed her company, but this morning, I had too much to do. Knowing that I had to be cordial, I looked at Kasey and then over her shoulder at Andrew and asked, "So, what's on tap for the week?" Andrew, who was number five in the list of our ten children, often reminded of me of Walter. He was much like him in stature, even had the beginning of the same bald spot on the top of his brown head. He has always been respectful to me at both work and home, even though I wasn't his biological mother, and he probably never dreamed I would end up being his boss. He had taken a layoff package from the airline he had been working for and was only supposed to work for us for a few short weeks, helping us get caught up on some graphic work. But he did such a great job that we ended up asking him to stay on, making the job full-time and permanent.

Kasey turned her chair to let Andrew answer first, but there was nothing except silence. "Hey, she was talking to us," Kasey said as she threw a wad of paper at Andrew's back. It fell to the stained concrete floor. The room was brown, much like my dining room, but the floor was a mixture of brown and black stain that resembled marble, but the white drop-in ceiling kept the large, rectangular room from feeling heavy. Kasey and I sat at the wall opposite Andrew. The only bad part about our location was the elevator on the opposite side. All day we heard it go up and come back down. Needless to say, it became a bit hypnotic around four in the afternoon, as people in the upstairs office were leaving for the day.

"Huh? Ah, what?" he asked, turning around and pulling his earbuds out. "Sorry. Good morning," he greeted me before immediately turning around again and putting them back in. Andrew's desk faced the wall beside the door. It was probably the best location in the room to effectively tune us out. It always amazed me that we could come and go, and he would be none the wiser.

Suddenly, Andrew turned back around, pulled a bud from one ear and asked, "Did you put that ad out yet?"

"Not yet, but I'll do it as soon as I get back from my meeting," I replied, hoping I would remember. We'd become so busy that we needed another office assistant, and it was my job to find one. After all, we couldn't call ourselves a luxury medical office if the phones weren't answered immediately or calls weren't returned in a timely manner.

The next few days were more of the same. My to-do list continued to grow almost as quickly as the interruptions came:

"Judy, can you help me with the stress-test machine? It's acting up."

"Judy, how much did we spend on marketing last month?"

"Judy, another call. Do we want to change our credit card processing company?"

"There's an agent who wants to get their author on the radio show."

My one saving grace was the radio show we did on Wednesdays. I always enjoyed researching potential topics, writing the show, and finding guests, but most of all, I found joy in simply spending time with Walter and Dr. Anderson. The two of them were complete opposites, not just in stature, but also in personality. Dr. Anderson was tall and very thin. He loved riding his Harley Davidson in jeans, boots, and a leather jacket. It was like his alter ego, or perhaps maybe even his true self. Walter, on the other hand, used to be an avid chess player and talked much like one, always thinking of possible ramifications to his comments or decisions, both personal and business. Considering how different they were, it's a miracle the two remained partners for almost three decades.

The three of us always learned something from the guests who came on the show. And over the years, we also learned a great deal about each other and ourselves. Once, when we discussed the importance of good communication between parents and children with Fran Walfish, a famous Hollywood psychologist, we discovered that we weren't nearly as good at communicating with our own kids as we thought. Then, there was the time we discussed drug interactions and side effects, and Dr. Anderson piped up with, "Believe me, if I have a four-hour erection, I'm not going to the ER. I'm calling everyone I know and then getting it engraved on my tombstone!"

The radio show has given us all a great deal of personal and professional gratification. I would love to send letters to all my former teachers who wrote, "Talks too much," on my report cards, letting them know what I do now. Kind of a, "Look at me now! And you thought talking too much was a bad thing!"

"So, what's the show on today?" asked Dr. Anderson as he strolled into the office on Wednesday, wearing a pinstriped suit with a shiny pink tie that matched the handkerchief in his jacket pocket. It was obviously something his personal tailor had put together. I had known Dr. Anderson a long time, about twenty years. I remembered when his idea of dressing up was wearing his dark Wrangler jeans with his dress cowboy boots, back when he still resembled the Texas A&M Aggie on the outside as much as he still did on the inside. They say you can take the man out of the country, but you can't take the country boy out of the man.

"Aging. Or rather, how not to age," I replied rather unenthusiastically as I glanced up from my computer screen.

"Well, we could do that one with our eyes closed," he said cockily as he quickly grabbed a patient's paperwork and headed into the exam room.

He was right. People traveled from all corners of the globe to consult him and Walter. Preventative and proactive medicine was their specialty. People want to live longer and healthier lives, and some are willing to go to great lengths to make sure that when they do get old, they do it gracefully. When Walter and Dr. Anderson decided to go into anti-aging instead of the same old family medicine practice, I often thought it may have been a little self-serving.

By the end of the show that afternoon, I was talked out. That often happened after two hours of non-stop conversing without a second of dead air. As I removed my headphones, I looked at each of them and said, "Age to Perfection."

"What?" asked Walter.

"The title of the next book: *Age to Perfection*. We already did *Stay Young*, so I thought it would be good to focus more on how to stay healthy as we age. Come on, we're all gonna age. Besides, look at how many people are living past a hundred these days."

"I like it," said Anderson as his hazel eyes grew wide. He paused, then continued, "You know, if we make it that long, we're going to need second, third, or even fourth careers." His eye brows raised to the top of his long narrow face as he finished with, "Hell, we may even need that many wives, too."

I gave Anderson The Look, the one that says it all. The careers thing, sure, but more wives? Walter and I were each other's second and final spouses. I guess his comment struck a chord with me. I might have been second, but I was definitely final.

"Not me," Walter said quickly, shaking his head as if to deny any sort of agreement with Anderson's statement.

"That's right. Not you," I replied sternly with a grimace. "Oh," I said, "the full title should be *Age to Perfection: How to Thrive to 100 Happy, Healthy, Wealthy and Wise*."

"We're not financial advisers—drop the wealthy," said Walter.

Then he patted my knee and half-jokingly said, "We'll expect the rough draft by next month."

The idea for the book was twofold. I had been searching for a title and topic that would fit with my job of marketing the practice, and *Age to Perfection* seemed to be a perfect match. The subtitle, *Happy, Healthy and Wise*, was more a part of my own personal quest, perhaps inspired by the obituaries. I'd noticed that some people were happy, some people lived happily and healthily, some were even wise, but far too many people seemed to just live, period. They weren't thriving, they were merely surviving. I wanted to find out why and how some people aged happily and wisely, while others just seemed to age. I knew that if I could discover their secret, maybe, just maybe I could not only live longer, but live my life to the fullest.

"Happy Friday!" Kasey said cheerfully as her thick blonde hair draped around her face like a lion's mane, a perfect frame for her piercing blue eyes. She had on brown slacks and a cream top with a print of big bright flowers. The fabric was one of those modern polyester blends that look more like silk but doesn't make you sweat the way silk does. "Any big plans for the weekend?"

"Unfortunately, it's Friday, and I still need to dig my way out of this stack of work," I responded. I didn't want to take my work home over the weekend, much like my own mom always had. I could still picture her so vividly, sitting on the couch, in her burgundy robe and panty hose, drawing up spreadsheets with a pencil and a ruler, long before the days of Excel. She always wore her panty hose, even at night. I only remember seeing her bare legs once as a child. They were extremely fair and smooth, an image that stuck with me, perhaps because it seemed so much more natural given her fair complexion. I longed for the day she would retire. Maybe then, just maybe, I could get to know her.

I even wondered if retirement meant she would buy jeans and maybe even a pair of tennis shoes instead of the skirts and blouses she wore day in and day out.

Just as I sat down, Andrew spun around in his chair and asked, "Any applicants for that position yet?"

Crap! I thought. I still needed to write and post the ad. "Actually, I'm going to write the ad up right now," I assured him. "Don't worry. Besides, we're always flooded with applicants. The key is to find just the right person in a stack of unqualified, undesirable, unemployed, or underemployed resumes."

Ten voice mails, thirty-five emails, and one impromptu meeting with a salesperson later, I finally sat down to write the ad. I knew exactly what I wanted, so coming up with precise, accurate wording that would effectively screen applicants was critical.

"It's done. Do you want to hear it?" I announced to anyone willing to listen when I finally finished.

"Of course," Kasey said as she tore off a sheet of paper from her notepad and tossed it at Andrew's head to get his attention. He pulled out both of his ear buds, turned around to face me, and leaned back in his chair. I was certain that his chair was broken, as he always leaned it back way too far. I often imagined him toppling over backwards and making a complete fool of himself. I felt certain that it would eventually happen, so I liked to picture it and practice not laughing too hard. Just in case.

I had to hire just the right person, someone with a smile that warmed the room, but an attitude that commanded respect and trust from each patient. In my mind, it was a cross between the girl next door and a bombshell with brains. It may be sexist, but I knew it had to be a woman. Medical receptionists in the South are almost always female. Besides, our patients would never feel comfortable calling a young strapping male and asking for a refill of their Viagra. Oddly enough, they never minded asking the ladies for it, . . . "Needed: medical office assistant. Must be physically fit and wellness-minded. Free of tattoos and body piercings. Non-smoker. Must be able to carry themselves in a professional manner. Blah, blah, blah. The rest is just about the benefits we offer, hours, and all that jazz."

I looked up to see both Kasey and Andrew staring at me like I had two heads. "You can't say that!" exclaimed Andrew.

"I just did. It's posted and has probably already been seen by hundreds of non-qualified people," I responded. "This is Texas, a right-to-work state. I can definitely say all that. You know how much I hate tattoos and body piercings. Besides, think about it, most of our executives have dress codes against them at their own corporations."

Andrew knew I hated tattoos, but I'd never really told him why. It's almost too painful to talk about, but when I was a little girl, I admired my Uncle Frank, my dad's brother, so much. He was big and strong and always smiled and played with us kids. His brown wavy hair was just long enough to give balance to his large family nose, which came from our German roots. Being the cool uncle, he even snuck us in to see *Grease* at the drive-in. He was married to my Aunt Dawn, whom I also adored. She was so beautiful with her long blonde hair, blue eyes, and faint freckles across her cheeks. I wanted to look just like her. They were such a cute hippie couple back in the 70s. He even had her name tattooed on his arm.

One day Uncle Frank changed in a big way. I'm not sure if it was drugs or alcohol or both, but something went terribly wrong. They got divorced and all of us kids were crushed. To the horror of us kids, he went out and got a tattoo of the devil—right over my Aunt Dawn's name. I was sad and frightened all at the same time. The Uncle Frank I knew would never do that. The Uncle Frank I knew was kind, loving, and fun.

Not long after, he purchased a new shiny motorcycle. He was so proud of that thing, even taking pictures with us kids sitting upon it, just behind him, showing off all our biceps. Uncle Frank was cool, but unfortunately, he had a fatal crash on that bike, leaving my Dad and my grandparents devastated and my cousins fatherless. The crash was so severe that my dad had to identify my uncle's body by his boots and the surgical pin in his index finger. Now, every time I see a tattoo it reminds me of a loss of innocence replaced by evil, darkness, and loss.

Chapter Four

~

Serendipitous

Sometimes I imagine God sitting up in heaven, watching us, eating popcorn, and saying, "Watch this!" to the angels who look on with unending amazement. His master plan for serendipitous meetings often caused a domino effect that had the ability to change us forever. But the best part about such meetings was that they happened when you least expected them.

"How's the new book coming, Judy?" asked the other Judy in the office. She was lean and muscular, but a real girly-girl, always in heels and a classy, colorful dress. Her hairstyle had probably never changed much over the decades, but the bangs and long blonde curls she wore suited her well. The two of us had a running joke that you had to be named Judy to work at our office. Somewhere along the line, I became Judy 1 and she became Judy 2. She was also one of the best hires I ever made. Not only was she our Fitness Director, but she also answered phones and booked appointments. You name it, she could do it. She was older than the other applicants by at least a few decades, but she possessed a warmness that could set anyone at ease, especially an uptight patient.

"Umm, yeah, about that," I said putting my purse on the desk and leaning over on it with a look of defeat. If I could find some time to write, that would be great. I just need more hours in the day. By the time I get home, cook dinner, and visit with Walter and the kids, I'm spent."

"Don't worry, I know you'll get it done and it'll be wonderful," she said, tilting her blonde head in an understanding manner. Her teeth were pearly white, but the size of her smile was much smaller than Kasey's, and her voice was calmer, too. "Oh, and here's a stack of more resumes. I hope we're getting close to a hire." Her voice always tended to end on a high note, and she could make even the most dreaded tasks sound like fun. Some people find this kind of optimism annoying, but I liked it and even found it motivating.

As I walked past the diplomas, straightening them almost without looking, I stared down at the top resume. "You've got to be kidding me," I mumbled under my breath. "Another Judy? Nope, three's a crowd."

The nurse looked up as I walked past her, talking to myself. She probably said something to me, but I didn't hear it. I had plenty of work to do, and my mind was already on it.

For the next few hours, I sat at my desk, sifting through a multitude of resumes. Any resume with a typo went into the trash. No cover letter: into the trash. Bad spacing: trash. Finally, I came to one that struck me as odd. The applicant had job-hopped a great deal, listing ten employers over the five years she had been in the workforce. "Listen to this," I said. Both Andrew and Kasey were all ears. "*Luscious*. Seriously, someone named their kid Luscious. Why would somebody give their kid a name that sounds like she comes with her own pole? How does she expect to get any respect? Can you imagine her answering the phones? What if one of our CEO patients' wife calls? 'Hello, this is Luscious,'" I said in my best phone-sex voice.

By that point, several other employees had gathered in the doorway, listening. The nurse shook her dirty-blonde head. She stood there in her skirt and cowgirl boots, an outfit she knew I wouldn't approve of. I have always been picky about the way employees dress. Sometimes their idea of what's professional didn't always jibe with my idea, or anyone else's idea, of professional attire. I often told them that if they looked in the mirror, smiled, and thought about how damn sexy they looked, it was time to change their outfit. "It's amazing you ever hired any of us. You're looking for perfect. Perfect doesn't exist. I feel lucky I got past that trash can," she said, pointing down at wire-rimmed basket that was overflowing with rejects. I knew I needed to talk to the nurse about her attire, but right then I needed to stay on task.

Once I had rummaged through the stack of what seemed like hundreds of resumes, I had five truly qualified applicant resumes on my desk and an avalanche of papers under my desk.

The next few days were filled with emails, meetings, fixing the EKG machine, and trying to carve out time to write. In addition to my normal duties, I also now had to squeeze interviews into my busy schedule, which was a bit of a headache.

Applicant number one was too soft-spoken. There was no way she could handle working for me, let alone for Dr. Anderson. Between the two of us, we would have eaten her alive.

I don't remember much about applicant number two, which was enough to cut her out of the running for the position. If she didn't make a good impression on me, there was no way she would make one on our high-profile patients.

Applicant number three was very tall and thin, like a model that had just walked off the runway. She didn't smoke, drink, or have tattoos, but she had a quirky personality and an interesting sense of style. Her eyelashes were about three inches long and circled her wide eyes like a lion's mane. Her hair was cut in an inverted bob, with one side much longer than the other. It was a huge distraction for me, due to my obsessive-compulsive tendencies. I wanted to grab her head and tilt it to even out the sides, or better yet, grab the scissors for a more permanent fix.

She wasn't at all what I expected from her perfectly crafted resume and cleverly written cover letter, both of which were without a single typo. On paper, she seemed ideal, but during the interview, she earned herself the nickname "Creepy Girl," and a ticket to the door without a job offer.

Perhaps I inherited my rather direct interview style from my strict mother, but I've found that it's a great way to see how candidates react to pressure, or rather, interrogation. I once read that you can learn all you want to know about a job candidate by asking a few unexpected personal questions. Most of the time, I can guess the answers in advance, but this woman's responses were like none I'd ever heard.

"Tell me your top three favorite movies," I said. Historically, I've gotten the same responses again and again: *Forrest Gump*, *The Notebook*, *When Harry Met Sally*, and *The Matrix*. Of course, Creepy Girl went off in a completely different direction.

"Oh, I like this question," she said, looking relieved. She finally made eye contact for the first time, but only for a brief moment. The rest of the time, her eyes had been darting around the room as if they were following a fly in the air. She even wrung her shaky hands with such force that I felt as if she might pull her skin off. "Every Disney movie ever, *Zombieland*, and *Silence of the Lambs*. Oh, actually, *Silence of the Lambs* is tied with *The Shining*."

Yuck! I thought, finally asking her what adjectives her friends and family would use to describe her. She would have been better off being a little less honest. But staying true to form, she replied, "Argumentative, quirky, curious, and philosophical."

Not exactly the ideal attributes for a new hire. Then she looked right at me, wringing her hands and blinking more times than a politician. I think she was waiting for me to say something, but I was in shock.

Are you freaking serious? I thought. *I have a twitchy serial killer in my presence!* I had never met anyone quite like this girl. I kept looking down at her well-crafted resume and thinking, *Is this really the same person? Had she never been coached on how to interview?*

Her eyes continued to scan the room, looking at the door, the walls, the ceiling. Perhaps she was searching for a quick exit strategy or praying that this interview would end. I imagined God up there, laughing as He rocked back and forth in His theater seat, thoroughly pleased with himself. *Okay, God,* I thought, *don't choke on your popcorn.*

I continued to make small talk, knowing that there was no way in hell I could hire this girl. I had visions of her conversing with our patients and letting it slip out that she had once murdered someone or that she had a pet snake that she liked to take for walks through the cemetery at night.

After the interview was over, I walked her to the door and gave her the usual, "I'll let you know." To this day, I'm not sure why I didn't just tell her right then and there that she was simply not a good candidate for the job.

"Gonna write today?" Walter asked at the dining room table as he stared down at the morning paper. He was in his blue suit, a white shirt with blue stripes, and a shiny silk tie with a pink, blue, and silver pattern. His hair was still slightly wet from the shower. I hadn't even finished the first page of obits, and there he was asking me about the book.

"Gonna try," I replied, "but I have to get out of the office on time. At the end of a ten-hour day, there's simply nothing left. Besides, I need to gather all my research and that takes time. Real time. Time I don't seem to have enough of."

"You'll get it done. I have faith in you."

Ugh. There's nothing like pressure to get the creative juices flowing.

Walter is a get-it-done kind of guy, a workaholic himself. He grew up poor, of Slavic descent, so any success he has achieved was through his own doing. In his quest for productivity, he always expects things to be done and to be done right the first time. Some people are driven, but he takes drive into overdrive. He's not only an incredible family physician, but he also understands business—a combination that's rarely found. Perhaps my workaholism is what attracted him to me. As they say, "Birds of a feather . . ."

It wasn't ten minutes later that I walked into the office to be greeted by Judy 2 in her tall black high heels, dangling jeweled earrings, and fitted red dress. She asked with a smile, "How's that book coming, Judy?" Pressure—there it was again. From the top of my head to the tips of my toes, it was as if I was being zapped back into reality, as the energy was sucked right out of me.

I sighed. "I think I really need to find a writing assistant. This book is going to take a lot more time and effort than I had anticipated. I don't know why, but I have a feeling it's going to be great if I can ever get it off the ground."

Judy 2 touched my shoulder and smiled. "You will," she assured me. "You will."

Where do I even find a writing assistant? I wondered rhetorically. As I walked away, I hollered back, "Another light is out down by the break room."

For a brief moment, I regretted the idea of the book. Why had I decided to take on more work? Here I am, struggling with the guilt vs. the satisfaction of workaholism and then I go and make more work for myself. *Maybe I should just table the book?* I thought. *Pick up the idea again when things are less hectic.*

For some reason, Creepy Girl continued to stay on my mind, even though we had hired someone else for the position. Even stranger, her resume floated back to the top of the mountain of papers littering my desk. Normally, I put the resumes of those we interviewed but didn't hire in a file labeled, "Applicants Who Failed."

I looked back over all her crazy answers that I had jotted written down on the back of her resume. When I rescanned her qualifications, something caught my attention. She had a degree in English and minors in creative writing and philosophy, graduating Magna Cum Laude. She had even won awards in writing. Suddenly, it all made sense. She wasn't creepy at all; she was going to be my new writing assistant! All that quirkiness may not be good for patients, but I was willing to bet it was good for writing. Maybe she admired people like Stephen King for his incredible storytelling abilities . . .

Ironically, I opened my inbox later that day to find an email from her. It started, "Thank you for the interview. I am confident that I would be a good fit . . ." Her email was lengthy, but very well written.

I replied: "Thank you for following up. While the position you applied for has been filled, I do have an opening for a writing assistant. I am working on a book and I feel your experience would be a huge asset." I was half fearing she would put a hex on me, half hoping she would be thrilled for the opportunity. But she quickly accepted, and I was happy to finally make some progress regarding the book.

Fridays became my writing days. Fridays and any other time I could squeeze in, that is. Writing the book had finally reached the top of my priority list. Creepy Girl no longer seemed creepy, and I felt compelled to refer to her by her actual name, Emily.

"Thanks for meeting here," I said to Emily as we settled into a table at the Southlake Library for our first meeting since that interview about three weeks prior. This location was perfect, since it kept me away from distractions at work and prevented her from having to come face-to-face with the girl who beat her out for the office position.

Her dark blue pants and light-colored t-shirt seemed to be much more comfortable than the fancy interview outfit I'd seen her in before. I didn't even mind her crooked hair. Besides, when she tilted her head to one side as she looked down to read, the sides almost appeared even. She looked me squarely in the eye, "Okay, here's a calendar I put together. We can add additional sessions and deadlines for specific milestones," she said confidently.

Is this the same girl I met at the office? I wondered. She was so prepared and didn't seem nervous at all. She was obviously in her element.

"Great! Well, the book is called *Age to Perfection: How to Thrive to 100 Happy, Healthy, and Wise.* Here are copies of studies I have printed out, the names of articles and books I want to reference, and, well, you get the picture," I said, handing her a stack of materials I had gathered during the Fridays before our meeting.

After about two hours of sifting through everything and making a list of additional materials to find, she looked at me and asked, "Are you freezing in here?" She looked around and behind her before frowning. "I can't believe I didn't bring a sweater or something."

"Oh my gosh, I know!" I exclaimed. "I didn't want to start off by complaining, but this place is like a meat locker."

In the meetings that followed, we came more prepared with

coats and scarves. Emily even showed up each week with a coffee for her and a hot chocolate for me.

One day, as Emily cradled her cup, the steam floating up to her unbelievably long lashes, she said, "You look like the wheels are turning." I was glad the steam didn't melt the glue off her lash extensions.

"They are. I have an idea. Are you up for the task of your life?"

"Yes!" She said with anticipation.

"Your assignment is to find as many people as you can over the age of one hundred. I want to interview 'em and find out what makes 'em tick. We've been doing all this research, but I feel like we missed the mark. Why don't we just ask the people who have been there and done that?"

"I'll find those people before we meet next week," she assured me enthusiastically.

You have got to be kidding me, I thought. She obviously believed this would be easy, but I knew better. I didn't just want people who were over one hundred; I needed people who could actually communicate. *Good luck with that.*

The next week, we were back at the library, and it was especially cold that morning. Morgue cold. Emily was a few minutes late, which was not like her. This time, I came prepared. I had long pants, a sweater, and a throw. I was ready to hunker down and get some serious work done.

She arrived with her usual coffee and hot chocolate in hand, though I noticed she had upgraded to Venti size. I suspected this was an attempt to butter me up prior to confessing that she hadn't been able to locate anyone over the age of one hundred who was willing, or more importantly, able to carry on a conversation with me. She was going to ask for more time. I was glad to see that she was ready to work, too, as evidenced by her layers of clothing and the jacket slung across her arm. I found it funny that she had the body of a runway model, but often dressed so slouchy for our writing sessions. Her sleeves were pulled over her hands, stopping at her knuckles, and her clothes were often a size too big. She liked to wear earth tones and black, like goth, but a somewhat more grown-up version. I knew she cleaned up well, after all, her interview outfit had been professional and well-tailored.

Instead of blurting out that she failed the assignment, I listened in amazement as she announced, "I've found a few people, and one in particular says she can meet with us next week." Emily sipped her coffee. "I can't believe she's a hundred. Getting onto her social calendar was almost impossible. She's spunky—girl's got more of a social life than I do."

I couldn't believe my ears. To think that Emily's resume had almost landed in the failure folder! A big smile filled my face. "What's her name?"

"Lucille. Lucille Fleming. She lives about fifteen minutes from here."

I didn't know why, but at that moment, even the sound of Lucille's name made me feel happy. I sat with my hot chocolate, taking it all in as Emily described their lively phone conversation. The day that Emily walked into my office was not some kind cruel joke; it was serendipitous. It was the kind of thing that made me want to give God a high-five.

Chapter Five

⟨ ✦ ⟩

The Tour

"Good morning," I said to Judy 2 as I entered through the wood-framed glass door of the office the Monday after I first met Lucille. Most staff entered through the back door, but I always preferred to come through the front, so I could see exactly what each patient would see when entering the office.

"Girl, you're early. It's just me and you. Can I get you anything?" She said as she came from behind the black granite-topped desk into the reception area. She stood there next to a headless, armless, and legless statue that sat upon a pedestal in the corner. When I brought that statue into the office for the first time, we named him Chester Peterless. It's one of the inside jokes between us charter members of the staff.

"I tell you what—let's walk back to the break room together. I'm going to grab a cup of green tea."

It wasn't until we reached our destination that I realized I hadn't even examined the lights or glanced over at the diplomas to see if they were straight. My mind was obviously preoccupied with my encounter with Lucille. "Things are good," I told her.

"The book is coming along, Emily is working out, and I met the most incredible lady."

"Oh, that's great. What lady?"

"I had Emily find people over one hundred for me to interview."

"Where the heck do you find them?" she asked in amusement.

"I know, right? That's what I thought, but Emily found some. One is even local, and I got to spend some time with her. Judy, you're going to think I'm crazy, but I felt like I knew her. I didn't want to leave. I know it sounds creepy, but I can't stop thinking about her. It's like she's an older version of me. No—that's not it, but something like that."

"Wow, and what a great idea for the book. I mean, these people know what it takes to live a long time. No better resource than the actual source."

"Exactly," I replied with a nod of my head.

"How's your mom? Have you talked to her lately?" She asked, almost sheepishly. Judy knew that I longed to spend time with my mom, but she was always busy.

"Well, now that she's retiring, I figure my time has finally come. Maybe she and I can get away sometime for some mother-daughter time." I sighed, thinking about all the times as a child when I'd asked my mom to do things with me, but always got a "we'll see" or "maybe." Now that work was out of the way for her, I was willing to push it out of the way for me, too.

Judy and I walked back up the hall, splitting off to head to our own areas of the office.

I sat at my desk, simply thinking. I didn't open my computer or go through the piles of work on my desk. I just sat there, staring off into the distance and replaying the visit with Lucille in my head. I thought about her outfit, her apartment, and that dress from her birthday party.

Eventually, Andrew and Kasey arrived, and the day officially started. And the day after that. And the day after that.

But something about Lucille stayed with me for the next two weeks. I couldn't get over the way she had hugged me when we left. It was a real hug, not the kind you give someone you've only met once and will likely never see again. I wanted to go back and visit her again, but I couldn't figure out how to ask without weirding her out. She knew me as an author, but I wanted to get to know her as a friend. After all, how could I possibly gain some of her great attributes without understanding her story? Perhaps she could mentor me in this thing we called life.

Finally, I came up with a plan and picked up the phone. "I thought of a few more questions; is there any chance I could stop by on Friday for a visit?" I asked, gripping the receiver and hoping she would agree.

"Sure!" she said enthusiastically. "Of course you can. Anything in particular I should prepare answers for?"

I wasn't expecting that. I didn't actually have any more questions; I just wanted to see her again. "No, I want you to be spontaneous," I replied, trying to sound legitimate.

"Okay, sounds good. See you at ten?"

"Yes, that's perfect." I hung up, making a mental note to come up with some good questions.

Friday rolled around, and after my early writing session with Emily, I drove to Lucille's place and walked back down that long hallway to Lucille's apartment door. "It's Judy," I announced loudly, but trying not to yell, as I tapped on her front door. There was a wreath affixed to the wooden surface, similar to the ones adoring the main doors to the building. But Lucille's was made of brown twigs covered with greenery, flowers, and topped off with a wide bow made of floral print. I stood there, all dressed up, waiting for her to answer. I was excited, not really nervous, just happy to be there.

"It's Lucille," she responded cheerfully as she opened the door, smiling widely.

She was all dressed up again: flowing pink skirt, silk blouse, a ribbon in her hair and another around her neck, and a beautiful white flower on her lapel. Just like the last time we'd met, her apartment was completely tidy. The kitchenette was clean and organized, with only a bunch of green bananas sitting out on the counter, waiting to ripen.

Before I could sit down, she said, "Let me show you around the place. Do you have time?"

"Yes, of course," I said quickly, my face flushing with pleasure. I had scheduled an hour and a half for our meeting, hoping and praying that she would let me stay that long.

"Great," she replied, grabbing her cane and heading toward the door. She guided me to a somewhat hidden elevator near the laundry room. The walls were tan and the art so-so, nothing special, just framed prints, and the carpet was brown and practical, probably in order to hide any stains. I seemed to be making mental notes about the contrast between the common areas and Lucille's lively, well-decorated apartment, which was full of color, bold patterns, and lots of detail, much like Lucille herself, though I only had an inkling of it at the time. "We'll take this one," she announced, raising her cane to push the elevator button.

"I like that trick," I said with a giggle.

Almost in unison, we pointed at the buttons and blurted out, "Yuck!" We were indeed kindred spirits. Even just thinking about all the viruses and bacteria one could pick up from shopping carts, elevator buttons, and ATM keypads grosses me out. If I wasn't careful, I could slip into obsession over it.

"That's the pool table room, where we play cards," she

informed me majestically as we stepped out onto the first floor. "I play bridge. Lots of bridge. Not just any bridge." She looked me in the eye and very seriously added, "Duplicate bridge."

I knew I was supposed to be impressed by the way she said it, but I had no idea what duplicate bridge was. "Wow," I said, smiling and very convincingly. "That's great!" I later learned just how difficult duplicate bridge was. It was more of a tournament-style bridge that was played in teams. Since each team plays the same hands, the game is more reliant upon skill than luck.

As we walked down the hall, she started telling me about how much she liked living there and about all her friends. "Everyone's so nice. There's a group of us, and we really cut up. Let's go in here and sit down. This is our café," she said, performing a Vanna White arm swoosh. The room had several cherry wood tables and chair sets, the tops of the tables covered in crisp, white tablecloths. Some tables were missing traditional chairs so that wheelchairs could be placed in those spots. There was a coffee bar along one wall and the back wall overlooked the back porch and the grass-filled courtyard. She directed me past a few other residents who were sitting and chatting. She waved to them all and announced with excitement, "I have a visitor. This is Judy. She's writing a book and interviewing me for it." Her nose lifted a little higher into the air as we made our way to a table in the corner. "Let's go over there," she said, adding rather loudly, "So we're not distracted." We sat at the table the furthest from the door.

I realized that she had planned to go to the café all along. I was her show-and-tell for the day, and I was totally okay with that. In fact, I was more than okay—I was amused.

We sat and chatted for quite some time, remaining there long after the others had left. She told me about her two sons and her grandchildren, and she even shared a little gossip about the other residents who had just gotten up to leave. She eventually looked at me very seriously and said, "Now, what did you want to ask me?"

Ask her? I thought, my mind floundering. *Oh, crap, I forgot to think of any questions!* I fumbled with my notebook, which I had really only brought to make our visit look more official.

She quickly figured out that I wasn't prepared to ask her anything in particular and came to my rescue: "It's okay, Judy, you don't have to ask me anything. You don't have to have a reason to visit." She reached out and placed her warm aged hand on my forearm. "You can come see me just because."

"Really?" I asked, sounding like a little kid. I was so excited by her offer. I couldn't wait to hear her story. All her stories.

"Really," she replied in a soft voice.

After that, we just made small talk, and she showed me around the rest of the facility. When it was time for me to go, we went back up the front elevator and down the long hall to her room. "I hope you can come see me again soon."

"How about next Friday?" I offered, hoping I wasn't pushing my luck.

"Sure, next Friday is perfect," she said as she gave me a big hug goodbye. As I made my way back down the hall, she hollered enthusiastically, "See you Friday!"

I left feeling like my insides were smiling just as much as my face was. Lucille was my new friend, and she was excited to spend time with me, too. Time was such a precious gift, the one gift I had always longed for from my parents but had never really gotten. Something about Lucille was special, like no one I'd ever met before. I liked the way she dressed, her smile, her infectious love of life. She seemed to take notice of those she lived with and knew a little something about each and every one of them. She was even interested in getting to know more about me, my family, my job, and all the things that interested me in life—the real me. I wasn't used to fielding so many questions about me and my life. Many of my friends liked to talk about their lives, but they rarely asked me about mine. As I drove home, I thought to myself, *It doesn't matter that she's old. True friendship knows no age.*

Chapter Six

❦

Gift of a Lifetime

"Excited about your trip to Utah?" asked Judy 2 as she entered my office wearing black slacks, black high heels, and a white silky shirt that tied on one side. As usual, I was in long before Kasey and Andrew, and raring to get to work. Since I'd begun visiting with Lucille each week, all the work I wasn't doing on Fridays was being pushed to late nights or weekends. The workload hadn't changed, just the time in which I did the work. But somehow it all seemed worth it.

"You bet!" I replied taking my computer out and plugging it in. "I don't know what's harder: when your kids are young or when they move off to college." Luckily, my daughters, Katheryn and Brittany, had decided to go to the same school. Katheryn was studying animation, and Brittany was working toward education and theater degrees with a minor in sign language. We often teased Brittany that she was going to teach deaf kids to act. Out of the ten kids, these were the mine out of the his, mine, and ours. They couldn't be more different if they tried. Katheryn was always the tough girl, protecting her older sister Brittany, while Brittany was often afraid to try new things. Once I took them both to my dad's place up in Michigan in the winter, their first real experience with snow. Brittany came in after only a few minutes, her thick round glasses fogged up as she complained, "This is the worst day of my life! I am allergic to snow." She held up her hand exposing the space between her glove and coat to show us how red it was.

As much as they were polar opposites, I was surprised that they'd decided to go to school in the same town—and at the same school. It was a relief to us as their parents—at least they would have one another nearby. They loved each other, and we could count on them to stick together as long as they weren't living together . . . and driving each other crazy.

"How's Lucille? You two are developing quite a friendship— Friday after Friday, just like clockwork. It's good to see you get out of the office and focus on something other than work."

"Oh, she's great! I love going to see her," I gushed. "No offense, but it's the best part of my week. It's incredible how much fun we have together in that little apartment of hers. It's like some sort of momentary retreat from life. It's hard to explain, but it's like the stress of life just melts away—even if it's only for an hour or so."

I may have sounded a bit overly effusive, but the fact of the matter was that Lucille was rapidly becoming my best friend. Sometimes our conversations were about history or current events, but they were never about deadlines or climbing the corporate ladder. They were about life, pure and simple. It's amazing to me that the human experience is the same regardless of what decade you grow up in. Everyone has had their fair share of disappointments and achievements. Things they wanted to do, but for some reason didn't, or things they did that they regretted. And I could ask her anything, anything at all. She even asked me a few things nobody ever seemed to care about before, like, "If you could do anything at all in life, what would it be?"

The following days seemed to fly by in a whirlwind of planes, trains, and automobiles. At least Provo, Utah, is known for its hospitality. If you have to move college kids around, Happy Valley, as that area is often referred to as, isn't a bad place to do it. The town is known for its simplicity because of the Mormon culture. If you live in BYU (shared with UVU) housing, which is pretty much every apartment complex in the area, you were held to strict codes of conduct, which included no alcohol, and no couples of the opposite sex fraternizing in the bedrooms. It just made it a safer experience for everyone. On the flip side, most of the students get married while they are still in school, so there is also plenty of family housing. It's not unusual to see a young married mom or dad attending class with a newborn nestled in a pouch around their neck. Being a convert to the Church of Jesus Christ of Latter-day Saints (LDS) faith, it was something I had to get used to, but it didn't take long. I loved and had longed for a community that emphasized family as a priority. It was good to see that some of my children had embraced it also.

The ten days flew by and I was back in Texas, back at my desk, ready to face the mounds of work that had piled up. I wanted to power through it so I could go see Lucille. The first email I opened that morning was very different from the typical messages that come from our website's Contact Us page:

"This is the family of Lucille Fleming. We are trying to get in contact with Judy Gaman. Please have her call us as soon as you get this."

These words sent chills down my spine, piercing my very being. My heart began to beat so fast and so hard that I could see the front of my blue blouse pulsating. My thoughts began to race: *What if she died? This isn't the way it's supposed to end. Why did I go out of town? I was only gone ten days. How could things change so quickly?* Somehow, even though I didn't know what had happened, I began to imagine the worst.

I felt heavy with grief. Reaching for the black-corded receiver on my desk, I pulled the phone base quickly toward me. It took several tries, as I dialed and misdialed again and again in my anguish. It was like that familiar nightmare, where you try to run but you keep falling down. Frustration, anger, and fear all washed over me in waves as I started to taste my salty tears. The thought of losing my new best friend was more than my mind and body could process. She had been the best part of my week for weeks on end.

"Hello, this is Judy Gaman," I said with a quivering voice when I finally dialed the right number. My hand gripped the phone tightly, and a cold sweat broke out, filling the space between my white-knuckle grip and the receiver. I started to ask the question that I feared the most. "Is Lucille okay? Please tell me she's not . . ." I paused, unable to bear the word, let alone the thought of Lucille dying.

To forestall the moment, I switched gears, explaining, "I was in Utah with my girls—so sorry that I didn't see this email sooner, but I called you just as soon as I read it."

"Lucille's okay now, but I must tell you that she gave us quite a scare," her daughter-in-law explained calmly, clearly sensing the panic in my voice.

A scare? I thought. *What exactly is that supposed to mean?* I hoped it wasn't too bad. Maybe they just couldn't get ahold of her and got worried. I tried to remedy my anxiety by conjuring up every simple explanation imaginable.

"She died while you were gone," she explained, sounding a little too nonchalant for something so serious.

Dying is much more than just a scare, I thought. *Why is she so calm?*

Before I had a chance to ask, she continued matter-of-factly, "But she's alive now."

Dead? Alive? What was going on? My fear was replaced with confusion, as my eyes widened, and my palms continued to sweat. I was pacing in a small area next to my desk, so small that I could only take one or two steps in each direction. *Does that mean she's still the same old Lucille, or is she simply alive in the most basic sense of the word?* I wondered as I continued to pace frantically.

It turned out that Lucille had been admitted to the hospital while I was away, as her blood pressure had become dangerously high. She'd just gotten the green light to go home when things took a turn for the worse.

"She was standing at the nurses' station, signing herself out, looking great, and talking to everyone," the daughter-in-law explained. "Suddenly, she said she needed to lie down. She meant business—she needed to lie down *right away*. A nurse offered her a wheelchair, but she insisted on lying flat immediately. Next thing we knew, she fell into the nurse's arms and died. The nurse lowered her to the floor and called a code."

I imagined her small, lifeless body lying on the floor, her face pale and lacking the usual radiance and infectious smile that made Lucille so special. Her colorful, flowing skirt would have been draped across the cold linoleum, her old Hollywood style in stark contrast to the institutional flooring. Her silk blouse would surely have been buttoned up to the top, with a flower in her lapel. She would have had a matching ribbon laced through her styled gray hair; her signature look. She would have smelled of Chanel No. 5, a scent that would have lingered long past the coroner's departure. Had she not survived, the world would have lost one of the greatest women who had ever lived, and I would have lost my friend, my best friend.

Even though I knew the story hadn't ended that way, this

alternate ending played out in my head like a movie that I couldn't turn off. It took everything I had to snap back into reality.

"I hate to say it, but I'm so glad she didn't have a DNR!" I blurted out, knowing that my comment was a little self-serving. DNR stands for Do Not Resuscitate, a common order among the elderly, especially for people over ninety. I had long been in favor of them and had a hard time understanding how family members could dispute these orders when parents or grandparents of a certain age had made that choice. Yet, there I was, defensive over a DNR order for someone over one hundred. It was proof that everything we believe is contingent upon our current emotional state.

"There *was* a DNR," she said, almost laughing it off. "Luckily, everything happened so fast that everyone just reacted without thinking about it, and before we knew it, she went from sudden death to sudden life." Her voice seemed to lift as if she were smiling.

Despite my feelings of hopefulness, I felt sick to my stomach when I pulled up to the rehabilitation facility. It was a long building, one floor that reminded me of all the nursing homes I had visited as a child. It was light brown brick with a long overhang at the entrance, so people could get in and out safely if it rained. I was worried that these recent events were a sign that the end was near for this extraordinary woman. Fortunately, this worry was relieved the moment I saw her.

"Hey there, Judy girl," she spouted when I entered the room. "It's about time you got here. Tell me all about your trip." She was in the bed with the head of the bed almost straight up and down. Her makeup was on and her hair perfectly perched on her head. She definitely didn't look like a dead lady.

I couldn't believe it. She had *died*, and all she wanted to hear about was *my* trip? "First, tell me about yours. That was quite a scare."

"Oh, that," she said as she shrugged it off with the flip of her wrist and a roll of her eyes. "It was nothing, and I'm going to be back on my feet in no time. Here, have a seat," she said, pointing to the nearby wheelchair. "Someone has to use that thing, and it's not going to be me!"

She and I were soon talking up a storm as though nothing had happened, placing bets on how soon she'd be able to leave.

After this experience, it was clear to me that every moment with Lucille was a gift. Time really was my enemy. From then on, every laugh, every smile, every tear, every story, everything was on borrowed time. In the nearly four years of Fridays that followed, our friendship grew deeper than I had ever imagined.

Chapter Seven

Almost Famous

I continued to visit Lucille every Friday. It was always just the two of us, nothing fancy. Then again, everything about Lucille was fancy. She made the simple act of spending time together feel like a special occasion. She would often set out her good china and offer me a cup of tea. Since I didn't drink black tea, she'd sent an aide out for some herbal tea to have on hand. The linen napkins were pressed, and the table set. She usually had a little something for show and tell too, like a photo of her as a young girl.

During our conversations, she always asked a lot of questions about my life. She would ask me about work and seemed to be fascinated with my various projects at the office. Of course, the office was the last topic I wanted to discuss during our precious time together. She always wanted to hear all about the show topics and guests. She was intrigued each time we had a celebrity on, but nothing impressed her as much as the fact that I was the author of a book. Not just any book: a book she was going to be a part of.

* * *

It was Tuesday and I had just returned from a meeting with a corporate client. "Some boxes came for you," Judy 2 said as she threw her arms in the air with excitement. It was as if she was sitting right there glued to the front desk, just to be sure and catch me as I came through the door. "They're pretty heavy, so I left them in the breakroom," she continued with a wink.

I ran down the hall and flung the breakroom door open. As soon as I saw the return address, I knew exactly what they were: copies of my book. Since we always published under our own imprint, we would order several cases from the printer in bulk. Excited, I unwrapped the top box as quickly as I could. I pulled a book out, held it up to examine the cover in person, stopping only to hug it to my chest. Then, as I always do, I smelled it. Nothing smells better than your own book, fresh off the presses.

Without even thinking, I ran out of the office, got in the car, and drove straight to Lucille's place. I didn't even stop to call ahead. I approached her door and went right in, not even bothering to knock. "Lucille, you have got to see this!" I exclaimed, barely able to contain myself.

She didn't have time to get up, just to swivel around in her chair. She was wearing a white blouse that buttoned halfway up her neck and a colorful pink wool shawl wound its way around her delicate shoulders. To top it all off, there was a white ribbon in her hair and a bright yellow flower on her lapel. "Oh, look at that!" she exclaimed, bouncing up and down with excitement. "Let me see my picture. Where am I?" Her fingers fumbled through the pages at lightning speed.

"Here, let me see it. I can find it quickly," I said, paging through the book, knowing exactly what page it was on. "Oh, here you are!"

"Grab a pen. I want to sign it," Lucille instructed. She reached over, took the book back from me, and signed her name over her picture. It was a simple black-and-white headshot, but she had the enthusiasm of someone with a full-page color portrait. Next to her little square photo was her top ten list of things to do to stay young. "Look at that," she said again. "Wait 'til I show all the girls!"

I left her with the book and kissed her on the cheek. "I have to get back to work. Sorry to run out, but I wanted you to be the first to see it." With that, I literally ran back down the hall, jumped in my car, and quickly drove back to work, hoping nobody noticed I had left.

Later that day, I was speaking with my PR agent and mentioned that I had been spending a lot of time with Lucille, and how excited Lucille was about the book.

"Do you think she would go on TV and do an interview with you?" she asked. "Good Morning Texas wants to interview you. I just got off the phone with them. I'm sure they'd love it if she came along."

"Oh my gosh, yes! I think that would be amazing," I said with excitement. It didn't occur to me until I hung up that perhaps I should have asked Lucille first.

After work, I drove back to Lucille's place. "Are you able to leave here?" I asked almost as soon as I walked in the door.

"Leave?" she asked, a bit puzzled by my question. She had just laid out her clothes for the next day. Everything, down to the ribbon and flower, was matched up and spread out neatly across the far corner of the bed.

"Yeah, like, can I take you places, or do you have to stay here?"

She laughed out loud. "Of course I can leave! Where are we going?"

"Good Morning Texas wants to interview me about the book, and my agent thought it would be great if you came along, too. That is, if you'd like to."

"What?" she screeched as she sprang from her recliner. I stared at her, mouth open. I didn't even know she could move that fast. "Yes, yes, I want to go! Of course I want to go." She turned and marched toward her closet. "What should I wear?"

Her closet was filled with colorful clothes in a myriad of fabrics, everything from fine silks to wool and polyester blends. She even had a long shelf full of different purses, one for every occasion. Tons of shoes, all heels, lined up like soldiers ready for the call to duty. The inside of her closet door served as a hanger for all her belts, some with shiny buckles and others that were all sequins. The only place I had ever seen more shoes was in my own closet. "Look at all your shoes!" I gasped. "We really are two of a kind. My husband calls me Imelda Marcos. She was the first lady of the Philippines, and she—"

"Had over a thousand pairs of shoes," Lucille said, finishing my sentence triumphantly.

"That's right. Looks like she might be a long-lost relative of ours."

Snickering, we began to shuffle through the clothes on the rack. There were so many to choose from and I could have stayed there all day, but soon I realized that it was getting late, and I needed to get home.

"The interview's next week; I'll call you with more details," I said as I hugged her goodbye.

Over the next few days, I started to feel nervous about taking Lucille to the interview. My mind raced with worries: *What if she gets tired? What if she needs to use the bathroom? What if she falls?* I had only ever seen Lucille in her own environment. Within the walls of Eden Estates, she was fine, but what if that changed when she was out in the real world?

Since I couldn't stop thinking about it, I called my longtime friend, Doreen. Doreen is from Australia. She has thick, jet-black hair and is exceptionally strong, both inside and out. We met when my son was only a year old. She started out as our nanny, then became my confidante, and over the years we developed a great friendship. I knew I could rely on her.

"I need your help," I explained after exchanging initial pleasantries. "You know that lady I told you about? Well, we're going to be on television, and I need a sidekick to go with us. Can you make it?"

"Darling, of course I'll be there," she said in that accent I admire so much. "Sounds like fun." I love the way she always dragged out the U in "fun," as though there were two of them.

A few days later, we pulled up at Eden to pick up Lucille. We didn't even get all the way under the *porte-cochere* before she burst out of the front doors, nearly running to the car. Doreen hopped out of the front seat to offer it to Lucille. "Your ride, my lady," she said, giving Lucille a slight bow.

Lucille's peach-colored skirt flowed as her heels moved quickly along the pavement. "Why, thank you," Lucille giggled as she climbed in. She had on a white satin blouse, turquoise heels, a turquoise wrap over one shoulder, and a matching flower on her lapel. She even had a matching turquoise belt to show off her tiny waist. A black ribbon in her blonde hair and a white ribbon around her neck completed her signature look. Lucille had three wigs: one blonde, one gray, and the other pure white. I was glad she wore the blonde one because it looked so good with her blue eyes.

"Lucille, this is Doreen, a good friend of mine."

"Oh, are you going to be on TV, too?" Lucille asked as her eyes widened with excitement.

"No, I'm your entourage."

Lucille's eyes grew wide and she posed, raising her shoulders and sinking her neck while pursing her lips gleefully.

"You see, Lucille, when you're famous, you have *people*," I added with a wink.

We all burst out laughing and started our trip to downtown Dallas.

Once we arrived, Doreen took Lucille by the arm and escorted her up the stairs to the station.

As soon as Lucille walked into the studio, it was obvious that she was the star of the day. We sat patiently in the green room where we could see all the action through the glass walls as well as on the screen in the corner. The production assistant came in and gave us all a rundown of what to expect. She spoke quickly, and I don't think any of us really paid much attention because of all the anticipation in the air.

Having done plenty of television interviews over the years, I knew this was going to be over in the blink of an eye. Everything was set up to be done in two shots: first, the host of the show and I would do a green smoothie demonstration while discussing the book and tips for staying young and healthy. Then we would walk over to where Lucille was seated and visit with her for a few minutes.

The crew was setting up the scene for Lucille's shot as we walked onto the set, and we noticed that there was some kind of fuss over the stool Lucille was supposed to sit on. A crewmember looked at her, looked back at the stool, and started to move it, saying, "I think we better get a different setup."

"What's wrong with that stool?" Lucille asked.

"Can you get up on it?" asked the gentleman, clearly assuming she couldn't.

"Of course I can! There's nothing wrong with me," she insisted rather indignantly. With that, she marched over to the stool and hopped right up on it.

"Wow!" He looked over at us, then back at the camera guy, with a surprised smile. "Okay, then. We're all set."

Lucille was a natural. She loved the limelight. All the way home, she recounted the experience over and over. "Next time, I want more time. I have so much to say," she said in a serious tone at one point.

"Look at that, Doreen, the talent is already making demands," I joked.

"You bet," Lucille said with a wink and a nod of agreement.

"So you would like a 'next time,' huh?" I asked.

"I could do this every week if you want," she said with a smile. Her tone turned to a little snobbish, "I'm practically a celebrity at Eden, you know. I told them all to tune in and watch." Then she sat up a little higher in her seat, her shoulders back with pride, and stared out the window as if she were very proud of her new accomplishment.

Not long after that, we were back on TV, this time recording an interview for The Broadcast, a show hosted by three women, one of whom was a local celebrity, Suzie Humphreys. I have always admired Suzie, an older woman who got her start in radio.

Lucille received her wish for a longer interview, all right; Suzie kept her on through two segments of the show. She asked her about everything, from beauty tips to nutrition. Lucille spent several minutes praising the importance of blueberries. At one point, Suzie asked Lucille if she ever thought she would live this long.

"No," said Lucille. "You see, about five months ago, I went into cardiac arrest and died. I died for three minutes." She went on to describe all the details of feeling faint and needing to lie down before she finally gave out. "They got the . . . the thing out," she said, searching for the word as she patted her chest.

"The defibrillator?" Suzie prompted.

"Yes."

"Tell them what you said when you came to," I piped up, but I couldn't wait for her and charged along with the story myself. "She said, 'That was a quick trip!'" The audience and television crew laughed.

Suzie leaned over and asked, with her heavy Texas accent, "Did you go anywhere? I mean, I've heard it said many times that when people have near-death experiences, they see a white light. Did you see such a thing?"

"No, nothing. I'm afraid I was . . . nowhere," she said as she held out her hands, palms up.

"Were you aware that you were 'nowhere'?" asked Suzie.

"No. No, I was not. I came to, and I said, 'You're hurting me'—you see, they were pounding me on the chest. This doctor said, 'Breathe, sweetie! Breathe,' and I said, 'I *am* breathing!'"

"And you said, 'Kiss me!'" Suzie added.

The crowd roared with laughter, and over the commotion, Lucille added, "Quick, before I die again!" The laughter continued for quite some time. Lucille was rocking back and forth as she laughed herself silly. On a forward swing, she said, "You gotta get it while you can!" Then she waved her hand in front of her face. "Did I just stay that?"

"Yes, you did," Suzie replied. "Right here on television for all these people to see." She waited a moment for the laughter to die down before continuing. "I think I know one reason why you've lived so long."

"Tell me."

"Because you love to laugh."

The interview continued for some time, and it was as if none of us wanted it to end, especially Lucille. When we started to leave, we were stopped at the door for lots of hugs from the staff and other guests. Lucille warmed so many hearts that day. She also found a new calling: she was now a longevity spokesperson.

On the way home, we were exhausted from all the excitement. Lucille was such a pro at these interviews. After we had been on Good Morning Texas, I realized she was strong enough to go out without any extra help, so this time it was just the two of us. My cheeks hurt from smiling and laughing so much during the interview. I felt like my face was frozen in that position. "I love you so much," I said as we drove, passing the tall buildings that stood as if at attention to the multi-lane freeway.

"I love you, too, Judy. I'm having so much fun. I can't tell you how much this has added to my life. Me, a little farm girl from Prince Edward Island, in a book and on TV. Now on TV twice." She sat back in the passenger side seat as if she were exhausted from all the fun she'd just had, but a wide smile was permanently affixed upon her face.

"You're going to need an agent," I giggled.

"Yes. Yes, I am," she replied, pretending to be snooty and star-like.

"I have one thing to tell you, and one thing to ask you."

"What is it?" she asked in anticipation, "Wait, tell me first, then ask me."

"Okay. First, I want to tell you that I'm going back to school to get my master's degree."

"Oh, that's wonderful!" she exclaimed as she patted my hand. "I'm so proud of you. You can do it, Judy. You're so smart," She said in a parental tone. Then, with a big smile she looked over at me and declared, "I'm going to your graduation. You know I'll be there for sure."

Lucille ultimately never made it to my graduation, due to the long flight and forecast of record heat and humidity. Regardless, those words meant so much to me. I was glad that she thought I was smart. I remember the first time Walter told me I was smart. My initial reaction was to say that I wasn't, but then I thought about it: *What if I am smart? What if I really could do anything I put my mind to?* When people you admire say you're smart, you actually start to believe it. Walter will never know just how much his confidence in me changed my life, and the same goes for Lucille.

"What are you getting it in?"

"Publishing. Since my undergrad is in health sciences, perhaps someday I'll get a PhD in medical writing. Then I can officially be the other Dr. Gaman. Dr. Judy for short."

"Yes! Dr. Judy," she repeated, trying out the title. She waited for a moment before changing the subject. "So, what did you want to ask me?"

"Feel free to say no, but I would like to write a book about you. Well, a book about you and me and our friendship." I looked at her quickly, wanting to capture her initial, immediate reaction.

"Yes! Oh my, a book about me?" Her eyes began to tear up. "Oh, what did I ever do to deserve this?" She smiled at me and then turned to look out the window as her tears started to fall. "She wants to write a book about me. Little ol' me. She thinks I'm important," she said quietly under her breath.

I was shocked that she should be so touched and surprised that I thought she was important, but I knew how she felt. After all, she made me feel important, too.

"Great! It's official," I said as soon as I could speak through the lump in my throat. "Well, we'll definitely need to spend more time together. Much longer visits."

Her head turned quickly back toward me. "Definitely!" she said, excited.

"How about every Friday I pick you up for a long lunch?

'Lunch with Lucille on Fridays.' I'm going to add that to my calendar."

"I'll pencil it in, too," she said in mock seriousness.

"Oh, you better pen it in." I replied emphatically with the emphasis on the word pen. "This is serious business, you know." I was so excited that she liked the idea, and couldn't wait to get started on our Friday outings.

She held my hand tightly as we drove the rest of the way home. She thought she was the lucky one, but I knew that it was actually me. I was so lucky to have her in my life. She was filling some void in my life in a way I couldn't really understand. I had never had a best friend or a mentor like her, someone who just wanted to spend time together.

When I got back to the office, I walked past the diplomas. They were all crooked, but I didn't have time to straighten them. I did, however, have time to look at the nurse and smile. "Having a good day, I hope?" By the way she stopped looking at her computer and sat straight up with a smile, I thought that she must have been surprised that I acknowledged her, instead of just rushing by.

I grabbed something from my office that was meant for Lucille and headed back over to her place. The smile from the morning never left my face. It seemed to be a permanent fixture.

When I got to Eden, the ladies Lucille had previously introduced me to were sitting and chatting among themselves in the dining room. They were dressed nicely, but nothing overly fancy, mostly slacks and blouses. Their table was near the entrance, right where they could see all the comings and goings of the other residents. Their plates were filled with fried chicken and mashed potatoes, and it looked as though they had just gotten started with their meal. I knew they were talking about me because they smiled, and then the one doing the talking raised her butter knife and pointed it right at me. I didn't have time to talk to them, though. I was on a mission.

I walked down the hall toward Lucille's room, feeling like I had never left. "Lucille," I said as I peeked into her apartment. She was napping on her perfectly made bed, still in her clothes from the morning. Her stocking feet were straight in line with her head, and her hands were folded over her abdomen.

She opened one eye but didn't get up. I walked over to the bed, touched her shoulder, and whispered, "When you get up, check your front door. I've left a little something for you."

I closed the door and started back toward the elevator. Just before I turned the corner, I looked back at the eight-inch gold star I had hung over her wreath. The center of the star read "Almost Famous." I smiled faintly and walked away. I could feel our journey was just getting started, filling me with anticipation, and I could hardly wait until the next Friday.

Chapter Eight

$\mathcal{C}\!\!\sim\!\!\sim\!\!\odot$

Miss America

When we pulled up to the Rosewood Crescent Hotel, Lucille's eyes widened as she leaned forward, forcing the seatbelt to tighten across her chest as she tried to take in the majestic hotel all at once. The hotel's neo-French classical design includes acres of Indiana limestone that was topped off with the world's largest cut slate roof on record. The ornamental cast aluminum metal on the balconies, trellises, and railings resembled sparkling jewelry set against the pale stone walls.

The restaurant we were going to have lunch at was seventeen stories up. Lucille was in awe of all the different types of marble that could be found in the lobby. From dark to light and back to dark again, these brown-toned slabs were layered around each other in a rectangular pattern as if one was unwrapping the next, a gift for the eyes. This was our third Friday lunch outing, and the one I was definitely looking most forward to.

"Are you a member here? Are we actually going to the Crescent Club?" she asked in surprise.

"No, I'm not a member. I just called up and said, 'Hello, this is Judy Gaman,' and *voilà*, they let me in!" Name-dropping my own name as though I'm someone very important is an ongoing joke with the people I'm closest to. The funny thing is that it actually seems to work. The trick is to simply ask for things, wholeheartedly expecting to receive them.

We rushed into the elevator with giggles and grins. As we rode it up, Lucille's smile grew larger with each passing floor. The doors opened on the top floor just as we managed to pull ourselves together. We didn't want to look too excited. We wanted to look like we do this every day. Ali, a dark-skinned handsome older gentleman with a full head of close-cropped salt and pepper hair, whose mission was to make our visit special, met us at the threshold. Little did he know just how special he would make it.

Wood paneling served as the backdrop to massive, old oil paintings. These paintings had borne witness to romantic dinners and big business deals over the decades. As Lucille looked around, I could tell that she was mesmerized by every color, texture, and scent. The hard wood on the walls, the detail in the inlaid wood floors and the white-coffered ceiling all showed such fine materials and craftsmanship. The scent of seasoned steak and grilled onions filled the air. I couldn't help but think that people must have felt this same way when they witnessed the grandeur of the Titanic, which sank the same year Lucille was born.

Ali walked confidently with a wide stride, looking as though he owned the place. He led us to the very window that makes the Crescent Club so famous. I had only ever admired it from the outside and seeing it from the inside was very different. Looking through that stately old crescent-shaped club window out onto the sleek Dallas skyline felt like looking through a portal from the past to the future.

A full-length white linen tablecloth flowed gracefully down to the old, hand-scraped wooden floor. Crystal goblets, the finest silverware, and ornate salt-and-pepper shakers looked like jewelry for the table. In the center, a simple silver vase contained two pink roses in perfect bloom, so beautiful, rich, and flawless in color that it was hard to believe they were real. As we sat like girls at a tea party, our silhouettes must have looked like something straight out of a storybook.

A lavish spread of the finest dining options, Texas style, filled the buffet. The perfectly seasoned sirloin was so tender you could cut it with a fork. Each bite seemed better than the last. It was a meal made for a queen, complete with a view of the land she ruled—if only for one day.

"There's something wonderful about getting all dressed up to sit down for a fine meal together," I said, thinking back to my childhood. "When I was little, around six years old, I loved tea parties. I would arrange my dolls and stuffed animals in a circle and serve them sugar water out of a miniature porcelain teapot with tiny hand-painted flowers. My mother gave it to me, and I treasured it. Each time I used it, I carefully washed it out afterward and placed it back in the original box." I sat there pondering how innocent life was back then.

"Oh, to be six again!" she said gaily. Preparing to share a good story, Lucille sat up straighter, and her face went from happy to serious. "On a cold winter day, when I was around that same age, my mom and I spent lots of time making fudge. That was always a real treat for us kids, since candies and sweets weren't easy to come by. This was a special day, though. I got all dressed up, and we went to see my older sister Pat at school for a Christmas party. I loved going to the school with Mom because I felt like such a big girl."

"I was like that, too, always wanting to be like my big sister," I added, and Lucille nodded in agreement.

"Well, after the party was over, Mom, Pat, and I went to visit our cousins and bring them some fudge. I was so excited to go visiting that I thought I would burst. I had that tingling feeling, as if I were going to bubble over with joy. When we were almost to the door of my cousin's house, my happy day turned to terror."

Lucille paused to sip her water. "You know I'm afraid of dogs, right?" I shook my head in the negative. "Well, this was the day that put that fear into me. Forever." Her eyes grew big with that word—forever.

"I had been dancing around as we walked, so I fell a few steps behind. Everyone else had already gone in by the time I reached the house. Before I could get to the door, a collie came out of nowhere. The next thing I knew, the dog was attached to my leg, severing a muscle and leaving ten different bite marks." I could see the goose bumps on her arms and knew this memory felt as real as when it had happened.

"That day, my life was saved by someone who was about to lose theirs. I always found that a little ironic. There was a woman on the second floor who was dying of consumption, you know consumption that was all too common in those days. Luckily, her bedroom window was open, and she used all the energy she had to get to that window and see what all my screaming was about. Once she saw the dog on top of my little body, she yelled through the house, 'Someone get that dog off her!'"

Lucille reached below the table and began to rub her leg. "Back then, you just did what you could. They poured iodine on my leg every day and put me on crutches for a few months. There was pain. Real pain. Now, even ninety-something years later, I'm still taken with indescribable fear whenever a dog approaches me. I just don't like 'em." Her face shook in disapproval.

As we finished our meal, my mind wandered back to my first brush with fear. I wasn't always a little girl in pretty dresses, toting a doll and planning tea parties. About half the time, I was digging up worms, climbing trees, and making mud pies. Maybe it has something to do with being a Gemini, but I have always had a pair of torn, worn-out jeans hanging next to a beautiful pink dress in my closet. I figure that the best way to avoid a stereotype is to always keep them guessing. I suspect that Lucille wasn't much different. After all, we were both June babies.

"I remember my first brush with fear," I said, thinking back to a summer day in Michigan when I was just old enough to start school.

"I loved to climb trees, and once, around that same magical age of six—that must be the theme of the day: six." We shared a smile of agreement before I continued. "I climbed to the top of a huge cherry tree in our front yard. As I climbed up, I could feel the bark breaking off under my fingers and heard it crumbling beneath my worn-out tennis shoes. I felt so proud climbing that tree, knowing I was going higher than I ever had.

"I climbed, hoping to pass that infamous branch that my older sister consistently reached with absolutely no fear, making me green with envy every single time." Lucille also had an older sister, so she understood the innate drive for sibling one-upmanship. "I was determined and just kept going, branch after branch, until I almost reached the top. The smaller branches had trouble holding my weight without bending. Then it happened: I looked down, and to my surprise, I saw that I had finally mastered the cherry tree and was far above my sister's record!"

Lucille reached over and gave me a high five.

"Instead of being happy, though, I felt fear, real fear. My entire body felt hot, and I started to sweat. I was filled with emotions I had never felt before. I was terrified that I would fall. I had no idea how to get down. My hands were dripping with sweat, and they started slipping on the crumbling bark. Then, just like the lady in your story, a hero came to rescue me. My older sister, the one I was hoping to impress, came running when she heard me crying for help.

"She tried to talk me down, but nothing she said could make me unravel my body, which was now snaked around the top of that tree, hanging on for dear life. She even climbed to the top herself, hoping to carry me down, but I clung to the branches too tightly. Besides, she was only ten and was too small to carry me. I knew it was hopeless."

Lucille shook her head in disbelief, her eyes never leaving mine as she took another bite of her steak and quickly swallowed. "What did you do? How did you get down?"

"Jennifer ran to the neighbor's house and brought back their teenage son, Junior, a tall, strong boy in high school. Junior climbed to the top of that tree like it was nothing. He grabbed me with one arm and climbed back down with the other." I said, still feeling that sense of relief as though it had happened just yesterday. "He and Jennifer saved my life that day, but something in me changed forever. I had tasted fear and the fragility of my own life for the first time. The innocence of being six was gone, replaced with the reality that things can change in an instant."

"Is Miss America finished with her plate?" Ali asked loudly as he bent over and kissed Lucille's hand. She blushed and replied with a smile that extended from ear to ear, "Yes, and it was terrific!"

Ali leaned in and whispered to us, his cologne with its hints of sandalwood wafting over us pleasantly, "See that bus boy over there? He is staring at you because I told him you're a former Miss America and that you have more money than he could imagine." Lucille lifted her arm and gave short, dark, and handsome Ali a high five. It was definitely high-five day. Ali winked as he started to walk away with her plate.

"Judy is writing a book about me," she said, completely ignoring the fact that Ali had a job to do. "She and I believe everyone has a story. Sit down, Ali," she said sternly, as if she were his mother. "Sit down and tell us your story," she said patting the table and smiling. She completely disregarded the reality that Ali could get fired for sitting down and fraternizing with the members of the club. *Besides,* I thought, *we aren't really members here anyway.*

Nonetheless, Ali couldn't resist her charming, motherly request, and sat down just as he was asked to. "I was born in Persia and came to the United States forty-five years ago as a student," he said leaning over, placing his arms on the table and looking directly into our eyes, making it obvious that this story was just for us and not the whole restaurant. "A friend of mine had come to Texas and said I should go, too. I had never even heard of Texas or seen it on a map. Being young and naive, I found a sponsor and boarded a twenty-hour flight to the great unknown. To make matters worse, I didn't know a bit of English."

Lucille and I found that last part hard to believe; Ali's English was so perfect, we couldn't imagine him speaking any other language.

His smile faded as he continued. "I never took into account how hard it would be to come to a foreign land without a network of friends or relatives. In addition, there was the culture shock that only Texas forty-five years ago could deliver." Pausing, he winked and added, "We don't have cowboys in Iran."

"Well, you're still here," Lucille said matter-of-factly. "It couldn't have been that bad."

Ali nodded and smiled. He snapped out of his storytelling mode as if he suddenly remembered he was at work. He looked around briefly, got up, and went back to work. It was as though he left us hanging. I was sure there was more to his story. After all, what made him stay? How did he get his job?

Lucille turned to me as if to brag. "I wasn't so fortunate when I came to the U.S. in 1929. Back in those days, it was a little tougher." I didn't have the heart to tell her that it was still pretty hard; I just let her talk. "Lucky for me, I had an uncle in the States willing to put up the five-hundred dollars. It was called a 'nuisance fee.' If you stayed in the country for a couple years and didn't cause any trouble, the person got their money back. If you weren't a good citizen, though, you had to go back to wherever you came from, and they lost their money. Back then, five-hundred dollars was a lot of money to lose, so I made sure to finish nursing school and behave myself, so my uncle would get it back. Nobody wants to be deported and disowned at the same time."

We continued making small talk, looking out over the skyline, and finishing up with our taste testing of various desserts. When there is a dessert menu, you can't eat just one. Lemon tartlets, chocolate mousse, and fresh berries with heavy whipping cream and chocolate shavings—how could one possibly choose?

I could always tell when Lucille's mind went back to her childhood: her face would start to change a bit, and her eyebrows would dance around her forehead, keeping perfect time with the beat of her thoughts. "As I got older, about eight to twelve years old, I had a lot more chores to do," she began. "On top of my homework, I was in charge of all the lamps in the house. We didn't have electricity back then, so one of my jobs was to clean the kerosene lamps. They would get all black from the flames, so that only a little light could shine through. Every night, I had to wipe each lamp down with newspaper to remove the residue. Then I had to trim the wicks. It was a real dirty job," she said, shaking her head and looking down at her hands. "These hands would be filthy."

I looked at her hands now, clean and perched upon a white linen napkin as she dined in style.

A twinkle came into her eye. "It wasn't all work, though. We also made time to play and entertain. One night, there was a knock on the door, and a woman and her children were standing there in the cold Canadian winter air. My dad, being the gentleman he was, invited them right in with his big, welcoming smile. I don't even know who they were or why they were there.

"Dad had a knack for music, and as they sat down, he pulled himself up to our pump organ. That organ was beautiful, the nicest thing we owned. It had been handed down through my mother's family, and we cherished it. It had a mirror, beveled glass, and a place on each side for a lamp. I had to clean those lamps, too. The seat was red and fit for a king. And my dad sat at it just like royalty. He started to play and sing. I remember it like it was yesterday."

With that, Lucille started to sing right there in the club:

"You can talk about your learned men, your wit and wisdom rare,
Your poets and your painters, they get praises everywhere.
They're good enough to make a show, but will you tell me how
The world would ever do without the man behind the plow."

My jaw dropped in amazement, and I applauded and laughed when she finished. It was as if she had taken me back into the past, right into the heart of that cold Canadian night. I imagined Lucille and her family all huddled in that small room, the music filling their heads like a carnival for the senses. It was probably cold enough to still see their breath at times, but I doubt they would have cared—the love in that room was surely enough to warm an entire city block.

Ali made his way back over with a smile on his face. I think he enjoyed the song, too. We could tell that he had more to say by the way he walked with such purpose toward our table. We were glad he was coming back to finish his story, because he'd left us hanging.

He sat down as if his body was melting back into the chair. His face began to change back into storytelling mode. He began to speak earnestly, as if it were very important for him to finish his story. "I told my friend that I wanted to go back to Persia. But he reminded me that a ticket out of the U.S. does not guarantee a ticket back in if you change your mind. It was a statement that weighed heavy on my heart and mind. I was tortured with indecision, so I decided to ask God what I should do. My choice either way would affect my future and the future of unborn children.

"I waited and waited, but God still didn't answer me." Ali's face reflected the emotional turmoil he must have experienced. "Then one day, I was very depressed. It was the kind of depression where you feel almost numb. I was sitting on a bench at the street corner looking pretty bad, as if the life had drained out of my body." We all shared a knowing look, then Lucille motioned for him to continue.

"I was sitting there feeling lost and confused, when a cowboy walked up. He was a real Marlboro man, like the one I'd seen on the billboards. He placed his hand on my shoulder and said with a real Texan accent, 'Buddy, I don't know what type of problem you have, but you need to hang in there.'" Ali's eye released a single tear that traced the wrinkles in his cheek. "Jesus came to me as a cowboy. I tell you, when God wants to send you a message, He can do it with all types of messengers. It doesn't matter if you are Catholic, Baptist, Methodist, or any other religion. God is everywhere, and everywhere is God. Sometimes we just forget to look for Him."

I suddenly realized how deep this discussion had gotten and how right Ali was. As he continued, his face lit up, "I stayed in Texas, and now I have a beautiful wife and daughter. My daughter works in law. Life is better than I had ever dreamed it would be. I have been at the Crescent for thirty years, and I have met a lot of people. And today . . . today I met Miss America." He reached down and kissed Lucille's hand once more. The tears were gone, and a genuine smile wrapped around his face.

"Let's take some pictures of you girls," Ali said, noticing my camera. We took picture after picture, posing in front of the oils, in the stately chairs, the two of us together, Lucille and Ali together.

As Lucille and I walked out to the elevator, I looked back one last time at the table centered in the crescent window. It had already been bussed and draped with clean linen, as though we had never been there. It had happened so fast, it felt like the whole luncheon had been a dream. The only thing that convinced me that it had actually happened was seeing those two perfect pink roses sitting in the center of the table, backlit from the sun, a symbol of our friendship, so perfect that it was hard to believe it was real.

Chapter Nine

❦

Starry Night

Many Fridays came and went as we made memories, shared a laugh or two, and reminisced about our pasts. But, it was during the next outing that we shared our deepest, darkest moments, the moments that we had never shared with any friend before.

Then, next Friday, I pulled up at six o'clock sharp and immediately spotted Lucille peeking through the panes of the front door, looking for me. I parked, ran around the car, and opened the door for her. "Looks like they let you leave at night, too," I said with a smile.

"And I don't even have a curfew," she said as if she were bragging.

The restaurant was just a few minutes down the freeway from her place. We pulled up to the lighted building, and she looked at the fountain out front, all aglow. "This looks pretty fancy."

"The food is terrific. Prepare to eat way more than you should," I cautioned her.

The restaurant was filled with waiters in old-fashioned Brazilian clothing carrying skewers of meat from table to table. Lucille looked over at the massive salad bar that sat in the middle of the room and asked, "We can have anything we want? Anything?"

"Anything. I'll fix you a plate from the salad bar, and you can turn your little card to green. That's how they know to offer you the meats. When you're full, you turn it to red."

"Well, they should get this system at Eden," she said, turning her card to green. Within seconds, she was bombarded.

"Chicken?"

"Sure."

"Lamb?"

"Okay."

"Tenderloin?"

"You guys need to slow down. I can't possibly eat that fast," she said to the last waiter, as if to scold him.

"Lucille, turn it to red," I reminded her, placing her salad on the table.

"Oops. I forgot," she said, smiling with her cheeks stuffed with food. It was the first and only time I witnessed her talking with food in her mouth.

After we had exhausted the main course, a man wheeled a cart over that was filled with desserts. "Which one would you like?" he asked.

She looked the cart over carefully, asking lots of questions, like this was the hardest decision she had had to make in quite a while. "That one. Carrot cake."

As she put her fork in the cake, she looked at me almost dismissively and said, "You know, my dad had a sweet tooth. If my mom made a pie, she would have to give him a slice and hide the rest. Otherwise, he would eat the whole thing." I guess that was her way of saying she was planning on finishing it. Obviously, a genetic defect and not gluttony.

She was right, because she finished every meal off with

something sweet. Sometimes she would even wrap up a cookie or two, carefully placing them in her purse for later.

She finished her cake, sat back, and somberly announced, "My mom had a stroke when she was eighty."

"Really?" I replied, knowing this may be a hard story for her to share.

"Yes, and it was bad. It put her in a coma. She lay in bed for two days, and my father couldn't do a thing about it." Her eyes began to blur as if she were fighting a tear. She paused for just a moment and then continued. "There was a huge snow storm, and the nearest hospital was too far away."

"I bet he felt helpless." I couldn't even imagine being in his place. It wasn't as if he could pick up a phone and dial 911, there was nobody to turn to. "What did he do?"

"Eventually, our neighbors realized that they hadn't seen any activity over our way from their house. Even when it snows, you see people moving around. One of them came over once the snow had stopped. Dad explained what was going on, and before he knew it, the neighbors had gotten a school bus and made it into a makeshift ambulance."

"They got her to the hospital? Did she live?" I knew that was a loaded question, but I had to know. I sat there imagining the neighbors all working together in the snow.

"It took about three hours, but they got her there. As mom tells the story, she actually heard them tell my father that she would never walk or talk again." Lucille's eyebrows went up and her lips pursed a bit before she added, "That only made her more determined. Within two and a half months, she was both walking and talking."

I felt proud of her mom. I didn't even know her, but I realized that Lucille must have gotten her strong and determined spirit from her mother. "Did you go see her?"

A frown of shame clouded her face, something that I wasn't used to seeing. She looked down at her coffee cup. "No. No, I did not. She had two daughters that were nurses, and neither of us went to help."

I was almost afraid to ask the question, but I really needed to know why. "I'm not judging you, but I'm curious. Why?"

"I didn't go because I couldn't." She paused quietly as if she were reflecting upon that moment in time. "I was suffering from postpartum depression and had been for a while. Of course, they didn't know what that was at the time. It didn't even have a name back then. It was the darkest period of my life." Her eyes had filled with tears, but none fell out, not yet at least. I didn't want to see anyone. I even made my kids lie and tell people I wasn't home. I've always felt bad about that. My poor boys suffered just as much as I did." A single tear fell from the corner of her right eye.

"How did you snap out of it?" I guess snap out of it sounded a bit raw and uncaring, not at all my intension.

Her energy went up just a bit as she started her story. "Well, I finally decided to go to Prince Edward Island to see my parents. The boys were so thrilled. We packed our bags and headed to the airport." Then, as fast as her energy had gone up, it came back down, "We got all the way to the terminal, and then I backed out. I just couldn't do it."

"They must have been devastated," I said, leaning in and holding my cup of warm green tea tight with both hands. I imagined being their age and going through the motions of vacation on—nope—vacation off.

"They were. My husband, Joe, just picked up my bags, and we went home. The boys must have come into my room every hour, on the hour, that night, asking if I was better yet. The next day, we went back to the airport."

I found myself holding my breath and silently hoping she had gotten on the plane, not just for the boy's sake, but for her sake, too. "Did you get on the plane this time? Please tell me you did."

"I did. I got on that plane." She said, hitting the edge of the table with the tips of her fingers. We shared a brief smile. "I was so depressed that I don't remember much of the trip, though." She shrugged her shoulders a bit dismissively. "When we got back home, the priest came by to see me. I think Joe must have told him I wasn't doing very well."

"Did he give you a blessing?" I asked.

"No. He took one look at me and told me to," her words slowed down a bit for emphasis, "get a job."

"Get a job? Seriously?" I giggled.

"Seriously. And he was right." She stated emphatically. I went back to nursing, and day by day, I seemed to get better. I was cured." Then the smile that I loved so much came back across her face. I knew that she must not have shared that story too many times before, if ever, by the relief on her face. It was as if she could put it behind her now.

I thought about my own mom. She had gone to nursing school while she was pregnant with me, and I couldn't remember a time when she wasn't working. It's such a part of her identity that if asked, "what's your mom like?" I would have to answer that she was nurse before saying anything else.

Even when we lived in Michigan, she taught nursing students at night. One time, she let me go to class with her and bring my doll. She was teaching the students how to put a cast on a broken arm that night, and she let me cast my doll's arm. I loved that night. It was good to spend time with her and see her in action. I think Mom liked having me come along that night too, because she brought it up for years to come.

After this conversation with Lucille, I had a revelation.

Maybe being a wife and mother hadn't been my mom's calling after all. I had always dreamed about her being a stay-at-home mom, imagining her sewing and cooking, and picturing her singing around the house. That was just my fantasy, though, not hers. What if she had been like Lucille? What if she had been miserable staying home? Perhaps she needed to work. Perhaps work was her therapy as well.

After some silence at our table, I looked at Lucille and shared something that only a very few people know about me. "I feel your pain when you talk about being so depressed. I went through that, too. Mine wasn't postpartum, but it was bad. Everything seemed to be falling apart all at once. My first marriage was in shambles, and I'd had a huge fight with my sister. Not a little one—the kind that takes years to recover from." I stopped abruptly, suddenly realizing I had opened Pandora's Box. Did I really want to share this? Now? Right here in the restaurant?

"Did you hide out in your room, too?" Lucille asked with enthusiasm as if she was hoping I would say yes.

"I wish I could have. I had a job, so I had to keep plugging along. Things were really dark, especially inside my head, so I decided to see a psychologist for help." I took a deep breath as I realized there was no turning back now, I was definitely going to tell this story.

"Did it work? How long did you have to go?" She asked leaning in and waiting for my answer.

"Oh, I only went once," I said rolling my eyes a bit. "I asked for an emergency appointment, and when I got there, I was in tears. I kept blubbering and trying to tell him about all the things that were making me crazy. I *felt* crazy, you know. Never felt that way before or since, but it was bad."

"He helped you in one visit?" she asked, sounding impressed.

I had to laugh a little at that question. "No, he didn't actually help me at all. I remember him being really rude, but that could've just been me hating everyone at that moment. I stormed out. He tried to stop me, asking if I intended to harm myself."

"What did you say?" Her eyes grew wider.

"I didn't know how to answer that question. I was too freaked out." I took my hands off my tea cup and said matter-of-factly, "I knew I didn't want to be locked up, so I looked at him and said NO."

"Then what did you do?" She asked with both hands out to the side, palms up.

"I got in my car and drove." I looked away for a moment to hold the emotions back. I could feel the memory coming back as my body grew warmer. "I don't even know how I got there, but I made it to our church. I was Episcopalian back then. The main cathedral was locked, so I went into a small chapel on the side, called St. Mary's Chapel."

"Oh, we have those in the Catholic Church, too," she said, reaching out to touch my arm.

My mind drifted back to that chapel. It was small, with cold, hard surfaces. The dark tile floor, the brick wall behind the altar, and the hardwood pews offered little comfort that day. I stared at the little boxes on the wall, boxes that contained the ashes of those who had left this earth. I envied them. I wanted to disappear into that wall, too. The emptiness of the room gave me solace. The last thing I wanted was to see another human being or for them to see me.

"I sat there and cried and cried. I don't even know how long I sat there; it seemed like hours. I prayed that I would get better. I prayed for peace. I prayed until I didn't have any tears or snot left. Then I got in my car and drove home."

"Did you feel better? I bet that really helped."

"It did, but what happened next was nothing short of a

miracle. I had a sign from the other side, something that helped heal me almost instantly."

"What was it? Did God talk to you?"

"Not exactly, but I got the message. My great-grandpa was Catholic, like you. When he died, my mom gave me a wooden circle with a picture of Christ's face embossed in metal in the middle, and it hung on my wall for years. I was the only one home, so I yelled out to God, 'Are you listening?' Just then, that plaque of Jesus came flying off the wall and landed on my tile entryway floor. The wood separated from the metal."

"What did you do? Were you afraid?" From her expression and wide eyes, I could tell she would have been. Then she scooted to the edge of her chair.

"Not really." I said calmly as I reflected back on that moment. "It was strange." I remembered that moment so clearly that I paused to watch it play out again in my head. "I got down on my hands and knees and searched for the three tiny nails that held the pieces together. When I found them, I hammered them back in, one by one. When it was all done, it was like a switch was flipped inside me. I knew, really knew, that everything was going to work out."

"Did it?"

"It took time, but yes, it did. You know, I don't tell that story to many people," I said, looking down at the tablecloth for a moment, my eyes filling with tears. Who was I kidding, I had never told this story in its entirety to anyone. It was always too painful to recount.

"I'm glad you told it to me. You're my best friend, Judy. You can tell me anything, anything at all." She said with a smile as she shook my forearm with her strong, clenching hand.

I knew that. I knew she could tell me anything, too. It was the strangest feeling in the world.

We stayed at the restaurant so long that it was completely dark outside when we left, and the expansive Texas sky was filled with stars. As we drove out of the parking lot, Lucille looked back at the glowing fountain one last time. "I wish they could see that," she said quietly. "I sure miss my parents." She said sadly, "It's funny how so much time's gone by."

The evening was emotionally draining for both of us and we were tired, but it was a good kind of tired. We didn't say much the rest of the ride. I walked her to the door, and she pointed at the keypad that was to the right of the door. "I have a code to get in. And unlike most people around here, I can actually remember it," she said proudly. "Good night, Judy." She hugged me and kissed my cheek.

"Good night, Lucille."

As I drove home, I looked up at the stars again. I wondered if our ancestors are up there cheering for us. I wondered if they know the trials we face. I like to believe they do. I also like to believe that every once in a while, they also give us a push in the right direction.

Chapter Ten

Wiggin'

One Wednesday afternoon, I stopped by Lucille's apartment just to check on her and see if she needed anything. It hadn't even been a week since our last meeting, but I already missed her smiling face so much. It was a beautiful day outside and the sun was shining, the air crisp.

I knocked on her door and opened it at the same time. "It's just me," I said.

"Oh good! Glad you stopped in," she said, seeming less surprised than I thought she would be. She finished brushing one of her wigs and set it back on the Styrofoam head. She was wearing a yellow top and a multi-colored flowing skirt. Her bangle bracelets sounded like chimes as she straightened the wig on its stand. "I *really* need a new wig," she blurted out excitedly.

Great, I thought with a smile. *That means she plans on being around for a while. Those things are expensive.* "I'll take you," I offered with a smile. Trying on many different hairstyles without having to commit to a cut or dye job sounded fun.

"We're going wiggin'!" she sang, doing a little dance of excitement around her living room. We both instantly caught a case of the giggles, sounding like two schoolgirls squealing about a boy. *I must be getting old*, I thought, *because we're just going a couple miles down the road to a store that sells fake hair.*

"You know, I went to that wig shop years ago to look around," I confessed. "I really wanted to try one on, but I was intimidated because I didn't know the first thing about wig etiquette. I was reaching for a long blonde wig, and a stern saleslady appeared and informed me that she would only assist me if I was a serious buyer."

"That's rude. You should have told her that you were serious."

"This may sound bad, but I actually considered making up some story about having cancer, but I refrained. I remembered something that my mother once told me: 'Never tell a lie because it just might come true.'"

"So, did you try one on?"

"Nope. As soon as the saleslady looked away, I slipped out the door. I was too embarrassed." Then I looked at Lucille and winked. We continued our small talk about clothes, shoes, and the ladies down the hall. Before I knew it, an hour had flown by. "See You Friday," I said giving her a hug before heading out the door. I needed to get home to start dinner and her dining room was going to close soon.

Friday finally rolled around, and we planned to go to the wig shop first and then have lunch. As we drove there, I thought about how, this time, I was going wiggin' with an expert. Suddenly, it hit me: I was about to see Lucille without her wig on. This was very rare, as few people ever saw her without that wig. In one of our previous visits, she had told me that she kept it on her bedside table at night while she slept, in case of an emergency: "If I need an ambulance, it's right there. A girl shouldn't be caught dead without her hair!"

I couldn't help but wonder how much hair she had left on her aging head. Was it snow white? Was she completely bald? I hadn't thought about what was under her wig until that moment. What a gift this was going to be, a gift of friendship and trust, where all guards were down and everything was real. I don't think I'd ever had a friendship like that before. In fact, I don't think many people ever will. It's almost as if the whole world is afraid of showing who they really are. We spend most of our time hiding behind the mask of who we think other people want us to be instead of creating real, intimate connections.

I glanced over at her sage-colored iridescent skirt and pink top. She had a gorgeous black flower in her lapel, a matching black ribbon around her neck, and another in her hair. Her hands were folded together, and she bounced up and down in her seat, clapping in excitement. I smiled at her with both my head and my heart.

It was just a short drive to the store, but we managed to have a deep discussion about current world affairs, including the issues with Russia and Syria. This was before Russia and Syria were daily topics on the news. There is nothing quite like hearing the opinion of someone who has lived through more wars than anyone else around. When Lucille was born, Russia was Russia, but it was a monarchy; then it became the communist Soviet Union; and then it went back to being Russia again, but as a democracy. She also knew Germany before, during, and after Hitler.

Toward the end of our conversation, she said, "I have learned to just leave it all up to God. A few months ago, we had a guest speaker at church. He showed up in sandals," she added with a look of disapproval.

I mentally giggled to myself. *Only a staunch Catholic would be scandalized by a man's choice of footwear. Many other churches are going with a come-as-you are policy. Besides, didn't Jesus wear sandals?*

Lucille continued: "The man told us that we should think about all the things that are troubling us, write them down on a piece of paper, and bring them up to the altar. So, I thought about all the things that had me worried, and I wrote them down. As I walked up to the altar, I said, 'God, I'm too old to be troubled with all this, so you're going to have to take over.'" She shrugged her shoulders and smiled. "I felt better almost instantly."

Perhaps we should put a transcript of the nightly news on the altar. I bet that would solve most of the world's stress issues, I thought.

Aloud, I said, "I heard something this week that really resonated with me." She was the one that had brought up God, so I figured it was safe to share. "It happened during World War II. A mother was devastated to send her son off to war. Like most women, she filled her time with working in the factories supporting the war effort. Her job was to make life vests for the sailors. With each vest she sewed, she prayed that it would protect whichever soldier it found and keep him from harm's way. She also prayed continuously for her son and kept the faith that God would bring him back to her alive and in one piece."

"Prayers are good, but that poor mother." She said, looking down and shaking her head.

"Her son was in the Navy, and his ship was eventually sent into battle. The ship sank, and almost all the sailors drowned. It seemed certain that her prayers wouldn't be answered."

"Oh no," Lucille said, raising her hand to cover her mouth.

"They found her son, though, the sole survivor of the wreckage. He was wearing a life vest that was traced directly back to her factory and her very hands."

Lucille and I shared a look—the look that moms give each other. It was obvious that we both felt overwhelming compassion for both the son and the mom. Our eyes were filled with tears, and I had a lump in my throat that wasn't just due to the story.

You know you have a best friend when you can discuss politics and religion in the same car ride and still like each other at the end of it.

As we walked into the wig shop, I spotted two wigs, one pink and one purple, which were proudly displayed up front, just in time for Halloween. "That's it," I teased. "Just think of what the girls back at Eden would say! I call pink."

This time, the shopkeeper didn't ask if we were serious buyers. Instead, she was smiling and eager to help from the moment we walked in. We pranced around the shop, comparing wig after wig. Picking out wigs made me feel like a kid in a candy shop. There was a menagerie of styles, colors, and lengths to choose from. The saleslady even took us back to a special room with salon chairs, large mirrors, and plenty of lighting. I felt like a star that was about to go on stage for her big debut.

"She's over one hundred, you know," I informed the saleslady, pointing to Lucille.

With her heavy Asian accent, she responded, "No . . . that cannot be true," making a face of disbelief.

Lucille sat up straight in the chair, shoulders back as if she were a rooster ready to crow. "That's right. I'm going to be 102 soon!"

Soon? I guess eight months is soon enough when you're 101. Then, suddenly, it hit me: this was it, the moment of truth. Lucille was about to take her hair off. I was nervous; I wasn't sure if she wanted me to look or turn away. Curiosity got the best of me though, and I had to look.

She pulled her wig off and announced, "Look at this!" We both let out a big belly laugh as a long, unruly stream of white hair fell across her head like a bad toupee. The rest of her scalp didn't have much hair, but what she did have was white and beautiful. Without her wig, she looked quite different. For the first time, I saw the real Lucille, a frail-looking woman who appeared to be her actual age. It was a little frightening, not because she looked old, but because I was reminded of the reality that she was living on borrowed time. I was struck less by her appearance and more by her trust in me. I got to see what she saw when she looked in the mirror at night, what she saw behind closed doors, and in that moment, I knew we were now best friends at an even deeper level.

She lifted up that string of unruly hair, as if to measure its length. Then she looked in the mirror and back at me, "Looks like it's time for a haircut," she blurted through her giggles.

I started to giggle too and before we knew it, we were both laughing, acting like two teenagers as we tried on red, brown, silver, and blonde wigs of all shapes and sizes. Each time we put on a new wig, we were completely transformed. We would look in the mirror, laughing, look at each other, and then move on to the next wig. It was as if our souls left our bodies for a while and danced around in the pure bliss of true, raw friendship.

"I love a good prank," she said with a devilish smile.

"Me too! What do you have in mind?"

"Why don't you buy a bunch of different wigs? Then every time you come over, we could tell all the Eden girls that you're one of Judy's sisters!"

We erupted into another fit of giggles.

Eventually, after trying on numerous styles and colors, Lucille decided to purchase a new wig in the same style as she had before, but in a different color.

"Seriously?" I asked, surprised that we had spent so much time just for her to play it safe.

"Look, when you reach my age, you know what you want. I just had to make sure, that's all."

There was a little poetic justice in that trip. In the end, I bought two wigs, shampoo, a wire wig stand, and a little net to hold my natural hair in. I was officially a "serious buyer."

I left that wig shop changed, not because of the new hair I was proudly displaying atop my head, but because of the truths I learned that day. Truths about trust, about friendship, and about what constituted real beauty.

As I dropped Lucille back off at her place I looked at her outfit and the perfectly placed wig atop her head, complete with her signature ribbon. I thought, *Lucille is just as beautiful without her hair as she was with it.* It never really was about her stylish clothes, perfect hair, and matching accessories; it was about the spirit deep within her. It glowed brighter than anything on the outside. I blew her a kiss goodbye as I drove away. Smiling to myself, I drove home almost as if on autopilot as I reminisced about the events of the day.

Chapter Eleven

⌒∽⌒

No Place Like Home

Several weeks had passed, and fall was encroaching on winter, the weather getting cooler, the crisp air a welcome change after the long, hot Texas summer. I stopped in to pick up Lucille for our usual Friday outing. "How about the Four Seasons for lunch?" I asked nonchalantly as Lucille climbed into the car. The sun was shining, the birds were chirping, and another beautiful day was unfolding.

"Oh, the Four Seasons in Las Colinas? Yes, I think that will do," she said a little sarcastically as she smirked and winked.

Walter's other office is located directly across the street from the hotel, so he and I frequented the restaurant inside quite often. Las Colinas is just a fancy name for Irving, a city that Lucille and her husband Joe lived in from 1954 until 1961. Somewhere in the town's history, those north of the freeway wanted to be referred to as Las Colinas. I suppose it was to increase their property values and differentiate themselves from the older, run-down part of town.

"So much has changed about Irving since we lived here," she said, looking around as I exited the freeway and turned right on

MacArthur. "MacArthur Avenue used to be lined with trees and land, but now it's fast food restaurants, apartments, and gas stations." She said as she shook her head in disbelief. "Joe and I loved living here."

"I wish I could have known this town back then," I said. "You know, when Walter said he wanted to build a medical complex over here, the hospital laughed at him and said nothing would ever be built on the north side of Highway 114. Boy, were they wrong."

"Walter has vision," Lucille observed. "That's why he's been so successful. You're lucky, you know." She was right: Walter was definitely a visionary. Over the years, many colleagues have benefited from his foresight.

Soon the hotel, with sprawling golf course, was in sight. As we pulled onto the property, I waved at the security guard, who motioned us through with a smile.

"Look at that, he didn't even stop you." Lucille continued, "Judy Gaman, here." She made a waving motion, pretending to be a celebrity.

I had to chuckle at how impressed she was. "Lucille, I hate to break it to you, but they wave everyone through."

The driveway was lined with luscious plants and a mixture of flowers. The pansies were yellow, purple, blue, and just about any color you can imagine and the red roses were in full bloom. The car windows were up, but it was as if we could smell them anyway. "Can you imagine the watering bill for all this?"

"Hello, Mrs. Gaman. Good to see you again. Will you be dining with us for lunch?" asked the bellman as I exited the car.

Lucille leaned over and whispered, "I told you they knew it was you."

Another bellman opened Lucille's door and took her hand as if she were a queen. "Welcome, pretty lady. Glad you are joining us today."

Lucille smiled, taking it all in as we entered through the expansive wooden doors that opened to the high-ceilinged foyer. Tall, clear, glass vases filled the stately table in the center of the room. Each vase was filled with white orchids, simple and elegant.

"Look at that," Lucille said with a big smile. "Now that's impressive. Here, take my photo." She leaned up against the round table and smiled from ear to ear.

I couldn't help but notice that the solid white orchids, so plain and understated, were in stark contrast to her colorful outfit, flowing skirt, ribbons, and flashy jewelry. Yet, somehow she looked like she belonged there, a perfect addition to the scene.

Once inside the Café on the Green, Lucille glided across the floor to our table. The cane chairs and granite-topped table were nestled alongside the wall of floor-to-ceiling windows, giving us a view of the sunny sky, green grass, and birds passing by. Nature was so close, it was like we were dining on the luscious lawn just outside.

"I'll go see what's on the buffet today," I told her, pushing away from the table.

"Oh, of course," she said, still staring out the window. I loved seeing her take it all in.

When I returned, I informed her, "Lucille, they have a great line-up, a meal fit for a king. Anything you want, it's there. Take your pick: crab cakes, mahi-mahi, steak, grilled tomatoes, chicken, three kinds of soup—"

She stopped me mid-sentence. "And they have this *every day?*"

"Yes, every day."

"This was a great choice, Judy. Let's come back tomorrow, too!" She laughed and squirmed in her chair with excitement.

I scurried back to the buffet line and filled our plates edge-to-edge with a feast of flavors. I knew it was more than either of us could possibly eat, but everything looked amazing and the smells were incredibly tempting, making it hard to decide, so I got a little bit of everything.

As I set the plates down, Lucille's eyes grew wide as saucers. Then she raised her gaze back to me, pointing her tongue and resting it on her upper lip, while her face formed one of those guilty-pleasure smiles.

We ate in silence for ten solid minutes, tasting everything, before she dabbed the corner of her mouth with her napkin and broke the silence. "You know, my dad built our house with his own hands." She said with a thoughtful look in her eyes. "I can still remember every inch of it. The house sat on one hundred acres in Glenn Fanning, Prince Edward Island. You entered through the covered front porch and then went into the kitchen." Her right hand was moving as if she were directing me through the porch and turning into where their kitchen would have been. "The kitchen is where we spent most of our time, especially if we were busy working at the table."

"I remember sitting there for hours, knitting our own socks. Back then, socks went all the way up," she said, pointing to the very top of her legs. "Dad would shear the sheep and take the wool to the mill. Then the wool would come back in long strings of white that Mother could spin on her wheel. My son still has that old spinning wheel."

"That's so great that you kept it in the family."

"Mother would dye the wool in a big pot over the stove and then string the yarn outside to dry along the wire fence that divided our property from the neighbor's. Once it was ready, it was up to us to knit. We knitted for so long, I felt like my fingers would fall off. It took about a week to make just one pair."

I sat listening intently, thinking about how easy I'd had it my whole life. I couldn't even imagine spending a day making socks, let alone a week. I guess when you didn't have clothes to wear, you did what it took to make them. Humbled, I stayed quiet and waited for her to continue.

"You know, that house was beautiful, but it had cold wooden floors until mom decided to make a large carpet for our living room."

"Wait, your mom *made* the carpet?" I asked incredulously as my hand dropped and my fork chimed as it hit the table.

"She sure did. She used her loom, and it took an entire year. We were all so excited. I remember it so well. It was beautiful." Lucille extended her arm and moved her hand back and forth in front of her eyes, like she was looking right at it. "She dyed the wool, so the carpet would have stripes of red, green, and black. Boy, we thought we were in high cotton once we had carpet." She smiled and continued to eat, making her way past the veggies and over to the perfectly cooked salmon. "Talk about high cotton," she said, poking the salmon with her fork.

She took a bite of carrots, paused, then looked at me and said, "That house was a long way from my school. We had to walk three miles each way. Dad was always resoling our shoes because we wore them out."

"Why was your school so far away?" I asked.

"Oh, that wasn't the school we were supposed to go to. There was another school that was closer, but one time I made the mistake of saying 'them's good' about something. My mother asked me where I had learned that expression, and I told her that my teacher said it often. Well, that was the end of that. We were transferred to the other school. My mother was not going to put up with bad grammar."

I chuckled, thinking that Lucille must have gotten her feistiness from her mother. I envisioned her mother up at that school giving the teacher a piece of her mind.

"She was a tough lady, my mother. Her name was Bridgett. Bridgett Kelly. I never told you this before, but she was a distant relative of Grace Kelly."

"Really? Grace Kelly? Did you ever meet her?"

"No, we were poor, so she didn't have much to do with us. Social classes didn't mix much back then." Lucille paused, then added, "My mother was a nun."

"Wait, your mother was a nun?" I sat there, a little confused. "I thought nuns couldn't marry."

"Yes, she was. I'm lucky to be here. When my father, John Reville, caught her eye, she found a new calling."

I suddenly felt a little guilty about how happy I was that the nun thing hadn't worked out for her mom. *What if Lucille had never been born? What if John had not stolen her heart?* I wondered. It was another testament to how the universe has a way of working things out.

"She was feisty, all right," Lucille continued about her mother. "Once, it was rumored that they were going to drop one of the L's from the name 'Kelly.' My mother made up a little saying—'Don't knock the L out of Kelly; if you do, a Kelly will knock the L out of you!'"

I laughed. "Bet she didn't learn that at the convent!"

"Probably not," she agreed, smiling. "Mother started teaching after she gave up being a nun. That's probably why she was so strict about what we learned at school." As she lifted her fork, capped with a piece of steak, she smiled. "I sure loved that new school, despite the walk. In the morning, we would all bring something with us: meat, potatoes, onions, or carrots. The teacher kept a big cooking pot right next to her up front. In the morning, she would put all the food we had brought into the pot, and it would cook all morning while we learned."

"I bet it smelled great in there," I said.

"You bet it did. The whole school, which was only two rooms, was filled with the aroma of homemade roast." Her nose went up, and she sniffed the air, as if she were smelling the old schoolhouse all over again. A faint smile crossed her face, and her eyes closed.

"I bet you brought the potatoes?" I asked, already knowing the answer. Since her father was a potato farmer, I doubt she would have brought anything else.

"Sure did. Except for school meals, we mostly lived off our land. So many of our dinners consisted of onions and potatoes—that was it." She looked over her plate, which was now almost completely empty.

I thought about how this little farm girl from Prince Edward Island, whose clothes were plain and shoes worn, had made such a wonderful and colorful life for herself. I also realized that we would now consider her young life poor and underprivileged. But in my eyes, she wasn't poor at all. She had the privilege of watching both her parents work hard, sometimes working alongside them. She learned something new every day, and the memories she made now spanned a century.

"Shall I bring you a hot chocolate, Mrs. Gaman?" asked our waiter, breaking into my reverie.

"That would be great. Lucille, would you like a decaf coffee?"

"Sure," she replied. After the waiter walked away, she looked at me and said, "He knows you don't like coffee. Now that's service."

The waiter quickly returned with our drinks. He was a tall young man, slender and with tan skin. Lucille looked at his nametag but couldn't quite make it out. "What's your name?"

"Lasantha," he replied.

"Like lasagna?" she said with a laugh.

"La-san-tha," he replied, not quite as amused as she was, but still friendly.

"What's the origin of that name? Where're you from?" I asked.

"Sri Lanka," he said with a smile.

"That is crazy. I ate at a Sri Lankan restaurant not that long ago. Before that, I had never even heard of Sri Lanka."

"They cook everything in—"

"Banana leaves," we said simultaneously, then pointed at each other and laughed.

"How did you know she likes hot chocolate?" Lucille asked him, slightly suspicious.

"Oh, we know everything about our special customers," he said smiling. The whites of his eyes captivating against his dark skin.

"Judy, you're a special customer," Lucille said with a wink. "I don't know how they keep up with everything, though."

Lasantha shrugged and said, "We actually have a board in the back with who's coming in for the day. If they are regular customers, we put notes up there, so everyone knows a little something about them. For example, I know that Mrs. Gaman here is gluten-free; that she likes hot chocolate, not coffee; and that she also likes those little gluten-free Brazilian cheese balls that we make for her since she can't eat gluten."

I smiled in amazement and chuckled a bit. Then I looked up at him and asked, "You've been here a long time, haven't you?"

"Twenty-two years, right here at the Four Seasons. I served in the Gulf War; I actually came to the United States to go to aerospace school. I took a job here, my first job, and loved it," he said proudly. I guess he wasn't as young as I'd thought. He looked good for being close to my age. "My only problem is that I can't eat out anywhere else."

"Why not?" Lucille and I asked in unison.

"I find myself critiquing every little thing—the food, the service, the napkins, you name it. Working somewhere like this kind of spoils you," he said. With that, he excused himself and walked away to tend to another table.

"You're on the board, Mrs. Judy Gaman—gluten-free cheese balls, please," Lucille said in a snooty voice with an almost devilish laugh.

"Enough. Let's get back to where we were. You were telling me about that new school."

"That three-mile walk was a doozy. That's six miles a day, you know." She said pointing at me as if she was looking for sympathy. "We often caught rides with those that passed by. In fact, one day, a nice gentleman stopped his buggy and offered us a ride. I was so excited because my feet were tired. Canadian winters can be harsh." Her body shivered as if it could still feel the brutal winters against her skin.

I thought about how cold it must have been for those kids in such brutal weather. I couldn't even imagine my own childhood being so tough. My biggest complaint at that age was having to stand in the Michigan snow at the end of our driveway for about ten minutes, waiting for the bus to come.

"The nice man stopped the horses, so we could climb up. Just as we got settled on the bench, he put one arm up to rest it on the back of the seat, while he held the reigns with the other. As he did that, his arm brushed my shoulder." Lucille's eyes grew large, and she leaned forward. With a quiet voice, she said, "We didn't know much about the facts of life back then." Suddenly, her voice grew louder, and she exclaimed, "I thought I was pregnant!" We both burst out laughing. "I wasn't sure how you got pregnant, but I knew a man had to touch you." We continued to giggle like little girls.

"That's so funny. When I was little, I was terrified of being pregnant, too. I had no idea how you got that way, but I knew I didn't want it. One of my sister's friends was pregnant, and I watched her get really big. I swore she was going to blow up and spew everywhere. It really freaked me out. After that baby was born, they talked about the delivery in detail. I was so grossed out that I wanted to throw up. I promised myself I would never have a baby."

"Good thing we grow out of those fears. I can't imagine life without my boys," she said, leaning back in her chair and pausing before continuing on with her story. "But that day, I was so glad to get home. There's no place like home. I loved our house, even if it wasn't very big. The five of us shared the two rooms upstairs, with my parents in one, and me and my sisters in the other. Our beds were made of straw."

"Ouch. Straw? Didn't that poke you all night?" I asked, crinkling my nose.

"No, and it was surprisingly warm and quite comfortable," she replied as though offended by my facial expression. "We had sheets and blankets and a puff blanket."

"Puff blanket?"

"Oh, that was the best part. It was like a comforter, but it was stuffed with puffs of wool. That night, though, even the puff blanket couldn't comfort me. I cozied up under the blankets and worried myself to sleep, vowing never to take another ride home from school. And I didn't, not for a long time."

After a pause, Lucille asked, "What was your house like growing up?"

"Well, our house in Texas was very different from the one we had in Michigan."

"Smaller?"

"No, lonelier," I said, reaching for a cheese ball. "These are good, aren't they?"

"Oh, yes," she replied, grabbing one for herself. "But I have to tell you, I'm stuffed."

"Ready to go?"

"No, of course not. I want to know why your house seemed lonely."

I swallowed hard. That was something I preferred not to think about, let alone share. In 1981, my life changed dramatically, and everything I knew went south. Literally. A big move altered the course of my life forever.

"We're moving to Texas," my mom announced unemotionally one day, as though she were discussing the weather. She never asked our opinion, she just informed us. That was kind of her style. And as kids, we never questioned, we just *did*. That was the style she had chosen for us.

A few days after this sudden news, I sat in our basement in Michigan in an orange, crushed-velvet swivel chair. Long blonde pigtails framed my round, dimpled face. I hated my dimples because people pinched them, but I also loved them because people said they made me look cute. I wore my pink, terrycloth, one-piece short set with white strap ties at the shoulder. Pink seemed happy and bubbly, like me. At my feet sat all of my friends from the neighborhood, school, and Girl Scouts. Each girl held a gift she had brought for my tenth birthday party. I felt like a queen overlooking her kingdom as I opened one gift after another. I must have said, "I love it!" a dozen times as I smiled from ear to ear, exposing my dimples in their finest form.

Soon enough, I had opened everything. The floor was littered with pink and purple wrapping paper. It looked like a tornado had hit the room: a mother's nightmare, but a birthday girl's dream.

The conversation soon turned to my coming move. "You're so lucky," said Becky. "I hope you get a horse. Everyone in Texas has a horse!"

"Horses! Horses!" my friends started to chant.

"Time for cake!" my mom yelled. In response, the girls raced through the paper, ripping it to shreds under their hurried feet.

I was excited about our move as well, even though I had never seen the house we were moving to. Mom went down to Texas to pick it out on her own and was either too busy to take pictures or simply forgot. I decided it would just have to be a mystery, like those Hardy Boys and Nancy Drew Mysteries that my older sister Jennifer used to read.

As I blew out the candles on my cake, my very best friend, Nicole, leaned over and whispered, "Wish for a pony."

Nothing can rain on a child's wish like the dark cloud of divorce. I didn't really understand the forecast, so I wished for a pony.

In many ways, my upbringing was typical for my generation. Most of us had working parents, and many of us were the products of divorce. Maybe the X in Gen-X referred to an algebraic equation; as latchkey kids, we were left to solve our own problems and find our own solutions, constantly solving for X.

A bad divorce, a single-parent home, and an insatiable need for attention: these were the hallmarks of my generation. Get up, get over it, and get on with things. It's too bad that one of those longhaired, bad-boy bands of the 80s never used that in a song— surely a missed opportunity for a platinum album.

"I didn't see my parents much. You see, instead of my mother's face in the morning seeing me off to school, it was usually George Washington's staring back at me. She always left my lunch money on the table with a note. Instead of a kiss on the cheek, it was 'XOXO' at the bottom of a note. A sign of the times, I guess."

"Where was your mom?"

"Mom was always at work. She was a nurse. A darn good nurse, and her life reflected every bit of that profession. It just was who she was—or is who she is, I should say."

"Was she there when you got home?"

"No. Hey, did I ever tell you that our house served as the soup kitchen for Johnson County, Texas, during the Great Depression?"

"Really? That house has a lot of history." I could tell she was impressed by the way she raised her eyebrows.

"The walls creaked, and the floorboards seemed to speak, just waiting for someone to listen. And I was always listening." I looked out the window and choked back a tear. "School ended around three, and then I was back home again, though my mom wouldn't be home for hours. By high school, my older sisters had all moved out."

"Were you afraid?" Lucille asked. Her face seemed sad or concerned as she leaned in for my answer.

"Not really. I always thought that the creaking noises could be old ghosts that were there to keep me company. A neighbor kid once told me that an old man had once died in my bedroom. Once I got over that shock, I actually hoped for ghosts. As long as they were friendly, maybe I would have someone to talk to. Maybe they were watching over me, like pseudo-parents."

"I'm sorry," she said with a frown.

"Don't be. Hey, let's go. I need to walk off all this food."

"Okay," she said with a smile, "but I don't think that's possible."

As I pushed back my chair from the table and stood up, I had a thought. *Time is all I ever really wanted. Time with my parents, time to get to know them and let them get to know me. Isn't time all any of us really wants? It's the only thing we can't buy, but the one thing we need the most.* I was grateful that Lucille was giving me time, especially since her time on earth was knowingly coming to a close. Nonetheless, she chose to share some of her precious time with me.

On the drive back to Lucille's place, I was hoping to change the subject, but she wouldn't let me. "What kinds of things did you do together? I mean on the weekends." I could tell that our conversation was resonating with her, by the way she brought it up. She blurted it out as if she had been wondering how to ask me. Before I could answer, she was on to the next question. "What about your dad?"

I stared straight ahead, never taking my eyes off the road. "I often had to love my parents from a distance. Spending time together was never much of an option. With my mom, I liked to wait up to tell her good night. She worked long hours, and, being the boss, she was on call 24-7. I remember when beepers first came out. I was so excited that I had a way to get Mom's attention at any given time. But within a week, I realized that her employer provided it for their own benefit. The sound of that beeper eventually made me want to throw up." Just talking about it again with Lucille made my stomach churn in a way that was jarringly familiar.

She wasn't going to let me get off that easy. She asked again, "And your dad?"

"Most of our time was spent on long distance phone calls. This was back in the day when you paid by the minute to talk to someone outside your area code. The farther away, the higher the charge. Mom didn't like me running up our bill, so I often prayed and hoped he would call me. Those calls were few and far between."

"Did you write back and forth? That's what they did in my day."

"Not really. I think I still have three of the four letters I ever received from him. Dad was never much of a writer, so most of the time, I just imagined what his life was like. I wondered if he missed me and if he wondered about my life, too. I sure thought about him a great deal. The more time passed, the more I had to use my imagination." At that, I had to stop. I had spent years pushing these feelings down. I think this was the first time I had ever verbalized my loss of connection with my dad. Even my own children had never heard me share this disappointment. I don't think I even expressed these feelings to Walter. "Enough about me. Yuck, I hate talking about this stuff. Besides, I can't really complain. I had a house, food, and clothes, and I didn't have to walk miles in the snow to get an education."

"Hey, look at that," she said pointing at what appeared to be an open field to the right of the freeway.

I looked over but couldn't figure out what she was pointing at. "What?"

"Nothing. Just trying to change the subject," she said with an understanding smile.

After I dropped Lucille off at her place, I started thinking about how hard she'd had it growing up. I loved her stories, and I imagined myself living her childhood. Hers represented everything I'd really wanted from my own childhood. She'd spent time learning from her parents and working the farm together. I knew it was hard work, but there was a trade-off.

I remember eating many meals alone at the kitchen table, most of which came from a can or were microwaved. I would sit there for hours while I poured over my schoolwork, bending my head over one book, then another. Back then there was no internet, no social media, just me, my homework, and the ominous sound of the creaking boards of our old house. I would have given up all the material comforts I was raised with, walked in the snow for miles, and owned just one pair of shoes in exchange for a home that wasn't quite so lonely.

Chapter Twelve

The Simplicity of Apple Pie

Lucille and I spent lots of time together before Christmas, but then we had to break our routine for a little family time. Lucille had gone to California to see her family and as usual, all our family came to our home for the holidays.

Ten days without a visit with Lucille seemed like a lifetime. It wasn't Friday just yet, but Friday seemed so far away, so we decided to have our Friday girls' day on Wednesday that week. I was ready for some old-fashioned family time, the kind she'd described in our previous visit.

I pulled up to Eden Estates, hopped out of the car, and, like always, opened the passenger door like a chauffeur picking up a celebrity. Lucille emerged from the building's big white doors with an ear-to-ear smile, gleaming like a star. Her arms opened wide, and we embraced more like old friends who had been parted for years, not days. She was picture-perfect in her long, pink wool coat and a black leather belt to accent her waistline. Her look was finished off with a pair of purple velvet high heels. She was definitely overdressed for a day of baking pies.

This New Year's Eve was going to be quite special. She had mentioned before that she wanted to spend some time with me and my girls so she could teach us how to bake apple pies the way her mother had taught her. I didn't know which was more exciting: the anticipation leading up to it, or the day finally arriving. *How lucky I am*, I thought over and over, *that this wonderful woman wants to spend time with my children and me, passing down something that was important to her and to her mother so many years ago. Something so simple, yet so profound.*

The simple things in life are what it all really boils down to. This thought resonated in my mind, especially after a Christmas celebration where everything seemed to be about big presents and rushing from one event to another, with no time to enjoy what really mattered.

"Since the theme is simplicity, how about tomato soup and grilled cheese for lunch?" I asked.

"Fantastic! That sounds wonderful," she said with a smile.

We drove to my house, where Lucille sat in the place of honor at the head of the table, where Walter always sits.

"The only thing fancy about today," I said, lifting a crystal champagne glass filled with apple cider. "To a great year!"

"To another year of adventures together," Lucille replied

"To health and happiness," added my daughter, Katheryn.

"And to grilled cheese," said my other daughter Kaitlyn.

It was so good to have the girls home from college. Even though Brittany and Katheryn were as different as night and day, they both loved to cook. Kaitlyn, our youngest daughter, also loved to cook, but was always especially good at baking. They were just as excited about Lucille coming over as I was.

It doesn't matter what year, or even what decade it is, humans seem to have the same aspirations year after year. Somehow, as the months go by, we tend to lose sight of the big picture and focus on all the insignificant details that bog us down and dampen our spirits. *Not this year*, I thought. *This year, I am pledging to soak up every minute and remember that every day is a gift. The goal is to turn those days into memories, memories that can cheer me up when I'm down, memories that I can tell my children and grandchildren.*

"Did I ever tell you kids about how we purchased our groceries?" Lucille asked as she looked around the table at Brittany, Katheryn, Kaitlyn, and Little Walter. "First, we would gather the eggs and pack them up, careful not to break them. Then Mom would write out a list of what we needed from the store. My sister Pat and I would head down to the store with the eggs and the list."

"Wait, you *took* eggs to the store? That's backwards," Little Walter piped up. He was born in 2000, so this was all so foreign to him. Although he was known for his extreme intelligence, there were some things you just didn't read about in textbooks.

"That's right. And when we arrived, we would hand them over to the man at the store. He would carefully inspect them one by one. Then we would give him the list of items that mother had prepared. We were always hoping that there would be enough credit from the eggs to get everything on the list."

"What happened if there wasn't?" asked Brittany. She was the practical one, always asking the "what if" questions.

"Well, then we had to take something off the list." Lucille's eyes were clouded with disappointment for a moment, but then lit with excitement. "Sometimes there would be a little change left over. Once, the man at the store handed us a nickel after we got our groceries, and Pat and I looked at each other, so happy. We knew exactly what we wanted to do with that nickel, so we asked the man to add a candy bar to our order." She smirked as she reminisced. "We shared that candy bar the whole way home. Oh . . . it was so good."

"That's funny. You got excited over a candy bar," Little Walter said. Being the youngest, he never really had to do without something. Anything that wasn't handed down to him from his older siblings was purchased without a second thought.

"I'm excited that the candy bar was only five cents," added Katheryn.

"We were so proud of that candy bar. I can still remember how good it tasted. We were also glad that our other sister, Peggy, wasn't there."

"Yeah, then you would have only had a third of it," Kaitlyn said.

"But when we got home, mother asked if there was any change."

"Did you tell her?" I asked.

"We cringed, but we 'fessed up that we had spent it on a candy bar and that we ate the whole thing on the way home." I could tell that Lucille was thinking about her mother and that she still remembered what it felt like to disappoint a parent. "She said it was okay this time, but that we couldn't make a habit of it. Next time, she wanted us to bring her that nickel. Can you imagine how important a single nickel was? Well, that's what it's like when you don't have much. And we didn't have much."

The kids were hanging on Lucille's every word. Little Walter was even sitting propped up on his legs, so he could be higher in his chair and closer to her. I sat there thinking about how many childhood stories she must have, which led me to thoughts of my own parents. I wish so much that they would sit around, telling their stories to my kids.

"Don't you have a funny candy story, Mom?" Katheryn turned to me and asked. "Have you told Lucille about it? Lucille, you have got to hear this one."

Ironically, my story took place when I was about the same age as Lucille was in her story, around eight or so. Over the years, I had told my kids this story several times, and I was glad to see that at least one of them remembered it and found it worthy of repeating. Perhaps one day, it would be a story they would tell their own children.

"Well, growing up, my best friend, Nicole, was never allowed to eat sweets. In fact, she would come to my house just to have a bowl of what she referred to as 'regular cereal,' not 'grainy cereal.' Of course, by 'regular,' she just meant, 'sugary.' Her grandparents lived next door to us in a small town in Michigan, and since her stepdad was busy getting through medical school, she spent a lot of time at her grandma's house.

"One day, I told her about the 'Granny store,' a little red building with a half door and a lady inside with no legs. Granny, as we called her, wheeled around in the store, gathering the candy for the kids, who were her biggest fans and most loyal customers. I'm not sure what was more intriguing: going to see someone without any legs or going to get as much candy as we could carry back on our bikes. Both are quite amazing when you're that age.

"What made the Granny store even more exciting was that it was in forbidden territory, past the border of where we were allowed to ride our bikes. I never understood how my parents came up with these imaginary borders, but I could only ride as far as the first cross street. The Granny store had to be at least four blocks past that.

"Anyway, Nicole and I had no money, but that didn't stop us. Where there's a will, there's a way, so we looked for something of value that we could sell. And what could be more valuable than those beautiful, shiny vegetables that Nicole's grandfather had so painstakingly cared for over the months?"

"You're about to find out that my mom was no angel," Katheryn said with a grin. I don't know why, but Katheryn always loved the stories where I was doing something wrong. Perhaps it's because she was my most mischievous child.

"We grabbed Nicole's red wagon and began to harvest. Once the wagon was full, off we went, down the long driveway and into the subdivision nearby. We went door to door selling the vegetables one at a time, convincing each customer that the proceeds were going to a great cause. If I remember right, the eggplants brought in the most money, since we charged by the size. Once we had made our stash of cash and the cart was empty, off to the Granny store we went."

"It's kind of like your eggs, Lucille, but you had permission to take the eggs," Little Walter added, giving me a disapproving look.

"We walked up to the window to make our purchase. Nicole peered over to get a glimpse of Granny. Once she saw that Granny's legs stopped at her knees, she clasped my hand in fear. She swallowed hard and then blurted out her order. Granny wheeled around the room, gathering the items and placing them in a brown paper sack in her lap. Then she headed back to the window to finish our transactions, and off we went."

"I bet you had a bunch of candy," Lucille said with a guilty grin.

"We did, and we must have eaten about half of it before we got home."

"They got busted," Katheryn blurted out with a smile.

"Nicole's grandmother was onto us, and boy, were we in trouble! She was standing outside waiting for us, and not only did she take away our candy, but she also locked us up in the boring piano room for twenty-four hours!"

"It was like something out of a scary movie. Nobody missed

them either," Little Walter added. He probably couldn't even imagine that. He'd grown up with nannies in the house, so if we weren't looking after him, someone else was.

"Back then, all adults seemed to have the right to punish all kids. There I was, locked up next door, and my mother, just a vacant lot away, was none the wiser. As a matter of fact, she was none the wiser for about twenty years. Getting in trouble at a friend's house meant getting it twice as bad when you got home, so complaining about my punishment would not have been in my best interests."

"Kids these days get away with so much," Lucille said.

"I know. Trust me," I added, looking over at my kids.

After all our reminiscing, we headed into the kitchen. Lucille loved my kitchen because of its size. Everything in Texas is big, especially the houses. My kitchen was indeed roomy, but I hated how dated it was. We had redone the kitchen when we moved in thirteen years ago, but the Home Depot cabinets, floors, and laminate countertops were only supposed to be temporary.

"Look at these," I said to Lucille, holding up a pair of white chef's jackets.

"Wow, this is serious. You have real chef jackets?"

"Those are our Gaman kitchen jackets," Katheryn proudly informed her. "Sometimes we all get in here and cook together. The jackets were a gift to the whole family a couple Christmases ago."

At that moment, I felt proud. Those jackets meant that we were dedicated to cooking together. I just needed to find the time to cook together more often.

"See, our names are even on them," I said, pointing to the 'Mom' that was embroidered on the front of mine. "Oh, and I have a Kitchen Aid for the dough!" I was thinking I was going to impress Lucille by making the process a little easier.

"A what?" she asked, looking at it, sitting on the counter. "Well, we have no need for that. All we need is our hands and a wooden spoon. I have made apple pies my whole life, and that's all it takes."

At first, I was shocked that she had dismissed my idea to save time and effort, but I soon realized that she was right. We weren't in a hurry, and we wanted to experience the entire process by getting our hands a little dirty.

I handed her a peeler for the apples, the kind with the fancy swivel blade. She looked at me, raising an eyebrow. "A knife, please. Just a knife."

We all sat around the table, peeling apples and chatting away. I completely lost track of time, never once looking at the clock on the wall. I didn't have that familiar nagging feeling that I needed to do something else. I just enjoyed the moment without thinking about work.

"Look at this," Lucille said at one point, raising an apple peel that was one long, single spiraling strand.

"That's cool," Katheryn responded.

Before we knew it, we had peeled twice as many apples as we had intended.

"Flour, shortening, and ice water. All mixed by hand with a wooden spoon," Lucille instructed. "It's simple, but you have to get the proportions just right."

"How old were you when you made your first pie?" I asked.

"I was ten years old. Mother was sick, and she needed me to bake a pie. She hollered the instructions from the bedroom to the kitchen. I whined, 'I don't know how. This is too hard.' But she told me in a stern voice that I could do it and I *would* do it. And I did. Just like this."

I could imagine that moment, little Lucille complaining and her mother not hearing of it. Perhaps she got her own perseverance from moments like that with her strict mother. Now, grown-up Lucille seemed so happy to take on a challenge. I guess her mother was right.

Once the pie was in the oven and had been baking for a bit, I asked, "Can I turn on the light to see how it's doing?"

"Of course."

"Just wanted to check. Didn't want to use too much modern technology," I teased.

Lucille slapped me on the arm and rolled her eyes in response.

As the crust turned golden brown, the aroma of apple pie filled the room like a warm, loving hug. Perfect pies and a perfect day.

When it was done, and we were able to taste it, she judged it with an appreciative, "Hmmm," closing her eyes as if she were back in her mother's kitchen again, tasting apple pie for the first time.

The kids followed with their own, "Yummmm."

Lucille took off her chef's jacket and replaced it with her long pink coat. She made her way around the room, saying her good-byes to the kids. Joyfully, she headed out the door.

As I drove Lucille back to her place, she turned to me and said with a sweet smile, "I had such a great time today. Thank you for letting me cook in your kitchen. I love you, and I am so glad that we made this Wednesday our Friday."

After I dropped her off, I drove home wrapped up in thoughts about the day and with a smile on my face. I was at peace, and life seemed less complicated than it had even a day before. I was thinking about how perfect that crust was. Flour, shortening, and ice water—that was it. *Perhaps life is like that*, I thought. *The fewer ingredients, the better. Maybe I tend to complicate things a little too much by focusing on efficiency over form, and I definitely look at the clock too often . . .*

A few days later, I found a sign at the store made out of copper. "SIMPLIFY," it read—one word that seemed to say it all. I bought the sign and hung it up above the clock in my dining room. Simplification was my new goal. Little did I know, God was up there with his angels settling in with a big bowl of popcorn, ready to watch the unraveling of my newfound peace.

Chapter Thirteen

❦

Vacations

Over the next week, I couldn't help but think back on that big move to Texas. Not long after my birthday party, a giant eighteen-wheeler, the biggest I'd ever seen, pulled up in front of our house. The entire contents of our two-story red brick home were removed and placed inside the truck. Everything, except the clothes we needed for the trip: my cat, Herman, and Bullet, the German shepherd that belonged to my older sister, Jennifer.

Herman was a large, longhaired black-and-white cat. He was some kind of mix and was my best bud. I routinely dressed him in doll clothes and made him ride around inside my toys, usually a baby stroller or occasionally Mom's wheeled blue laundry hamper. He even let me give him bubble baths. He was almost always a good sport about it. Occasionally he would give me a look of disgust, his ears slightly bent back, and eyes lowered as if he were to say, "Really? Come on!"

Bullet wasn't a pure-bred either. We hadn't even planned on getting him; he just showed up one day. His protective instincts toward us girls convinced Dad that we should keep him. He was a beautiful dog, with thick black and white fur and soft, floppy ears. He looked like a German shepherd, except for those ears, which were a dead giveaway that he was at least somewhat mixed. I'm not sure who loved her pet more, me or Jennifer.

To our surprise, Bullet and Herman were allowed in Mom's Lincoln during the drive to Texas. I don't know why, but she always drove a Lincoln. Perhaps that could be a line in her obituary; after all, it's something that was important to her. I could probably write a whole paragraph about all the Lincolns she owned over the years. They always had to have leather seats, not cloth. Why did everything else in her life seem negotiable, even if it had terrible consequences, but not the type of car? For her, a Lincoln with leather seats was an absolute necessity.

During that long drive, Herman lay on the front dashboard, soaking up the summer sun, while Bullet ruled the back. After twelve hundred miles with pets and food in the car, that leather smell Mom loved so much was gone. So was the smell of Dad's cologne.

It was another Friday and Lucille and I were at the Sanford House, a historic home-turned-bed-and-breakfast, which was known for its gourmet menus. The dining room had creaking old wooden floors and the tables were layered with full-length white linen tablecloths, topped with brown linen squares, and surrounded with carved antique wooden-and-silk chairs. The walls were adorned with various oil paintings that reflected the light from the crystal chandelier that hung from the middle of what was once a family's living room. Under the red-fringed drapes that cascaded glamorously to the floor, we sat, nestled in the bay window at a small table for two. Lucille was adorable as usual in her lime-green cashmere sweater and a white fox stole that wrapped around her neck, clipping in the front. There was no lapel for a flower this time, but she managed to fit in a matching lime ribbon around her neck and another in her hair.

"I don't have many memories of childhood vacations," I said, thinking back to all the hopes I had as a teenager. "We had had family vacations when I was really little, but I was too young to remember them. Once my parents divorced, that was it. From the time I was ten until I was an adult, I never had a chance to make those memories with my mother, and my dad was too far away. On a few occasions we would fly to see Dad, but things seemed so different and somewhat awkward. Mom was always working and had a million excuses why she couldn't take off. I know those excuses seemed real to her, but I honestly took them to mean that spending time together was just not high on her priority list. The family just seemed fractured, like nothing fit right anymore."

Lucille's eyebrows turned downward. "Oh no! That's terrible."

"I held a grudge over it for years, resenting any career move she made. Every time she changed jobs, I knew the vacation time she had earned would go to waste. I always felt as though she loved those jobs more than she loved me." I could tell that my pout on my face was matching the whine in my voice, but I didn't care. "I remember listening to the other kids talk about their plans for summer vacation or spring break and trying to shrink down in my chair, hoping nobody would ask me about my plans."

As I told Lucille this, all those old feelings came rushing back. My eyes started to water. Suddenly, I found myself asking Lucille the same rhetorical question I'd been asking myself for decades: "Why didn't she ever want to spend time with me? Why was making a memory together never a priority?" A single tear fell from my left eye, then another from my right as I choked back a sob.

"She loves you, Judy." Lucille said in a low, even voice. "I'm sure she was just doing what she thought she had to do." Lucille always spoke in such a comforting way. "Sometimes we just don't understand things in our past, so we need to keep looking forward." Her hand reached across the table and patted mine.

"You're absolutely right," I said, "I've always made it a priority to vacation with my kids. Not just big, fancy stuff, but little spurts of memories that come during road trips and three-day weekends. I made a promise to myself that my kids will have plenty of fun times to remember, and then tell their kids about. I can't change the past, but I can write a different future."

Hearing myself say those words aloud made me suddenly realize that perhaps my kids wouldn't write a resume obituary for me after all. Instead of my kids listing off accolades related to my profession, community involvement, and my love of the job, perhaps they would focus on the good times, the fun times, and the times I had spent and will spend with them in the future. Lucille opened my eyes to the world around me by coming into my life. She was teaching me that the best trophy was not the one that sat on the mantle gathering dust, but the one that carried on your legacy long after you're gone, the ones with two legs, a big heart, and part of your own genetic material. I could feel that this was just the beginning of our journey together, but I knew that Lucille was teaching me to focus on what was really important in life—what I already had.

She took my hand and looked me right in the eye. "For what it's worth, I love spending time with you. I know I'm not your mother, but you're like my daughter," she said softly as she squeezed my hand just a little tighter, "and I cherish every minute we have together."

With those words, it was like a giant eraser rubbed across my heart, wiping away all the pain in one smooth motion. Without even realizing it, I'd needed to hear that I was worth spending time with. I'd needed to hear that I was someone's priority. I wasn't looking for the kind of reassurance you get from a spouse—Walter offered me that—but the kind you get from a parent. I suddenly realized that all the vacations in the world, even if they had been to the finest and fanciest destinations imaginable, couldn't compare with the memories I was making each Friday with Lucille—memories that are imprinted on my heart forever.

After I dropped Lucille off, my phone rang. It was Walter.

He was speaking in his soothing, mellifluous doctor voice, the tone he used when he had something serious to say or bad news to deliver, a tone I'd heard many times over the years. "Judy, your mom was in today. We need to talk about it tonight."

"You can't do that to me," I said nervously. "Just lay it on me. What's wrong?"

He let out a sigh. "She really doesn't want us talking about it," he said, pausing as if to justify telling me anyway, "but she also doesn't know that you came to me about it first. You were right: it's pretty clear that she's in the early stages of Alzheimer's disease. That's not something that I can fix." Walter had done just what I asked: he gave it to me straight. I knew this new development was hard for him, especially since his own mom had died from Alzheimer's a few years back. For him, it was probably like reliving it all over again. "It's still early, and most people probably won't notice. Maybe they'll find a cure before it advances too far," he said, offering a token of hope. He knew this was my biggest fear.

It wasn't like he was telling me anything I didn't know, but in that moment, it became real and concrete. Perhaps it was his doctor voice, or the fact that he wouldn't ever verbalize that unless he was sure. Tears streamed down my face as I drove home. I was mourning those vacations we never took. I was angry that the job had always been the priority. I was even mad that she wouldn't go roller skating with me when I was little because she was afraid she would break a leg. "I break a leg; we don't eat," she would tell me. I'm quite sure that was a gross exaggeration, but nonetheless, I think she believed it. Little did she know I would have given up food for weeks if it meant spending time together. After all, what was food compared to memories? But most of all, I knew that in order for me to accept it and deal with Mom's Alzheimer's diagnosis, we had to talk about it. This was not just her journey; it was part of my life story, too.

Still, my mom is a private person, and talking about something like this wasn't her style. She'd never been comfortable with showing any kind of weakness. Even when she was temporarily sick in the past, she always replied to our concern the same way, with an "I'm fine" and an abrupt change of subject. Perhaps she felt like I'd be judging her, which was so far from the truth that it wasn't funny. It wasn't her fault, none of it, and I couldn't imagine what she must've been going through at that moment. Did she have regrets? Did she wish she would've worked less and made more memories instead?

I thought back to my theory about God. Was He sitting back, thickening the plot in my life's story? Did He send Lucille to me at just the right time? Maybe that gap in my heart, that desperate need for time and understanding from my mother, was going to be filled by Lucille. Then it hit me: *I could lose both of them in the next few years, and then what?* What would I miss about each of them? Would I have regrets that Mom and I never really built the type of memories I so longed for? I wanted desperately to love our relationship for what it was and not what I wished it had been. And Lucille—would I feel like her mentorship was complete, or would she wind up leaving too early, like a good book that's missing the last chapter?

Chapter Fourteen

Rising to the Occasion

The whole holiday season was hard, but after a few weeks of coming to terms with my mom's Alzheimer's diagnosis, I made a conscious decision to focus on the present, not the future. After all, I could die first in a car crash or freak accident. Then I would've spent all my time worrying over nothing. Nobody really knew the future, so why obsess over it? At least, that was my thinking at the time. It was a blessing that I hadn't recognized these few months as the calm before the storm.

"I have just the adventure for us. There's this amazing French restaurant in Dallas called Rise that is famous for their soufflés! The Bushes love it, and George and Laura actually have their own table there!"

Lucille grinned from ear to ear as we pulled away from Eden. "If it's good enough for the Bushes, well, it's good enough for me." A twinkle filled her eyes, and I knew she was excited to start our Friday outing.

The brisk February day was perfect, and the sunlight warmed our bodies through the car windows as we made small talk. As usual, Lucille was dressed to the nines, wearing an ensemble of pink and black. I had never seen anyone who could pull off pink and black so well, but her velvety black skirt against her silky pink blouse was tied together with the large black and gold beads that hung from her neck. Her pink lipstick matched her shirt as if it was made for it.

We pulled in and made our way to the restaurant's entrance. It was like entering a small cave filled with plants leading us to a heavy wooden door. The sun had been so bright that the dimly lit restaurant appeared to be almost completely dark. Lucille grabbed my arm as if I were her security blanket and leaned over to say, "My eyes have to adjust. I simply can't see a thing."

I could see just fine. In fact, I could see that all eyes had turned to her. As always, people looked at her as though royalty had just entered the room. She simply had that air about her. As she held on to me with both hands, I took my free arm and folded it across my body, my hand covering the top of hers, saying "Don't worry; I've got you. I'll guide you to our table. Just look around and smile—your fan club is here." She giggled, her grasp loosened slightly, and she stood tall, imagining that all eyes were on her.

The room was filled with tables and chairs in the middle and along one side. The other side had a long bench that stretched the length of the wall. There were heavy wooden tables in front of the bench and chairs on the opposite side. We were seated at that benched table where we could look out and see just about everyone else who was dining. Soon enough, people started coming over one by one to introduce themselves—something that I had experienced with Lucille many times. She was like a magnet. They must have felt what I'd felt the first time I met her.

A tall, thin, and stylish woman with long, flowing blonde hair stopped at our table to hug Lucille. She looked like she was about forty and was wearing an expensive, cream-colored pants suit with very high heels. "You're a star," she said, smiling at Lucille and batting her eyelashes. Since her face didn't wrinkle with the smile, I guessed that maybe she was actually in her fifties but hiding her age gracefully behind Botox and fillers.

Lucille smiled graciously, hugging her back. As the lady walked away, Lucille leaned across the table and whispered with a wink, "When you're old and wrinkled, you tend to get all the attention."

We laughed, and I replied, "Yes, but just remember: I'm your agent, Miss America."

Her eyes eventually adjusted to the dimness, and she looked around the restaurant, discovering that this was indeed a unique place. There was a large tree in the middle of the room, covered with small white lights. It gave the space a cozy and almost magical feel, but it also seemed to be the only source of the understated lighting. The far wall was covered in cobblestones, while another was draped with French linens for sale. A fourth wall was filled with books and various unique items. This shelved wall was the backdrop for the table that was usually reserved for George and his beautiful bride. "Maybe they'll come join us," she said, secretly wishing she could meet them.

We placed an order for marshmallow soup, one of the house specialties. It's a tomato-based soup that contains some sort of dumplings that float around as if they're marshmallows. When trying to decide between sweet and savory soufflés, we agreed that there was only one solution: we both needed to get one of each. Salmon and blueberry soufflés it was.

If you know anything about French cooking, specifically soufflés, you know that they take time and attention to prepare and cook. This was useful for us, as it gave us time for Lucille to continue sharing her life experiences with me.

After we ordered, she glanced over at the wall of French linens and smiled. "This place is like being in a different world." She looked around, basking in the ambiance; her head moved from side to side, and her eyes traveled from the floor to the ceiling. The environment seemed to trigger some connection in her mind. "Stepping into this place today reminds me of stepping into America for the first time. It takes a while to get used to, but then you can see what all the fuss is about."

She lifted her green glass of water to examine it closely. "Look at this. I wondered why it was so heavy," she said, pointing to the indention on the bottom. The glasses were made from recycled wine bottles.

Just then, the owner came by. She was a classy, petite blonde lady who carried herself with a sense of accomplishment. She had heard the buzz about a queenly centenarian being in her restaurant and came over and sat down with us. She shared a few stories about the restaurant, the food, and her love for what she does. The daughter of an Italian-American father and French mother, she spent plenty of time in France and around food—the best food.

A few more people stopped by our table, some even asking for a photo. One of them was holding a baby. As the baby girl came closer to Lucille, their eyes met. The baby smiled and became fixated on Lucille, reaching out to touch her face. Using both hands, she turned Lucille's face toward her, as if to say, "Hey, look at me!" As their eyes locked, I couldn't help but notice the contrast between those smooth, chubby hands, so new to this world, and Lucille's hands that bore a million memories.

This baby phenomenon is something I had seen time and time again. My theory is that those at the very beginning and those near the end of life hold a special bond. It's almost as if they're so close to heaven, they can speak to each other without saying a word.

After all the commotion was over, Lucille shifted in her seat as if she were settling in for a long haul. "John McDonald. That was his name. He was the son of the Honorable John A. McDonald," she said as she lifted her glass in sync with both her eyebrows. She was having her usual stiff drink: water, no ice. "He was the most eligible bachelor in all of Prince Edward Island. He was 5'10", had brown hair, and was fit as a fiddle, with muscles just about everywhere."

I was curious as to where this was going. John was not the name of her husband, so perhaps this was a crush or a wild love affair, but she didn't have that glazed-over look people get when talking about an old flame. Instead, her body language seemed matter-of-fact, as if she were telling me about her last bridge game.

"We didn't have much money. Nobody had much money . . . well, except the McDonalds. They had lots of money. We all went to the same church, and part of our Sunday entertainment was to see what stylish outfits they all arrived in. John always looked handsome in his finely tailored suits, and the girls always wore beautiful new dresses. After church one time, I remember sneaking over to their automobile to look at my reflection in it. Imagine, an automobile among all those horses and buggies!

"John had a sister named Mary. I really loved Mary—she was one of my best friends." She paused to take a sip of water, swallowing hard she added, "She died of the flu at age twelve. The family was so sad. His mother was devastated. Imagine, all that money, and it was still no match for the flu. Mrs. McDonald was so sweet to me when Mary died. She asked me to come over and pick something of Mary's that I would like to have. I chose a cameo locket that she used to wear. Her memory is still so close in my heart, as though it were yesterday."

I considered what I had just heard. It was hard to think about the death of a child, and how it would leave a scar on the heart of a young best friend. Although a child dying of the flu would now be the lead story on the five o'clock news, it was all too common back then, another example of the harsh reality of history. I thanked God every day for modern medicine.

"John and I dated. Everyone thought I was the luckiest girl in town. I had the most eligible bachelor wrapped around my finger—the finger of a potato farmer's daughter!" She laughed as she raised her hand, showing off her large, arthritic fingers, evidence of a working-class background. "He treated me really well," she said in a reflective tone as she gained a far-away look in her eyes. "He bought me ice cream. Remember, ice cream was a luxury back then. According to everyone else, I was lucky. I had it all."

"What happened?" I asked, a little shocked and surprised. John McDonald was her ticket off the farm and out of those dreary clothes she hated so much. Why wasn't Lucille Fleming, Lucille McDonald?

"I was my own boss. I always have been. I told John that I was going to America, so I could get an education," she said sternly with that signature brand of spunk that is so uniquely Lucille.

"So, you ended it? Just like that?"

"No. We wrote letters back and forth for several years. A long-distance relationship was considered good for a girl in school—less distraction," she claimed, waving her hand as if to dismiss the whole relationship.

The salmon soufflés arrived, and their savory scent filled the air, making our mouths water as if on cue. The soufflés were works of art, the top halves expanding out over the rim of the white ramekins with just the right amount of browning to the surface. Our stomachs groaned with anticipation. Lucille raised her fork and punctured the top of her salmon soufflé. "Love should be like cement—solid and unmoving. Not like a soufflé that falls in and then collapses." She paused and then looked up at me. "I just didn't love him, that's all."

The conversation died off after that as we focused on our food. It was so incredibly tasty, that melt-in-your-mouth, never-want-it-to-end kind of tasty. The soufflé collapsed on my tongue, giving off an explosion of delicately fishy flavor from the smoked salmon inside. It reminded me of the king salmon our Michigan neighbors would smoke after a long weekend of fishing on the Great Lakes.

Lucille slowly took the fork out of her mouth, pressing her lips hard down against it to ensure she got every last bit off. "I made it to Boston when I was seventeen. I didn't officially break up with John until I was twenty-three. A lot happened during those years. I was my own girl, all right, a girl who traveled a long way with just a suitcase full of a few clothes, five dollars my dad had given me, and that cameo locket."

"Were you frightened?" I asked. My body was starting to physically react to her story, as my heart began to speed up. Hearing it was like watching a movie that you become so engrossed in, you start to imagine yourself in the main character's shoes. I wasn't sure I could've ever been that brave, especially not at the ripe age of seventeen.

"Of course I was frightened," she said, her voice escalating. "The fear was almost blinding. I felt dark and sad, thinking about how I had left my family back home. I hadn't adjusted yet, so I couldn't see the future that was ahead. My older sister Pat had left for Boston three years earlier and had gotten a job at a hospital there. She was the one who came back to get me when I wanted to go to Boston, too. I remember sitting on the train, almost to our destination, when a big, burly man came and sat down next to me. He was incredibly intimidating as he rattled off questions like bullets from a revolver. I answered each one and then added,

'I have a job—I won't be a burden to the U.S.' I hoped the rest of my journey wouldn't feel so daunting."

The waitress placed the blueberry soufflés on our table. She made a hole in the top of each and began pouring a warm, purple sauce in. The soufflés caved in around it, shrinking before our eyes.

"I felt like that," Lucille said, then paused. "Deflated." Then she lifted her fork and pointed toward the heavenly dessert that was sending our salivary glands into overdrive. "I didn't eat for three days. Then I figured that three days was enough self-pity, so I went to work. Pat helped me get a job at Mass General, where she worked. I was paid $45 a month, plus room, board, and laundry. I felt like I was in high cotton."

Lucille lit up with excitement at that, almost as though she were reliving that exact moment. "I will never forget my first sight of Boston. The streets were busy, and there were people selling newspapers on the corner. I saw my first movie there—my first movie ever. After that, I was hooked, and I always saved enough money each month to see the latest picture show.

"When I went to work, I was what you now call a nurse's aide. My head nurses were stern but fair. When I got fitted for my uniform and apron, they had to custom-make mine because my waist was considerably smaller than the other staff members. Of course, that wouldn't be embarrassing now, but it was then. Now it would be a huge compliment.

"My first assignment was in the utility room. I was in charge of cleaning the bed pans!" She laughed at this and shrugged her shoulders forward. "It was a pretty messy job, but I figured I better make the most of it if I wanted to get promoted. So I did. I cleaned those pans so well that you could see your reflection in them, scrubbing and spit-polishing until there wasn't so much as a fingerprint visible. It became a joke among the hospital staff that my bedpans were so polished that the patients slid right off!" Her arm whisked through the air and we began to laugh.

She seemed proud of that job, as she sat up a little taller, her face and inflection lighting up as she continued. "It worked! I got promoted. They moved me to the men's ward when I was eighteen. My job there included asking each person if they had had a bowel movement that day. I was so embarrassed. I tried everything I could think of to avoid using the term 'bowel movement.' I would say things like, 'Did you go?' but was just met with responses like, 'Go where?' I even saw my first naked man there!" Her eyes growing wide as saucers, "I was so shaken, I ran down the hall back to the head nurse, shocked at what I had seen. I guess you could say I grew up on that ward." Her head shook back and forth slightly as she reached for her glass of water.

I was listening intently to Lucille's story but also wondering about my mom's first job. Why hadn't she ever told me her stories? Would they just fade away as her Alzheimer's progressed? Maybe I'd just never know. And the thought of not ever knowing—my children not ever knowing as well—made me suddenly despondent, my eyes welling up with unshed tears. Years back I'd given both my parents a memory book for grandparents, the kind they could fill with their memories and then give back. Neither one of them ever returned it to me. I used to think they were just too busy, but now after ten or more years, I had decided that it just wasn't important to them. It broke my heart. After all, how hard could it have been to simply sit down one afternoon and fill out a few pages? I would want my children and grandchildren to know about me. I would also be thrilled that they cared enough to ask.

Lucille continued, "As time passed, other people, including the doctors, started asking me what I was doing there. They all wondered why I wasn't in school. I would proudly respond that I was saving up to put myself through nursing school. I was happy to be doing this work; it sure beat picking potatoes and chasing hens!

"Pat and I finally saved up enough money, and together we made our way to the various nursing campuses to inquire about getting our degrees. Cambridge City, Cambridge Mount Auburn, and Beth Israel all accepted us, but Beth Israel said we could not be in the same class since we were sisters; I would have to wait a year. As much as we wanted to go there, we wanted to go on this journey together even more."

Wow. I thought, astonished. I couldn't even get my sisters together to celebrate our birthdays. I couldn't imagine us committing to something like that.

"Cambridge Mount Auburn said they would take us together, but we would first have to complete a chemistry class, something neither of us had done in school back in Canada. We graciously obliged, and soon we were part of the 1936 B-division nursing program. It took us three years, going to school year-round with no time for goofing off, but we made it. We graduated."

I smiled at Lucille in admiration. Not only did she give up what others would consider the easy path, she also held on to her dream for higher education and a better life. Lucille was never meant to be Lucille McDonald; she was meant to be every bit of Lucille Fleming. Just like the soufflés, she embraced the slow, but perfect, process. She rose to the occasion. And like our entrance into that dark restaurant, she held on to her dreams with both hands, gave herself time to adjust, and then took in all the world had to offer.

Later, as we drove down the busy highway, cars passing on either side, Lucille said, "Hey, what about your first job?"

"Ironically, I was a nurse's aide, too."

"Really?"

"Yes, while I was in high school. Getting a job at sixteen wasn't an option; it was a requirement in our house. Even though I had school and band most of the year, my mom expected me to find time to work and start building some experience. Luckily for me, she was the Director of Nurses at a nursing home about fifteen minutes from our house. They needed nurse's aides, and my best friend and I needed jobs."

"That worked out. Sixteen? That is young."

I put on my blinker and exited, going from one crowded highway to another. Texas highways are funny sometimes, with all the twists and turns that take you from one town to the next. Sometimes you even exit on the right to catch a highway you see off to your left. This was one of those times. As I peered down from the overpass at the highway that was now below us, I explained, "I was really excited to start working. As the youngest child, I was always envious of my older sisters. I desperately wanted to speed up the process, to have a job, a car, and a life."

My mind drifted back to that hot summer day when we started our training, literally the day after my sixteenth birthday. Nursing homes always seem to have a certain smell to them, but nursing homes in the summer have an even stronger smell. It's the antiseptic scent of disinfectant, usually bleach or pine, with undertones of urine and bad food. It didn't bother me, though, because that smell was also the smell of money. My own money.

"There was a mandatory training class where all the new aides learned to take blood pressure, turn and lift patients, feed them, bathe them, and anything else they might need. It was hard work. My best friend didn't last; she decided it wasn't for her. On the contrary, I took the training very seriously. I wanted to prove to my mother and to myself that I could do this. I was also desperate to get my own car, so having a paycheck was additional motivation."

"That's motivation, all right," Lucille agreed.

"Once I completed the training classes, I received a certificate. I had my first title: C.N.A., Certified Nurse's Aide. I started taking care of the residents right away."

Much like Lucille, the experiences I gained at that first job made me grow up fast, probably too fast.

"Do you see where we are now?" I asked pointing to a water tower that said Irving. Lucille nodded and winked. I shook my head a bit as I continued my story, "I will never forget my first shift leader, Pat. She was an LVN, Licensed Vocational Nurse, who had been in the military. She was strong and stood incredibly straight. I think she must have been discharged with an injury, because when she turned to look at me, she turned her whole body. It was as if her neck didn't work properly. I didn't dare ask her what was wrong. To her, I was just the boss's snot-nosed daughter whose mom got her a job."

"Did you find a way to get away from her? Work a different shift?" Lucille asked as she pointed out the exit sign for her street to be sure I saw it. With the construction, it's sometimes easy to miss.

"I wish. One day, she actually spoke to me in what appeared to be a normal tone. 'Judy, please go to Room 206 and get Mr. Brighton's blood pressure for me.' When I got there, I noticed that Mr. Brighton was asleep. I was torn between waking him up and letting Pat down. I decided my fear of Pat was greater, so I checked his blood pressure, trying very hard not to disturb him. I tried twice, but couldn't hear it. I even took my stethoscope out of my ears and turned the buds around, thinking I had them in wrong. Still nothing.

"Deflated, I walked back to the nurse's station. Being short, the nurse's station seemed so high. I felt like a child approaching her teacher's desk. Pat was talking to one of the medication aides, so I sheepishly waited my turn to talk.

"'Well?' she asked.

"'I couldn't hear anything,' I confessed, staring down at my white nursing shoes that I wore so proudly.

"'Try again!' she demanded, pointing back down the hall toward the patient's room.

"I walked back and tried again. Nothing. I simply couldn't hear anything. I felt like a failure. *How could this be so hard?* I asked myself. I had aced it in my classes. I stood next to the patient's bed and contemplated what to do.

"As I re-approached the nurse's station, the two of them seemed to be having a great time. I had never even seen Pat crack a smile, much less giggle. I had decided to just make up a blood pressure reading, but then I just couldn't do it. I had to admit that there was just no way for me to get Mr. Brighton's blood pressure.

"'I can't believe you,' the medication aide said. I thought she was talking to me, but she was looking at Pat. 'Don't be so cruel,' she finished with a grin, as she went back to counting her pills.

"'Judy, that man is dead. He died a few minutes before I sent you in there." She smiled devilishly and went back to work.

"I couldn't believe it. Then it hit me—I had just touched my first real dead person. I was completely creeped out and was somewhere between wanting to run away and wanting to stand there and throw up. Life completely changed for me in that moment. I suddenly realized my own mortality; a reality that felt totally unnatural for a sixteen-year-old."

"That is terrible, Judy," said Lucille. Her voice suddenly changed from feeling sorry for me to a slight giggle under her breath "But it also sounds like a prank I would pull. The difference between me and that nurse though is that I was at least nice to people, even if I liked to play jokes," she finished as she reached for the door handle.

"See you next week?" I asked.

"Friday!" she responded, climbing from the car.

I couldn't stop thinking about my time as a nurse's aide. In the months following that incident, I saw even more death. I carried on conversations with people who were in their right mind, and many who were not. I fed those that could not feed themselves, bathed and cleaned adults as if they were babies, and saw lots of nurses who had forgotten that these people were people—somebody's mother, father, brother, or sister.

My mom ran quite the tight ship. There was no time for slacking off and no room for error. Even though it was a tough job, it gave me a chance to see my mother in action, real action. She was always so mentally into her job, even when she wasn't at work. She even got mixed up sometimes, calling our house "the facility," especially when she wanted it cleaned up. She really only had one mode—work. Since I finally had her attention, I really wanted to make her proud. I was the hardest working aide in the place and took my job very seriously.

Then I did it: I messed up.

"Can someone help me?" I yelled from a patient's room.

There was a lady that needed to be transferred to her bed from her Jerry chair, a tall chair that had a table attached. To this day, I don't know how it happened, but I dropped her. I fell right down with her, almost landing on top of her. My guess is that her shriveled, contracted body somehow caught the chair, but I don't really know.

"I'm here, I'm here," said the charge nurse as she rushed in and saw me hovering over the patient's bloody body. Luckily, Pat was off that day and another nurse was in charge. Still, it meant a trip to the director's office to sign an incident report. Before I knew it, my own mother was writing me up.

"We need to report this to the family. The state also tracks all falls," she said stoically.

All I wanted was to go home and cry to my mom, but instead, my mom was the one across the desk from me.

She looked at me coldly and in a stern and disappointed tone she said, "This is why it's so important to transfer patients—"

"I know," I said. "I'm so sorry." My lack of attention to detail could have cost this lady her life. Luckily, it didn't. I felt like a failure as I sat there, my heart pounding inside my chest. My stomach ached from the stress of the event, not to mention the stress of disappointing my mom.

Through it all, I was hoping my mom would tell me that it was all okay, or that my apology was accepted. But that wasn't how it worked in business. She didn't acknowledge my apology, just handed me a paper to sign.

Although it felt like it at the time, this was not the end of the world or my job. A few months later, the Assistant Director of Nurses, Barbara, took a new job at a brand-new facility. She asked me to follow her there, and I did. I followed her again a few months after that when she left to take another position at the neighboring hospital.

I worked on the medical/surgical ward most of my senior year of high school. When the oncology ward was full, they often transferred patients up to our floor. That is where I met Mr. Robinson.

I will never forget his face and his smile. The first time I walked into his room, he said, "Well, hello sunshine!" His big grin and shiny bald head made him look like a celebrity. Ironically, he was calling me 'sunshine' when he was the yellow one. He was jaundiced from head to toe and didn't have a single hair on his body. He always had great stories to tell and a smile to share. He had pancreatic cancer with a grim prognosis, yet he was making the most of his remaining time.

At one point, I was off for a couple days. When I returned

to work, I grabbed my clipboard and headed straight toward his room. As I approached his door, I decided to surprise him. I jumped in front of the doorway, arms spread wide, and yelled, "Hello sunshine!" but my words echoed back to me from the bare walls and stripped bed. He was gone. Just like that. I stood there in the doorway in disbelief. I don't know how long I was there, but it seemed like a long time. I looked at the bed and imagined him in it, smiling back at me. The rest of my shift, I just went through the motions, lifeless and on the verge of tears.

As a teenager, I was learning life lessons that most people don't experience until years later. During those eighteen months that I was a nurse's aide, I felt my innocence slip away as I saw loss, illness, and family drama play out within those hospital rooms. I learned that life was not simple, it was filled with complicated twists and turns. I realized already that time was moving forward, ever so quickly, and that it would never slow down or rewind. I was getting exactly what I had wished for—I was growing up. It was too bad I had suddenly changed my mind about that. Growing up and getting a job wasn't exactly what I had pictured.

Lucille opened the door of Eden with her right hand and then held it open with her back. "See you next Friday," she said as she turned, waved and blew me a kiss goodbye.

Chapter Fifteen

Parting Skies (The God Story)

The usual spring rush at work was almost more than I could handle. I looked forward to having lunch with Lucille on Friday, knowing that I would be able to hit the pause button, even if it was just for a few hours of good conversation and laughs.

When Friday finally rolled around and I was driving to Eden Estates to pick her up, I noticed a few sprinkles starting to hit the windshield. The closer I got to her place, the larger the drops became. Lucille was never fond of going out when it was raining, probably for fear of falling on wet pavement.

My heart sank as the clouds grew darker; I was very much in need of my "Lucille fix" and couldn't imagine having to wait another week to get together. I was actually in withdrawal, complete with anxiety, and a serious craving for our time together. At that moment, the stressors of the past week suddenly caught up with me. I felt my eyes welling up with tears, almost a direct reflection of the water that ran down my windshield.

I had prayed that we would have a great time, but I apparently forgot to ask for good weather. "Dear God," I prayed solemnly in my biggest Texas accent—everyone knows God loves Texas—"please part the skies. You know as well as I do that rain could bring this Friday luncheon to a screeching halt. I really, really need to see my Lucille." I continued down the road with the windshield wipers going at full speed.

I had to admit, I felt silly at first, praying with such desperation for something that seemed so minor. How could I take God away from those tasks that seem so much more important? I was sure that somewhere, someone was praying for remission from their cancer or asking that a loved one's life be spared. But even through my slight guilt, I prayed that God would answer my simple request.

Something within me was changing. Spending time with Lucille was not just more enjoyable—it was suddenly more *important* to me than my work. It wasn't like me push work aside and focus on something completely different. When I was with Lucille, I was never thinking about work or my to-do list. I was simply living in the moment—probably for the first time in a long time.

Just as I pulled up under the porte cochere, the rain stopped, and the sun came out, as if on cue. Lucille stepped through the doors in a gorgeous black and pink outfit, dressed to the nines. Her black skirt came down to her ankles but flowed slightly behind her as she walked. Her pink silky blouse had a black flower on the shoulder to match the black ribbon on her neck and the one in her hair. She's the only one I ever knew who could sport a black flower and look good doing it. If there were such a thing as *Senior Vogue*, she would have been their cover girl.

She lifted her cane to the sky and wore a smile that radiated pure joy. I hopped out of the car and quickly ran around to open the passenger's door. She climbed in quickly, sweeping the side of her black skirt so as to not catch it in the door.

"Can you believe that? I thought for sure we were going to have to cancel our outing."

"I see it," I proclaimed proudly. "God and I had a little chat on the way over, and I ordered up some sunshine."

"He certainly listened!" Then she asked curiously, "Where are we going today?"

"There's a fabulous place in Dallas called Al Bernat's. I haven't been there, but I've heard it's amazing. I've been looking forward to it all week. Another culinary adventure is upon us!" I exclaimed as we entered the ramp onto the freeway.

"I just can't believe the weather. I mean, look at it," she said, twisting her head to get a better view. "The forecast said rain and storms, but the sky is blue, and the sun is so bright. God must really like you," she mused, staring up at the suddenly cloudless sky.

After our usual game of catch-up, which generally consisted of gossip about the senior center residents, Lucille became quiet. After about five minutes, she broke the silence with, "I wonder what God looks like. I think He looks like a man. What do you think?"

"I think He looks like a man, too."

"I've been trying to imagine Him and what He's like. Do you ever do that?"

"I do. I've actually thought about that a lot over the years, and I've come to the conclusion that He's a big, strong man with a very comfortable lap. Sometimes life just seems like too much to handle, and when that happens, I close my eyes and imaging that I'm climbing up on His lap, calling Him Daddy."

"Oh Judy, that's so great. I like that."

"Then He gives me a huge hug and tells me it'll all be okay. It's kind of weird, but I can actually feel that hug, and I swear it makes me feel better. Then I picture myself climbing off His lap and coming back down to reality." I thought for a moment about what I had just said. Maybe I had relied on God to be my father figure, especially during my tough teen years, because my own daddy was so far away.

"That's so nice," she said with a smile. "I think Jesus looks like a man, too, but I think the Holy Ghost looks like a spirit, not a man. What exactly do our spirits look like, anyway?" she asked seriously, as though she were on some sort of truth-seeking mission.

I found it somewhat charming that the person I looked up to as the most experienced and wisest person on earth was asking me about God and the mysteries of the universe. Still, I could tell by her intensity that this question weighed heavily on her mind. It was a little frightening, because I couldn't bear the thought of a Friday without Lucille. I was worried that she was asking because perhaps, she knew something I didn't. They say people often get curious about death right before they die. All I could do was hope that that wasn't the case.

I had no idea what spirits look like, but I gave her the best answer I could: "Well, I don't know exactly," I said slowly, "but I do know that our spirits are alive and well in Heaven until they are re-united with our bodies. I also know that our spirits know each other."

"I have always sensed that, too," she said enthusiastically.

"I believe our spirits knew each other before we even came here and we'll recognize each other when we return to Heaven. I also believe—well, this may sound crazy—but I believe spirits come here to protect us from time to time."

Her eyes lit up and she raised a finger as if to make a point. "Once I almost fell. I knew I was going down, but it was like someone or something lifted me up and said, 'No, you're not going to fall today.' I never could explain how I managed to not hit the ground that day."

I exited the freeway and turned down a main drag in an older part of Dallas. As we passed the businesses that flanked each side of the crowded four lane road, I realized that everyone was scurrying around on the sidewalks trying to fit in a lunch break before heading back to work. I was happy to not be rushed, but to simply be out for a leisurely lunch with my best friend with work and the office seemingly miles away.

As I looked over and smiled at Lucille, she turned and looked back at me seriously. "Do you think Joe will recognize me when I get to Heaven?" Her tone changed, and I could see that she was missing the love of her life, wondering if they would ever be together again.

"Absolutely! Beyond a shadow of a doubt. I think we'll all know each other. Since you will probably live to be two hundred, I promise I'll greet you when you arrive." I gave her a big cheesy smile, and we both burst out laughing.

So many of Lucille's friends and family had passed on; it was almost like she was stuck between two worlds. She paused for a moment to think, then blurted out, "This is how I'm going to greet you: 'JUDY! Yay! Hey, it's Lucille! Come here, girl!'" She was bouncing up and down in her seat, demonstrating her enthusiasm. Her voice was loud, and she was waving her arms, as if to motion me toward her. I felt comforted by that, like I could really count on her to be there when my day came.

"Promise?" I asked.

"Promise," she said with a big grin. She always had a way of making my heart laugh with pure joy.

I had never put much thought into it until that moment, but I suddenly hoped and prayed that my mother would recognize me in heaven, even if she forgot who I was before she left this earth.

After all, weren't we supposed to be put back together in our best form?

We pulled up at the restaurant and handed the keys to the valet. The entrance was in the back of the building and down several stairs—stairs that were wet.

"Umm," I said uncertainly, looking from the stairs to Lucille and back again.

"Umm, what? Let's go." She hiked up her black skirt exposing her black stockings and glided down the stairs, one step at a time. When she reached the bottom, she let go of her skirt, brushed the wrinkles out, raised her chin proudly, and said, "No problem."

We entered and passed the bar on the way to our table. A man who was about sixty or seventy, with a large belly, and balding was sitting on one of the stools. I could tell he was either still a business man, or recently retired by his dark slacks, collared shirt, and expensive Rolex watch.

"Did you see that?" I asked.

"What?"

"That man at the bar was totally checking you out!"

"Well, he's too old for me," she said with a wink and a smile.

We climbed into a long, high-backed brown leather booth and took in everything this high-energy, highfalutin steak house had to offer. The menu looked great, and we decided to share an ahi tuna tartare appetizer while we waited for her clam chowder and my liver and onions.

"My mother used to make liver and onions, and I loved it as a kid, but I've never seen it on a menu. This is exciting," I exclaimed. *Wait, what?* I thought. *I just remembered my mother cooking something other than holiday dinners! I guess my dad must have liked liver and onions, too.*

"How can you get excited about liver and onions?" she asked, wrinkling her face in disgust. "I don't like liver, but Joe used to eat it all the time. He loved it and was always talking about how good it was for you. I don't care how good it is for you; it's one thing I will not eat."

Our food arrived on white plates. The food seemed to pop right off the plates, both visually and aromatically. After a while, Lucille asked, "You know that boy John McDonald I told you about?"

"The one with all the money?"

"That's the one, but it wasn't his money; it was his family's money. He just got to enjoy it when he was young," she clarified. "He wasn't spoiled, but they sure were wealthy. He had enough money to drive my sisters and me up to Montague. Back when I was young, it was a big deal to have a car, and the ride was as much a thrill as the destination." A small grin spread across her face then. "Sometimes, he would just pick me up, and we would go alone. Then, when he dropped me back off, he would kiss me. Ice cream and a kiss," she said with a sweet smile. "The girls at school would always gather 'round and ask if we had kissed." She leaned in, looking at me with great intent, and in a very serious voice, said, "I never kiss and tell."

We finished our lunch and started to head out, but we were stopped by Mr. Al Bernat himself. He was a man of great charisma and great stature, almost like an old-world Hollywood guy. His hair was salt and pepper, with a little more salt than pepper. His blue eyes seemed to sparkle as he took the time to chat with Lucille and introduce her to his wife. They were the perfect Dallas power couple. Her hair was long and blonde, her body that of a model, but her smile was warm and welcoming. She greeted them both, then proudly and loudly announced, "I'm 101, and this is my author, Judy. She's writing a book about me." She stood tall and smiled from ear to ear as if she were eager to impress him. Both Al and his wife were gracious, and after some small talk, they invited us both back any time.

As we exited the restaurant, Lucille proudly hiked up her black skirt again, and we journeyed back up the steep stairs toward the valet. We headed back to Eden Estates under still-clear skies.

As I pulled out of the lot and back onto the main drag, Lucille asked, "Did I ever tell you about the time I was followed?"

"No." I replied in shock. "When was that?"

"I was married to Joe at the time," she recalled, staring out the window. "There was this man following me in a car. I turned left, and he turned left. I turned right, and he turned right. Wherever I went, he went. So finally, I stopped, and he stopped right behind me. I felt like someone had once told me not to get out of the car in these situations, so I didn't. The man came up to my window." She tapped on the car window and pointed to the top of it." I cracked it just a little and said with my best don't-mess-with-me voice, 'You're following me!' And he said, 'I know. There's something wrong with your back tire.'"

"That's weird. Were you frightened? I would have been." I could feel my heart starting to speed up just thinking about it.

"I was. I felt sick and knew he wasn't telling the truth. I don't know how, but I just knew. So, I told him, 'I'll tell my husband when I get home. Thank you.' That way, he knew that Joe was home and that he should stop following me. She paused for a moment, then extended her arm out and added, "Eventually, he went a different way."

"That's terrifying. I would have been freaking out. Cell phones weren't even around back then, so it's not like you could call anyone."

"I know, and I haven't even told you the worst part yet," she said.

I put my hand up as if to ask her to hold on as I got onto the freeway. Once I was on and in the correct lane, I motioned for her to continue.

"The next day or so, Joe read in the paper that there was a man raping and murdering women. He would follow them in his car and get them to stop and look at something that was supposedly wrong with theirs." Her eyes filled with relief at the knowledge that she had just barely escaped danger.

"You know our conversation about the Holy Ghost earlier? Well, I think that was the Holy Ghost protecting you from danger. *He* told you not to get out of that car. You are so fortunate that you listened. Otherwise, we might not be here today; you may never have made it to see 101." I looked over at her. "I love you. I'm so glad you're alive. I can't imagine a life where we never would have met."

She looked back at me, placing her warm hand over mine. She nodded, and as her eyes began to water, she said, "Me, too. Me, too." The rest of the car ride was silent.

The once-light skies started to darken again. I pulled up, let Lucille out, and watched her walk through the front door of Eden Estates. I paused for a moment, thinking that she was right: God must really like me. I pulled out, and a single drop turned into a downpour just as I reached the highway again.

Chapter Sixteen

❦

Not What It Seems

Little Walter loved Lucille and summer meant he could join us on a Friday outing. It wasn't like a normal thirteen-year-old to be so excited about an old person, but then again, he was no ordinary teen. He was smart—really smart. When he started reading at the age of two, we all attributed it to the "super juice" he was given when he was born prematurely. I guess if those meds could mature his lungs, it could also have done a number on his brain. Luckily for him—and us—he turned out to be charismatic as well as intelligent.

All the way there, Little Walter was asking questions. "Do you think she's ever had sushi before? What if she doesn't like it? Does she know I'm coming with you?"

"Do you like sushi?" I asked Lucille with a smirk as she climbed in the car. I figured that I already knew the answer. Sushi was a little too hip, even if she was the hippest centenarian I knew.

"*What?!*" she screeched. I took that to be a no.

I glanced in the rearview mirror just in time to see Little Walter burst out laughing. His blue eyes were sparkling in the sun that shone through the backseat window and his laughter and grin from ear to ear was priceless. Sushi had been his suggestion. After all, if she wanted to venture outside of her routine at Eden, there was no better way than to try all the things she had been missing within its walls. We knew all the local places but thought we would take a trip over to a Fort Worth sushi bar called Shin Sei.

As we approached the restaurant, I noticed that the exterior seemed anything but desirable. It was an old building in a sort of strip mall. The brick had been painted dark brown and there was a lime green stripe that divided the building in half. The weirdest part was that it wasn't divided evenly. The stripe was two-thirds down, making the entrance look truncated. Where you entered, a multitude of paned windows surrounded the door and went all the way up to the roof. It looked dark and dreary from the outside and after all the raving reviews I'd read, I felt the need to double-check that we were in the right place. Sure enough, we were. Little Walter held the door for us, and we entered a place that was very different on the inside. The modern industrial décor was mostly earth tones but included beautiful green ceramic bowls that resembled lotus flowers. They were so detailed that they had to have been hand painted and individually designed. It was as if they floated their way weightlessly up one wall leading to a loft of more seating. The Asian staff wore big friendly smiles as they greeted us and took us to a table in the middle of the room.

"I've never had sushi," Lucille promptly told the dainty waitress, making a face of disgust.

"Well then, how could you possibly know you don't like it?" the gracious lady replied with a small bow and a genuine smile.

"Well," Lucille started to squirm, "fair enough. I will *try* it."

Little Walter was in heaven. He sat up tall on the seat, placing his folded arms on the wooden table and smiling big. He was a huge fan of sushi, and if he had his way, we would have ordered one of everything on the menu. "Bet you never had anything this amazing before. I think I want to learn how to make sushi." He'd had sushi countless times before, but this time he was getting a kick out of introducing it to Lucille.

"Do you know how to use these?" I asked, handing her a pair of chopsticks.

"Let me do it; let me show her!" Walter insisted.

"Here, Little Walter will show you," I said.

"That's something I meant to ask you. . . .When are you going to stop calling him Little Walter? Look at him, he's so big and strong," she said quite insistently.

Matching her tone, I replied, "My dad was called Little John until the day my grandfather died at age 90. He'll be my Little Walter at least until he's 70! Now stop trying to change the subject."

I was worried that her aged fingers wouldn't be able to maneuver the delicate wooden sticks, but she caught on quite easily. I could tell she enjoyed the whole chopstick experience, even if she wasn't excited about the sushi.

It wasn't long before wooden boats full of sushi arrived at our table. It was beautiful, each item almost too pretty to eat. The salmon rolls were lined up like dominos and such a bright pink color. "Look at this," Little Walter said.

Lucille's eyes widened like saucers, half in surprise and half in what appeared to be disgust. Her nose even seemed to flare as she faked a smile.

"Yes!" Little Walter cried out as he leaned forward, placing one bent leg underneath himself so he could see it all. "Come on, Lucille, you have got to try this. You're going to love it!"

She grabbed a piece with her chopsticks and brought it toward her mouth. I was impressed that she was such a quick study. She grimaced, bringing the piece of sushi toward her mouth and then backing up again, unable to take the plunge. "Are those eggs? I can see the fish eggs!"

"You can do it, Lucille," Little Walter started chanting. I found myself joining in: "You can do it! You can do it!" Luckily, there weren't too many people around for lunch just yet. Even the staff seemed excited for her to take that first bite. It seemed like it took forever, but she finally did it. She never lost that grimace as she chewed. I could tell she just wanted to swallow and get it over with; or better yet, spit it out.

We all started clapping and cheering. I was so proud of Lucille for trying something new and getting completely out of her comfort zone. "Look at it this way: you just got a hefty dose of Omega 3s," I said with a smile.

Lucille moved on to the fried rice for the rest of her meal, leaving Little Walter to enjoy more sushi than he could have ever imagined.

"What was college like for you, Lucille?" he asked as he shoveled in another tuna roll.

"Well, for starters, all the students had to be single. We were not allowed to marry while in school. We also lived in homes—nurse's homes with a very strict housemother. She was very different from my real mother. For the first three months, we were only allowed to go to work and class. After that, we could go out, but we had to be home by ten p.m.—no exceptions."

Walter looked at her and said, "Ten?" as he shoveled in another piece. "That's crazy!" He chewed as fast as possible, swallowed, and then finished, "I can stay out later than that when I'm in high school."

Lucille looked at him and shrugged, "One time, I made the mistake of staying out until eleven. We were just playing cards, but when I got back, she was furious. She was convinced I had been drinking and even made me breathe on her, so she could see if I smelled of alcohol." She pointed at Walter with one finger and added, "Of course, I did *not*."

I wasn't sure if she put so much emphasis on the word "not" because she was offended or because she wanted to make a point for him.

"That doesn't sound like any fun at all," Walter said as he put down his chopsticks. "Living with all girls and a mean house mom." A visible frown came across his face. Being a teenage boy, he was looking forward to the freedom that comes with college life and this wasn't at all what he had imagined.

"There were plenty of fun times, though. Heartbreaks, too. Between the Harvard boys and the hospital interns, we could always find something to occupy our time," She said with a dev-ilish grin. As a matter of fact, I dated this one intern for a whole year. I really liked him, *almost* loved him. He was good looking, and we always laughed when we were together," she said with a faint smile. "He told me that he really liked me and wanted me to meet his parents. Of course, I thought to myself, *This is serious*, but I didn't want to show how thrilled I was."

"You never told me about him before. I'm guessing it didn't last," I said with a grin as I sat back in my chair crossing my legs.

"No, it didn't, but I tried. I made sure to dress conservatively. I wore a nice skirt, a sweater, and a gold chain with a cross on it," she said as she draped her hand across her neck. His mother was very gracious as she shook my hand and welcomed me into their home. I could feel her taking inventory of me as she sized me up and down. I remember sitting there and listening in on a conver-sation between him and his mother just around the corner. I felt a little bad for eavesdropping, but it was impossible not to listen with them so close.

"'I really like her,' he said to his mother.

"'I like her too, but she's Catholic. Did you see that crucifix? Honey, we're Methodist. I'm sorry, but no,' she said sternly.

"*No?* I thought. *What does she mean?* I was so furious and heartbroken. She didn't even take the time to get to know me, to really 'try' me as a potential daughter-in-law." She paused for a moment of reflection. "I realized that my heart was caught up in what was a sign of the times."

"What's wrong with being Catholic?" Little Walter asked so innocently.

"It wasn't like it is now. People didn't go to each other's churches. Every religious group was so convinced that *they were right* that there was simply no tolerance for those of other faiths." Lucille shook her head as she looked at the two of us.

I couldn't help but think about how ironic her story was. It was much like the sushi restaurant: she didn't want to go because she had never been. I had almost turned around before we even entered, just based on the exterior. It's amazing how prone we are to prejudice, even in simple things.

"That is terrible. Did you meet Joe after that?" I asked, curious as to when she finally met her husband.

"Oh no, not yet. I had to go through a few more heartaches before Joe came along."

I watched as she painstakingly ate her fried rice with her chopsticks. She seemed so proud to be able to use those chopsticks that she didn't dare pick up a fork, even if it meant eating one grain at a time.

Lucille set her chopsticks down and grabbed a sip of water before starting down the path of another story. "Dorothy was my best friend. We had such a good time together. She helped me forget about all my boy troubles," she said as her face lit up. "We went ice-skating on the Charles River where we met two really nice-looking boys from *Harvard*. Al Haskell was the boy that caught my eye. When we were done skating, he walked me back to the nurse's home. He was smart, and boy was he handsome! I forgot all about my woes, and we began to date. We dated for almost a full year. I was sure we were going to get married." Her face turned sad "but once again, I was rejected at the end because I was Catholic, and he was Methodist."

"I can't believe it! Again?" I said, looking at Little Walter and then back at Lucille.

"It was a bad year. Even being a student nurse had its bad times. In my last year of school, I was asked to scrub in with a doctor for an appendectomy. It was an emergency, and this doctor was called in to do the procedure. He arrived smelling like a brewery and flirted with me the whole time." She shook her wrinkled her face in disgust, "I wanted to throw up. It was not the same back then; girls didn't speak up, especially not about their superiors.

"After the surgery, I counted the instruments, and they were all there. The doctor, still in a drunken stupor, stuck around after I left. The next day, I was called into the office. It turned out that an instrument called a Balfour retractor was missing." She looked at Little Walter to explain, "That's the instrument that holds the abdomen open while you work inside." Then she glanced back at me, "I knew it was there when I left, and I told them so. It didn't matter; they were holding me accountable." This was the first time I ever saw her make a mad face, eyebrows down and lips pursed a bit. "I almost lost my spot in nursing school over that. By the grace of God, they kept me on. They said I was too hard a worker to lose.

"That's when I decided to just focus on my studies and on becoming the best nurse I could be." Her face went back to being happy again. "It really paid off. I graduated in 1936, in a big fancy hotel in Boston. I wanted my parents to be there so badly, but there was no way they could afford the trip. Back then, nurses wore pins and capes to signify their accomplishments. My cape had a beautiful orange lining," she said pointing to the orange fish eggs sprinkled atop some sushi on our table, "and I received a ring, too. That night, I felt like I had the world on a string." Her shoulders went back, and she sat up straight in her chair. "I did it. I became something, and the lobster dinner in front of me was proof that I had made it out of the potato field."

"That is awesome," Little Walter said as he leaned back and let out a sigh, a sign that he was finally full. Even he, the sushi fanatic, couldn't finish what we had ordered.

Lucille mirrored his gesture by pushing her rice toward the center of the table, "I was the first nurse they ever had who graduated one day and returned the next as the boss. I left the hospital in a brown uniform with a white bib on Friday and returned on Monday in all white. It was strange to be a colleague and fellow student one day, and then come back the next day as the head hancho. The other students were staff nurses, and now I was the one in charge. I guess they really did think I was the hardest worker."

Lucille smiled at our server as she started to clear our dishes. Once the server walked away, she continued, "I liked being the boss, but it came with a great deal of responsibility. When you're the lady in all white, the buck stops with you. Once, a student who was working under me lost a patient's false teeth. Since I was the head nurse, I was ultimately held responsible. It cost me an entire month's pay, $65. That was the last time anyone lost anything under my watch."

I laughed, because I could imagine the tight ship she ran at that hospital. She was probably as tough as my mom. The two of them in their white uniforms, hats, and capes would have been like twins, for sure.

The server stopped by to gather the remainder of the dishes and fill our water glasses. She looked straight at Lucille and said with a bright smile, "You see, sushi is good."

Lucille smiled back and nodded. I guess she couldn't bring herself to actually agree with the words. Once the server left she looked at us with a smile and changed her nod of yes to a definite back and forth no. We all chuckled under our breath as we looked around to assure ourselves that nobody saw her do it.

"You remember that instrument that went missing?" Lucille asked. "Well, that doctor eventually cleaned up his act. He returned it to the hospital and admitted that he had taken it." She sat up straight in her chair and put her shoulders back as if to boast, "He and the hospital *both* apologized to me."

"I'm glad he returned it, but you almost lost everything you were working for," said Little Walter in a very sympathetic voice. "That's just not right."

"That's true, but it all worked out in the end," she said, pushing away from the table so she could stand.

I was grateful that Lucille shared her stories of rejection, being framed, and, ultimately, staying strong. Not only was it good for me to hear, but from the way he engaged in the conversation, I knew it had made an impact on Little Walter too. Neither of my parents had ever shared stories with me that made them seem weak or vulnerable, but I wish I they had. There was only one time where I ever saw my dad as vulnerable. About halfway through my first school year in Texas, Dad showed up at our new house, which wasn't anything like the one we had in Michigan. It was smaller and was a ranch-style single story, with dark red brick. Our driveway was much shorter too, so you heard every car that came down the road before it even reached the house. I remember sitting on the couch for months looking out the window for his car, but it never came.

The day he finally pulled up, I was so excited that I jumped up and down so hard and fast that I nearly peed my pants. I always knew he would come back, and there he was, just as I remembered him. Or so I thought. That night, he was sitting on the couch in our living room in a pair of jeans and a light blue wrinkled short-sleeved shirt. The room seemed dark because the single light that hung from the ceiling wasn't very effective after dark, and the room seemed heavy too, from the emotion Dad was carrying.

As I got closer to him, I saw a tear fall from his blue, blood-shot eye and make its way down his unshaven cheek. Up close, Dad didn't look the way I remembered him at all; he looked sad, and as if he hadn't slept in days. He didn't even smell like his aftershave or hair gel that I remembered so well. I ran my fingers across the top of his head to make sure it was him. Nobody had a bald spot as shiny and warm as my dad's. Yep, it was my dad, just in a new form I'd never seen before.

"Why are you crying?" I asked as I sat on his lap and brushed away his tears with my chubby little hand.

"I miss you girls," he said as he pulled us both in close and hugged us with his muscular arms. Being a pipefitter, his body was like a giant piece of steel; people often called him "Popeye," after the muscular cartoon sailor. Jennifer sat on his other knee, and she started crying, too. Bullet was in the backyard, standing at the sliding glass door looking in. He seemed to sense our pain, as his head was lowered and his tail, which usually wagged at record speed, was still and wedged between his legs.

I had never seen my dad cry before, and the feeling it created deep in my stomach was strange. I wanted to throw up or run away and felt fearful and uncertain of everything. Steel doesn't bend, but my dad was suddenly soft with me, something I couldn't wrap my decade-old brain around. The only thing I knew was that I needed to fix the problem. I needed Dad to go back to the way I remembered him being: equal parts strong and tough, mixed with a liberal helping of happy and joking around.

"It's okay, Dad," I said as I caught another falling tear, "Just move to Texas. Then we can see you any time." I innocently smiled my biggest, ear-to-ear, dimple-to-dimple smile, certain I had the solution.

At my suggestion, he hugged us both tightly and said nothing. After a long pause, he said slowly, "My life is in Michigan. I don't belong in Texas."

Suddenly, my heart sank, and I felt like I was going to throw up for sure. The answer seemed so simple to me, but everyone else was making it all so complicated. Why wouldn't Dad belong wherever we were? Those words he spoke never left me. I often wondered what makes a person "belong" anywhere. Where did I belong, and how would I know it?

The way that Lucille shared her life so openly made me realize that I could be real with my children and that it wouldn't make me seem weak, but strong. There were so many lessons that I had already learned from Lucille, yet I knew instinctively that there were many more to come. With every lesson she taught me, she was making me stronger, both mentally and emotionally. It was that strength that would carry me through the events to come. Events that I never saw coming.

Chapter Seventeen

The Belgian Waffle

Lucille and I continued our regular Friday outings and before we knew it the first week of November was upon us. Lucille climbed in the car wearing a fancy black-and-white outfit. She looked classy and timeless. She always looked beautiful, but today she was especially dolled up.

"What's wrong?" asked Lucille as we pulled out of the entrance way onto the road.

"Wrong?" I replied.

"You're not fooling me. I don't see that sparkle in your smile today. You always have a sparkling smile."

I thought for a moment. *Always? Not really. Fridays? Yes, I do on Fridays.* "Oh, it's nothing. I'm just still a little mad at Walter from last night."

"What happened? I can't imagine it was that bad."

"Yes, it was. I was completely exhausted from work, and all I wanted to do was relax. I had a headache, Dr. Anderson was on my case about something, and I just needed peace and quiet. I finally sat down, and Walter came in and asked me what I was going to make for dinner."

"So?"

"So, I told him, 'How about you make dinner this time?' And he looked at me like I had two heads.

"'What am I going to make?' he asked. I told him that I didn't care. I suggested he make something easy, like pancakes. Breakfast for dinner. After all, I wasn't even hungry."

"Did he do it? Did he make them?"

"No! He walked away, and about an hour later, Little Walter came in, looked at me, and asked, 'How do you make pancakes?'

"I couldn't believe it! I asked him in a not-so-nice voice, 'Why are you asking me that?' And do you know what he said, Lucille?"

"No, what?"

"He said, 'Dad said he didn't know how to make pancakes and that you really wanted them. He told me to figure it out.' Can you believe that? He delegated it to our teenage son!"

Lucille chuckled. "You know, back in my day, a woman would never tell her husband to make dinner. Even if we wanted to, we didn't dare."

"Well, that wasn't all. I marched into that kitchen, started throwing things around, ranting and raving. I think I even said, 'He's at work all day, making life-or-death decisions, but he can't make a simple pancake. It's not rocket science!'"

There was dead silence, and then, as serious as could be, Lucille said, "You need to tell him you're sorry. Make up for it; cook something really good tonight."

I couldn't believe my ears. "Whose side are you on?" I said. I was so irritated that I found myself nearing 80 mph on the freeway.

"Yours. It's not worth it," she said as she flipped her wrist at me dismissively. "He's a good man. Who cares if he can't make pancakes?"

"Ugh," I moaned, even though I knew she was right.

Recounting the whole thing out loud did make it sound rather ridiculous. Beyond ridiculous, in fact; I sounded like an ungrateful witch. I slowed back down to 60 and got out of the fast lane.

"Thank you for letting me pick the spot this time," Lucille said, changing the subject as she stared out the window. She knew the route since we were headed back to Irving, her and Joe's old stomping grounds. When we reached the hotel, a smile spread across her face. "Oh, it's just how I remembered it."

We pulled in to the bricked circle drive of the Omni Mandalay, a hotel that is known for its modern Mediterranean style. We drove up under the clay roof overhang, supported by several large round columns. The bellman came toward the car, taking Lucille's hand and helping her out. "You probably don't remember me," she said to him, "but I used to come here quite often." He didn't reply, just simply smiled and gave her a slight bow.

Three deep steps stretched the width of the hotel entrance, and brass handrails led us straight to a row of glass doors. "I've been here before, too," I said, "but it's been a while. The hospital used to have their Christmas party here each year. Walter and I shared quite a few dances at this place."

I suddenly noticed that she had stopped abruptly, and I knew she hadn't heard a thing I said. "They changed the floors," she said, looking at me in dismay. As she stood on the brightly colored red and green carpet, which had obviously been changed since she was last there, she looked disappointed.

"Lucille, when was the last time you were here?"

"Well, Joe and I used to come here quite often. I came back once in 2002, but it just wasn't the same without him."

Since she hadn't seen the place in over a dozen years, I was certain that a lot more had changed than just the carpet. I knew the hotel was catering to the recent shift of people coming in from India and was now one of the top hotels for Indian weddings. Of course, that explained the colorful carpet and modern art. She seemed paralyzed as she looked around. "Yep, the piano is still here," she assured herself as she pointed across the room at a large maple wood piano. The piano was in the center of the room, surrounded by incredible amounts of green foliage and a fountain. The weather may have been getting colder outside, but it looked so tropical inside. "I hope they haven't moved the restaurant; it used to be downstairs."

Lucille grasped her black flowing skirt with one hand and the stair railing with the other. Her black-and-white shirt with white lace collar served as the perfect backdrop for the black-and-white cameo dangling from her neck and the white silk rose that bloomed on her shoulder.

Once her feet touched the brown carpet that met the wood-paneled walls of Trevi's, she let out a sigh of relief. "Okay. Better. I feel at home here. This is more like how it used to be."

As we were seated, she leaned over and asked me, "I know it's lunch, but I really want a Belgian waffle. Do you think I can get one?"

"It's a hotel, so my guess is yes," I replied. When the waiter approached, I made sure to ask in just the right way: "Lucille here is 102. She requested that we come here today. And one more thing: she also would like a Belgian waffle with blueberries."

"A waffle?" the waiter questioned, looking confused for a moment before catching my wink. "Yes, of course, a waffle. If Lucille wants a waffle, she can have a waffle."

"With blueberries?" she asked sheepishly.

The waiter made a slight bow to her, as if to say, "Yes, your majesty."

"I'll have the salmon," I said handing the menus back to him.

Her eyes lit up as he walked away. "Waffles! They're my favorite. Nothing makes you feel better than a waffle."

Lucille started gazing around the restaurant, assuring herself that everything was still where it had been. "Yep, there it is," she announced, pointing toward the wall of glass that leaked the midday sun across the brown patterned carpet. "The porch. That was there, too. Of course, they ought to spruce it up a bit like it used to be. See all those buildings over there? They didn't used to be there. It sure has grown up around here. Did I ever tell you how I met Joe?" She asked, changing the subject. I shook my head no as I sipped from my water glass, waiting for her to continue. "Well, when I was twenty-nine, I resigned as head nurse. It was a hard job, with students constantly rotating through. Every time we got a new batch of students, we had to start all over from scratch. Nobody had stayed more than two years before me, but I stayed for five. I really felt that I had done my duty, so one day I just up and gave my two weeks' notice."

"Did you have another job already lined up?" I asked, curious. My mother had taught me that you never resign without knowing where you're going next; otherwise, you'll end up broke and starving.

"Nope. I just woke up one day and told myself, 'California. The weather is good there. I wonder what life would be like there.' The next thing I knew, I was on a train. Just me, my one suitcase of clothes, and my locket."

Wow, I thought. *Who does that? It's one thing to move to a new country for a new life, but quite another to decide to move across the country just to see if you would like it there.*

"Did you have a place to live? How did you even know how to get around?" I asked, placing the soft, cloth napkin on my lap in anticipation of our meal.

"My Aunt Margaret lived in Los Angeles. She was married to my mother's brother, William Kelly. He was a successful architect who had worked on the design of the Golden Gate Bridge," she said, reaching for a sip of water. "I heard they had quite a nice house, and I knew she could help me."

"That's crazy brave, you know," I said with an approving smile.

Lucille just shrugged off my compliment like it was no big deal. "I boarded the train in the morning and slept the whole way, lulled to sleep by the rocking motion. When I woke up, we were in California. I stepped off the train, made my way to Cat Pharmacy, and called my aunt. She let me stay with her while I looked for a job and a place to live. Her house sure beat living in the nurses' home back in Massachusetts."

"I bet you were glad to get away from that," I said knowingly. Lucille and I both had an element of rebellion in our personalities. I couldn't imagine her staying in that controlling environment for five minutes, let alone a couple years.

"You bet. The sun seemed to kiss my cheeks, as if giving approval of this new chapter in my life. But that chapter didn't start the way I had hoped."

"Oh, no. What happened?"

"Well . . ." she said, drawing the moment out. Lucille knew I just loved a good story. "During my first two weeks there, I became really sick. I had a sore throat and a fever. Since it seemed to last a few days, I decided to go to the local emergency room. After the doctor looked in my throat, he asked, 'What do you do?'

"'I'm a nurse, I replied. A *registered* nurse.'"

"He looked at me with excitement. 'Great! We need a nurse. Soon as you're better, come back, and we'll put you to work.'"

"Well, that was great luck!" I hollered, a little too loud, but I couldn't help it. I was overtaken by her luck in finding a job so quickly.

"I know. Turned out I had strep throat. It was a good thing I went to that hospital. The doctor there didn't just treat me, he also employed me!" She said with a smile and a chuckle.

"Doesn't get much better than that. How long did you stay with your aunt?"

"Well, a week later, I was right back there, doing emergency room nursing, and that is where I met my new friend, Dottie. She was beautiful, five-feet-five, with brown hair and a great figure. Being the same size and having the same color hair, we were like twins. She asked me to be her roommate, and I said yes. Dottie was living with a nice elderly couple. When we pulled up, I saw the tall, white colonial house with big steps," she said as her hand waved slowly in front of her face, "a large porch, and columns that seemed to reach the sky."

As she spoke, describing the house as if she were seeing it again for the first time, I couldn't help but think what a culture shock it must have been, given her humble beginnings back on Prince Edward Island. She must have been thrilled to be in such a beautiful place, a place without the harsh winter weather. She would never again have to scrape snow off her windows like she did as a young girl.

"Dottie and I became great friends. I told her about all my woes with boys back in Cambridge. She was sympathetic at first, but I'm sure it got old. There were plenty of boys in California, but I just couldn't bring myself to go on another blind date." She took the napkin and blotted her lips carefully, as if not to wipe off too much of her lipstick.

"I don't blame you. I bet you didn't wear any more button-up blouses, that's for sure." I said, remembering her last blind date thought she was a different kind of girl, trying desperately, yet unsuccessfully, to get into her shirt.

She laughed and pointed at me as if I were right. "Dottie insisted that she set me up with someone her boyfriend knew. I wasn't one bit excited, but she wouldn't leave me alone about it. Finally, I broke down, but under one condition. She was to invite her boyfriend, Bob, over with this other fella, and she was not to tell them I was home. My plan was to take a peek at this 'blind date' through my cracked door. If I thought he was worth a shot, I would come out and introduce myself. This way, it wasn't a true blind date, and if he didn't pass my initial approval, I didn't have to commit."

"That's a great plan," I said with a smile, wondering why I had never come up with an idea like that.

"It worked beautifully," she replied with a smile and a twinkle in her eye. "Bob was in the army and was Joe's captain, so he knew what kind of guy he was. According to Dottie, he was quite the fella. Now I just needed to see if his looks matched his character."

"Character is good, but character and looks, now that's a keeper," I said with a wink and a nod.

"That's right," she replied winking back. "They came over, and I could hear them talking in the living room. I remember thinking that he sounded nice, and I hoped his looks matched his voice. I cracked the door open and got a good look at him. I was smiling behind the door as I first laid eyes upon this handsome pilot. I remember actually saying, 'Oh yes!' to myself as I flung the door open."

"I bet you changed your mind about blind dates," I said, laughing. "To think you almost passed this one up."

"I know! I quickly went up to him and introduced myself with a smile that went from ear to ear. He smiled back, so I knew the attraction was mutual. Then we all went out on a double date. I still remember exactly what I was wearing that night: a black dress, black hose, and a perfect hairdo. Both boys were in their uniforms, and I felt like a queen as we entered the nightclub. It had a sign that read, 'Only the Most Beautiful Women Can Enter This Place.' I felt beautiful, all right, and lucky. I could tell Joe was different, not like those other men. I saw him again the next week, and the week after that. We really hit it off. He was quiet and reserved but so handsome and polite, something I wasn't used to."

Somehow, I couldn't imagine Lucille liking someone who was quiet and reserved. She was such a ball of fire that I had always imagined her falling for a boisterous, life-of-the-party type.

Lucille's waffle arrived, full of blueberries and topped with clouds of whipped cream. "Now *that's* a waffle," she said, reaching out to grab the waiter's arm in gratitude. I took a forkful of salmon and polenta and drug it through the Meyer lemon sauce that was drizzled on the plate. It was so flavorful, and the salmon was cooked to perfection, not at all dry. After a few bites, she wiped her mouth with her napkin and continued, leaning closer to me.

"The third week, Joe and Bob asked Dottie and me to go to Mexico for a night of dancing. I was so excited. I had never been to Mexico, and I love to dance. It was a very long ride, but once we got there, we danced and danced until our feet felt like they were going to fall off. At one point, I turned to Joe and said, 'Maybe we should go home now.' To my surprise, he informed me that it was too late, and we were not going to go home. He said that the boys had rented a room for the night." Her face turned sour, a sure sign of her disapproval, and without skipping a beat, she put her hand out as if to open a door. "We entered the hotel room, and I was surprised that it was a pretty nice place: carpeted and with nice furniture. But nonetheless, we were standing in a hotel room with two boys. I looked around, then turned right to Joe and proclaimed, 'There's only one bed!'

"He replied, 'No, there's another area right over there.'

"I was relieved for a moment, but as soon as he mentioned it, Bob and Dottie grabbed each other and staked their claim to the little living room with its pull-out bed. Call me naïve, but I had been thinking that us girls would stick together. Instead, there I was, staring at Joe and that big bed." She rolled her eyes and then with a bossy voice, said, "I told him, 'Look here, I am not sleeping on the floor.'

"He turned back to me and said, 'Me neither.'"

"What did you do? I think he should have slept on the floor."

"I ordered him to go to the bathroom and get all the towels he could find. He didn't even question me; he just did what I said. When he brought the towels back, I rolled them up one by one and made a line that divided both sides of the bed. I looked him square in the eye, pointed my finger in his face, and said, 'Look here, buddy. Don't you dare cross that line.'"

"So, you both slept in the same bed?" I asked in shock.

"I don't think I slept too much that night. I lay there stiff as a board, with one eye open. But he was a complete gentleman, and he never did cross that line. In the morning, he woke up and said, 'Lucille, you're the kind of girl I want to marry.' It wasn't even two weeks later that he bought me a wedding ring. He knew the jewelry store owner, who opened the store up on Sunday just for us. Joe spent $250, which was a lot of money back then."

"That's such a great story. Good for you!" I said cheering her on. "I wish girls these days were more like you."

"Well, it worked. You know the old saying about the cow and the milk?" she said with a wink.

We simultaneously blurted out, "Why buy the cow, if you can get the milk for free?!"

When we finally stopped laughing, she continued. "When we went to talk to his parents, they were excited, but they had reservations. It turns out that I got Joe on the rebound. The other issue was that his family was Methodist, and I was still Catholic."

"Oh, no! Not again," I said rolling my eyes.

"Well, it worked out this time," She replied with a sign of relief.

We both sat back and laughed. It turned out that the good Catholic girl made a great wife for a Methodist after all. "Isn't it crazy how one sore throat led to a chain of events that changed your life forever?" I asked.

"It's so easy to look at small setbacks as being negative, but sometimes it's just a set-up by God," Lucille replied matter-of-factly with a small shrug of her shoulders, as if it were the most obvious concept in the world.

"Did you and Joe come here a lot? Why this place?" I asked as we were halfway through our meal.

"Before he died, we came here quite a bit. It was close to home, and the food was always terrific," she said, taking another bite of her waffle and shaking her head as if to say the food's still just as good. "You know, back then I was working at the University of Dallas as a nurse. I was probably the oldest nurse they ever had. I loved that job, but at one point, I had to make a tough judgment call. When you're in a tough situation, always do what's right, not just what's right for you."

"Judgment call?" I asked as I put my fork down and looked her in the eye. "What sort of judgment call?"

"The head nurse was really smart. She had a BSN, not just an RN, like me. I had a lot of respect for her—a real smart cookie. Then she had to go on leave so she could have heart surgery. She had every intention of coming back."

"Did she?"

"Eventually, yes," Lucille said, taking a bite of her waffle and pausing to chew. "Her boss approached me while she was gone and offered me her job."

"Did you—"

"Of course not. I told him that I would never steal a friend's job. I didn't care about the job or the money. I only cared about doing what was right."

I thought about how amazing it was to hear from someone who didn't care about the title or the money, but relationships, instead. "That's awesome. You're an amazing woman. I bet God smiled at you when you did that," I said, feeling proud to know her.

Lucille sat quietly for a few minutes. I wasn't even sure if she heard my "God smiling" comment. I could tell she was stuck on memory lane. She took a sip of her water and said, "Joe always took me to work and picked me up at the end of the day. After he died in 1992, that changed. It was two weeks after he had passed, and I knew I had to go back to work. I came downstairs, and there was no Joe to take me. I finished my shift, and there was no Joe to drive me home or ask me about my day," she said, her voice turning a bit melancholy.

"I can't even imagine. Like you and Joe, Walter is such a big part of my life. We work together, eat together, sleep together, and even breathe together." I reached out and grasped her hand. I was thinking about how Joe had held her hand for decades and now he wasn't there. There was no one to hold her hand.

The waiter stopped in to check on us and fill our glasses. He could tell we were deep in conversation, so he quickly made an exit so as not to disturb us.

"A week before Joe died, someone told me how great he looked. I guess you never know when you're going to go or when someone you love is going to leave you. I have replayed that moment over and over in my mind for years: the thump, the ambulance, all our friends and family appearing." Her eyes looked so sad and empty as she reflected. It was evident that the pain was still there.

"Heart attack?"

"No, an abdominal aneurysm. Six transfusions, and they couldn't save him," she said shaking her head back and forth in disbelief. "I remember the doctors coming out of the O.R. I asked them how he did and if he was okay. They simply said, 'No, we lost him.' Those words changed my whole world. After that, it was like being in a coma for at least three months. I hardly remember anything from that first year."

"I think God gives us a shot of numbing juice to ease the pain," I mumbled as I pushed my plate away, not really knowing what to say. I knew the kind of semi-coma she was referring to. I had seen it one too many times on my friends and relatives as their spouses had passed away. I've often told Walter that if he died, I would need a straitjacket and a padded room. I honestly think it would make me completely crazy.

"Little by little, He lifts you out of it," she said, slowly raising her arms up and then dropping them to grab her clutch. "Oh, I have something to show you, something that I still carry with me and read from time to time."

I took the small note she handed me and unfolded it. It was in a child's handwriting:

Dear Grandma,
    If you feel lonesome at any time tonight, know that we are thinking of you.

"Colter, Jim's boy, was nine when he wrote that. He has no idea how much that little note meant to me. I had stayed with a friend at first, but after a week, I knew it was time for me to go back to my own house. That little note helped me through some bad times."

I sat there, trying to grasp the magnitude of her experience and fighting my own emotions. I wanted to imagine myself in her situation, but every time I did, my mind quickly shut those thoughts down. She was describing the realities of life, but it was more than my heart and mind could handle. Walter had changed my life forever. He was part of my identity. How did people cope with losing half of who they are?

As we got up from the table, I noticed we had both finished every last bite on our plates. The restaurant was nearly empty. We must have been sitting there for at least two hours. We were so focused on our conversation that neither of us noticed the comings and goings of the tables around us. The waiter gave us a smile and wave from across the room as we left.

The ride back to Lucille's place was quiet and somber. She didn't seem sad, just reflective. "My advice to you, my sweet Judy, is to enjoy every minute of it," she said sweetly as she rubbed her hand on my arm. "Never take Walter for granted. Love him every day as if it were your last day together. You never know when it could be."

I opened her car door to let her out and give her a hug, but to my surprise, she asked me to come up to her apartment for a minute.

She went to her kitchenette and fumbled around a bit in a cupboard. I had no idea what she was doing. "Here, take these. There are a few really good ones in here," she said, handing me a few recipe cards. "Sweet and sour chicken: make that tonight."

It wasn't until much later that I found out Joe and Lucille's anniversary was November 4th, which explained why she'd spent extra time on her makeup and outfit that day. It also explained why she'd chosen the Omni for lunch.

Lucille helped me put things in perspective that day. I was no longer the pancake Nazi, and my whole fight with Walter seemed childish. I took Lucille's advice: I went home, made Walter a great meal, and served up some "grateful wife" for dessert. It was the best decision I could have made. The calm before the storm was coming to an end, and I was about to find myself perched helplessly in the eye of it all.

Chapter Eighteen

⚜

Best-Laid Plans

It was April, which meant spring flowers and perfect sunny days mixed with the occasional storm. March in Texas is kind of like life. It's beautiful, but you always need to be prepared for some serious rain.

My agent had arranged a seven-city book tour for Lucille and me, and we were excited to start our journey. A journey that would take us miles from home. Our first stop would be Memphis. Even the news anchor that would interview us seemed excited to finally meet Lucille in person after hearing so much about her. Everything was panning out beautifully.

It was mid-week and I had stopped in to see Lucille in the afternoon. We were sitting in her living room chatting when she announced, "I'm getting my eyelashes done! Not the kind that old people glue on in strips. Nope, I'm getting them glued on lash by lash." She batted her eyes at me in excitement.

I looked at her, imagining that she was a real Hollywood actress, thrilled to be on television again. She totally looked the part in her multi-colored flowing skirt and silky blouse and coordinating silk scarf. "That's terrific! I can't wait to see how great you'll look. Of course, you can't improve upon perfection, Lucille." My comment was met by a smile wide as the sea and a quick pat on the arm. "See you on Friday. We can plan our outfits. I can't wait—this is going to be a blast! Traveling with my best friend—it just doesn't get any better than that," I said as I left.

That weekend I felt a strange sense of unease. Even the cats were excessively over-attentive, brushing up against us, climbing all over Walter, and nearly tripping me on the stairs. The dog started to whine for our attention even more than usual.

"Your turn," I said as I rolled over toward Walter.

"I hate that dog. Why can't he let us sleep?" he asked as he climbed out of bed for the second time that night. "What is wrong with you, Buttercup? What do you want from us?"

We've always had a love-hate relationship with Buttercup (a.k.a. the million-dollar dog). As a puppy, he got out of the yard during an ice storm and was hit by a car. He spent two weeks in doggie intensive care. They put his eye back in its socket and re-inflated his lungs. Now he's deaf in one ear, blind in one eye, and not quite right in the head.

By Sunday night, I suspected that my uneasy feeling was due to lack of sleep. I've been sleep deprived before, but something was different this time. I can't remember ever feeling so clingy; I couldn't seem to separate myself from Walter. The two of us, the cats, and the dog simply moved from room to room together.

After driving to work on Monday, I walked in, plopped my purse down on the front reception desk and said to Judy 2, "I'm such an independent woman, but I felt like a little baby this weekend. I'm homesick, and I haven't even left town yet! I can't understand it; I've been looking forward to this trip for weeks."

Judy 2 reached over and gave me a hug and said, "I'm sure it's nothing. You're probably just nervous about taking Lucille so far away."

As I tried to settle in at the office, nothing felt right. Instead of tackling projects, I was just moving stacks of paper around my desk. I stood up, sat down again, and repeated this process over and over. I heard the office phone ring in the background, but I paid it no mind.

Then, our nurse practitioner popped her head into my office and said in a serious, urgent tone, "It's Walter. He needs to talk to you right now." I looked at her with big eyes and I felt the blood rush to my head. My initial thought was that something had happened to one of the kids. *Why didn't he call my cell?* I thought as I picked up the receiver.

As soon as I heard Walter's voice, though, I knew it wasn't the kids—something was wrong with *him.* "Judy, I'm having chest pain; I'm headed to the emergency room right now." His words sounded forced and his voice, breathless. He seemed shaken and tearful. When a doctor sees a patient with chest pain, they're calm and systematic in their approach, but when the doctor gets chest pain, it's immediate panic. I could feel that panic through the phone, and it was as if it had transferred itself straight to me. My hands grew sweaty and my heart began to pound. I was in our upstairs office at the time of the call. I was in such a rush that I couldn't wait for the elevator, so instead, I ran down the stairs so fast it felt as if I was flying.

When I got in the car, all I could think about was Lucille in that hotel, pining for the memory of Joe. If this was it, would I soon be in a mourning coma? What places would I visit to reminisce about the good ol' days? I was choking back the tears, trying desperately to stay positive, but desperately failing.

I arrived at the hospital emergency room and found Walter hooked up to oxygen, IVs, and monitors. *How could this happen? He's on the wrong side of that bed! He needs to be standing next to it, and someone else needs to be lying in it,* I thought with no small degree of alarm. His face was a color it had never been before. He had that red, purplish look that old men get when their blood pressure is too high. His voice was quiet and subdued, and tears were rolling down each side of his face in perfect sequence, only slowing to navigate the oxygen tubes before silently hitting the white pillow beneath his head.

I sat next to him on the gurney and placed my head upon his chest. The reality of the situation set in as he stroked my hair and said, "I want to talk to you about the will and the life insurance policies. You need to know where everything is . . . just in case."

"Don't say it," I said sternly through my tears as I sat up to look him in the eye. "I can't bear the thought of you not making it out of here." I know many widows who would love to have had that information before their husband's passing but having that discussion would have made things seem a little too final. As much as I didn't want to hear it, he told me anyway.

"These EKG strips look fine. Perhaps it's stress," the attending physician said when he came in to check on Walter. "Still, since we take chest pain seriously, I think we should admit you for observation."

"Okay," Walter agreed. He agreed so quickly that I knew something was wrong.

Walter hates hospitals. Even when he ruptured his Achilles' tendon years ago, he insisted on going home and coming back in the morning for the surgery. The fact that he agreed to stay this time without any argument spoke volumes.

"It's my heart, Judy. I know it is." He looked me square in the eye, tears slowly escaping from the corners of his eyes.

I knew he was right; he's always right about medical things.

Some dear church friends arrived within minutes. They asked Walter if he would like a blessing, and he tearfully nodded and let out a faint, "Yes, please." One of them anointed his head with oil, and then they all placed their hands over his head and began to pray fervently for his recovery. By this time, everyone in the room was in tears. The enormity of the situation was evident. The attending doctor may not have known something was wrong, but we all knew the doctor on the gurney knew differently.

"Give me your keys," said our friend DarLynn. "Let's make a list of everything you need to have brought here. Also, write down everywhere Little Walter needs to be. I've got this."

The love and support of our friends was so overwhelming. They just took over, like I was putting my life on autopilot. Walter later coined the phrase "Code M," his new term for what Mormons do when someone's in trouble.

That night on the telemetry unit, I finally understood why I had felt such separation anxiety all weekend. I thought back to the animals' strange behavior. It's said that animals can sense trouble long before humans see it. If I had doubted that before, I was a firm believer now.

That small, cold hospital room became our little cave for the night. I climbed up onto the twin bed and sat with my chest against Walter's back, my arm wrapped around my dear, sweet husband. "I love you so much," I said quietly.

He grasped my hand and prayed. Tears streamed down both our faces as our warm bodies melted together over the cold, hard mattress. I tried to touch each part of my body to each part of his, memorizing every single inch of this precious man that I love so much.

Over the years, I've had many friends who have lost their spouses to illness or accident. That night, I couldn't help but wonder if I was going to be the next widow, and if so, how I would possibly ever smile again. I envisioned being strong for the kids by day and then falling asleep each night in tears, lying in a pile of his unwashed clothes. I secretly hoped that nobody was doing laundry at home, just in case. I was not ready to give up his scent.

Thoughts like this kept flooding my mind all night long.

The next day, Walter had a stress echo, a sonography test designed to look at his heart while at rest and then again after he had walked on a treadmill. I had assisted in stress tests for years, usually for Walter's patients, but this was the first time I ever understood how a patient could be afraid of it. The cardiologist reviewed the informed consent document before we began, and the words "sudden death" took on a whole new meaning for me. When I read it, I felt instantly sick to my stomach.

"I'm not expecting to see anything. I think this may be related to stress," the cardiologist assured us matter-of-factly. His attitude suggested that he thought it was silly to even do the test, especially since Walter felt much better after a good night's sleep.

Walter, being the smartest doctor I know, respectfully disagreed. "I know that pain was not from stress. I really think that something is wrong with my heart." He went on to explain in doctor-speak exactly what he thought it might be. The cardiologist didn't respond with much enthusiasm, especially after Walter gave him a detailed review of the anatomy of the heart, as if the cardiologist needed it. It was amusing to watch these two professionals have a pissing match, but it was one I actually hoped Walter would lose.

Only minutes into the stress test, Walter suddenly blurted out, "That's it; that's the pain." Suddenly, his faced changed to that blotchy purple color again. My heart was in my throat.

The cardiologist quickly got him off the treadmill and onto the table to scan his heart.

"I'm not seeing the problem," he said after a moment, "but since you had pain, we'll have to do a heart catheter tomorrow to be sure. Again, I don't anticipate anything; however, if we do stents, you'll have to stay another day for recovery."

That whole day and night, I felt like I was in a bad dream, and that I would wake up at any moment and this would all be over. I knew Walter was afraid, too. When you live with someone for so long, you learn all their little tells, the small signs that mean, "I'm scared," or "I'm hungry," or "I'm mad." Whenever Walter's afraid, he hibernates. That afternoon, he slept a lot, only waking up for someone to draw blood or check his blood pressure.

"Your cardiac enzymes went up. Whatever happened on the treadmill was definitely your heart," the cardiologist said when he came by to check on Walter. "We'll know more tomorrow when we do the cath."

"I knew it," he whispered as he squeezed my hand.

Of course he did, I thought, but this was one time I wanted him to be wrong.

The next morning, we said a prayer in the hall, he on the gurney and me standing helplessly at his side. Then they wheeled Walter away, his head covered in a blue mesh surgical cap, his face still that indescribable color. I stood completely still as he rolled further and further away from me, but in my mind, I was running after him, screaming, *No! I don't like this! Come back, and let's just go home.*

Once they turned the corner and were out of sight, I headed toward the cold, silent, empty waiting area feeling completely alone. After some time had passed, I suddenly had the most terrifying feeling I have ever experienced. Nothing about my surroundings had changed, but I was so afraid that I started hyperventilating and my heart began racing. It was like being panic stricken. It was as if electricity was buzzing through my veins. I reached for my phone and called my daughter Brittany.

"I'm freaking out here." I said as I paced back and forth on the cold hospital floor. "I'm so glad you answered."

"What happened? What did they find out?" she asked peppering one question after another. Then her tone changed. She slowed down and very sweetly coached me along by adding, "Try to stay calm, Mom."

"They haven't come out yet. I was sitting here, totally fine, but then it was like a switch went off inside me and I went into panic mode." By this time, I was crying, and I could feel how hot my face had become. My blood pressure must have been up because I could hear my pulse in my ears.

Brittany was between classes, so I was lucky to catch her. Her familiar, soothing voice helped calm me down. I didn't want to hang up, but I knew she had to go. She needed to get to class, and I needed to "pony up," as they say in Texas.

After about thirty minutes, a ding from the elevator pierced the silence, and out came my good friend Melissah from church. Code M, right on cue. With her dark auburn, curly hair, freckled face, narrow figure, and piercing blue eyes, she looked like an angel walking toward me. She's always had great timing.

Just as she joined me on the couch for a big hug, the cardiologist turned the corner. His walk was different this time; there was no smile, no swagger. I was glad that I wasn't alone, because whatever he was about to say was not going to be good; it was written all over his face.

I started to rise, but he gestured for me to sit back down. He then pulled out a diagram of the heart covered with lots of arrows and numbers. I didn't really need to know the details; I know enough to know that when things are good, there's no diagram, no arrows, and no numbers. "He has three arteries that are blocked, one of which is 99% blocked. I didn't correct them today because we should consider open-heart surgery. It looks as though he had a heart attack. Probably yesterday during the stress test. That explains the elevated enzymes after."

Crack his chest?! You said you weren't expecting anything! I thought in a panic. Luckily, my outer voice never yelled those words; instead, I regained my composure and said in a small, reserved tone, "He's a smart and reasonable man. Let's get him coherent and see what he wants to do."

I could tell the surgeon was a little taken aback by my calm, steady reply. Then I lost my composure and started to cry. The enormity of the situation sank in. To this day, I'm not sure why I felt the need to apologize for being so scared, but at that moment, I looked at him and mumbled, "Sorry," gesturing to my red face and the snot running from my nose. "You see, Walter is by far the best diagnostician I know. No offense. It's just that I'm not used to seeing him on this side of a case. It's a lot easier to have a doctor for a husband than a husband as a patient."

I don't even remember what the surgeon said after that; I just remember seeing him walk away. He knew that Walter had been right about his own diagnosis, and now he had to tell Walter, a family practitioner, that he, a cardiologist, had been wrong. There was no swagger, no attitude in his step; he was just a humbled doctor walking back down the hall, contemplating a peculiar case. I thought about something Walter tells all his medical students: "Listen to your patients; they're trying to give you the diagnosis."

"Crack my chest?!" Walter cried out from the hospital bed. "No way!" He was supposed to remain flat, but he nearly climbed out of the bed with that news.

At that moment, I was thankful that I was not the one to make this call. This was something he had to decide, not me.

"I have had way too many patients with terrible recoveries and awful pain, not to mention the time off work. I can't just close my practice that long. What will happen to my patients?"

I kept my cool, but I felt that this was not the moment for him to be thinking about work. I stood at the foot of the bed and remained quiet while they spoke.

Walter continued his conversation with the cardiac surgeon, unconvinced. I stepped out of his room to quickly go to the restroom. As I was heading back, I ran smack into Jerry, an oncologist and a friend of ours. Jerry was in his fifties, fit, and soft spoken. He's always worn his straight brown hair a little long on top to cover his large forehead. His demeanor is calming, which is probably why he's always been so successful with cancer patients. "Judy, what are you doing here?" he asked, surprised to see me. We hadn't run into him in a while, not since one of our mutual friends, a cardiologist, had a big retirement party.

"You haven't heard? Walter had a heart attack during a stress echo yesterday, and he just had a heart cath. They want to crack his chest, but he isn't having any part of it."

"Has Mike seen him?" Jerry asked. Mike Rothkopf was the Chief of Cardiology at that hospital and also a friend of ours. Walter sends almost all his patients to Mike. Even Lucille saw him. To this day, I don't know why we didn't get Mike involved earlier. I guess everything just happened so fast.

Jerry immediately took out his phone and called Mike. After quickly explaining the situation, Jerry hung up and reported, "He's on his way." I was relieved. I knew that Walter would listen to him.

A few minutes later, Dr. Rothkopf arrived. Walter seemed exceptionally relieved to see him. "I heard you were in here," Mike said with smile and a love squeeze on Walter's big toe through the hospital blanket. Walter was still lying flat from the cath procedure, something he would have to do for a few more hours.

"Mike, they want to crack my chest. I don't think they need to do that," Walter said, diagnosing himself from his hospital bed. "I want your opinion. I need to know what you would do if you were me." Walter's respect for Mike had apparently gone up another notch: he was letting him call the shot on his own life-or-death situation.

Mike walked over to the computer in the room and pulled up the images of Walter's heart. "It's pretty blocked. It may be hard to stent, but it can be done. They can use multiple stents, putting some together for this bit here," he said, pointing to an artery that had a rather long blocked section. He turned to Walter and said, "If it were me, I wouldn't get opened up; I would get the stents."

I was shocked by Mike's recommendation but relieved at the same time. I knew that he'd never steer us wrong. After all, he was Lucille's cardiologist, and she was 102.

They carried on with their doctor-talk, comparing all the latest studies, outcome ratios, and so forth. Mike's opinion was all Walter needed to hear. It was all I needed to hear. It was official: stents it was.

The next day seemed like that movie *Groundhog Day*: we went back down the hall, said a prayer together in the hallway, and shared a kiss goodbye. But this time, we both felt very confident about the outcome.

"I was able to stent all of them but this one," the cardiologist said, pointing to a small vessel called the ramus.

"Is that serious? What happens to that one?" I asked, concerned.

"It's no big deal. Some people don't even have that vessel. He'll be fine," he said almost dismissively as he started to stand up.

"Okay," I said, simply feeling relieved that the ordeal was finally over.

In what felt like minutes, Walter was back in his hospital room, lying flat again. "I've got to pee!" he announced rather loudly and frantically.

"Sorry, honey, but you can't get up for four more hours. Let me grab the urinal," I said in the most soothing voice I could.

"I can't pee lying on my back! I have to pee standing up." His voice grew agitated.

"Nope, you have to lie down and stay down."

"I can't. I just can't," he said as he stood up and grabbed the urinal. "Don't look. Turn around. Don't listen, either."

Inside my head I was screaming, *Doctors make the worst patients!* I literally had to beg him to let me have the urinal, so I could flush it when he was done. "Everybody pees, you know. It's not like this is the first urine I've ever flushed."

"Well, it's the first time you've flushed *my* urine," he responded, climbing back into bed and lying flat again.

I didn't like the CCU hospital beds because they were definitely made for only one. I tried to sleep in the recliner next to him but kept jerking awake to check on him. It was day three of this ordeal, and I hadn't left the hospital. I had to stay right there, as close to him as possible.

Brittany caught a flight in that morning and picked Little Walter up from the house. I felt so relieved when they entered the room.

Out of the ten children Walter and I had, *Brady Bunch* style, Brittany was my oldest, and she was very reliable. She was not your typical twenty-two-year old. Although our blended family put her somewhere in the middle, she still kept the personality traits of being the oldest child. She stood there in her jeans, tennis shoes, and sweatshirt looking exhausted from the flight, "Mom, have you told Lucille?" she asked after the initial greetings were over. "Aren't you supposed to go out of town with her soon?"

"Oh my gosh!" I said as my eyes popped wide open as I grabbed her arm. "I haven't even thought about that. What day is it today?" Time seems to stand still when you're in a hospital; even the days and nights run together. "This isn't something I want to tell her over the phone. She'd be worried sick."

I was able to take Walter home the next day. He was a little grumpy and groggy, but it was good to be home again. All the animals seemed to be back to normal and happy to see us again. When I tucked us into bed that night, I laid my head on Walter's chest, finding comfort in the beating of his heart. I thought about how fragile life is, about how much that little sound meant to me. Should that sound stop, so would my life as I knew it. It was a terrifying thought. I had laid my head on his chest for years, but I had never fully appreciated the comfort the sound his beating heart could bring.

The next morning at the breakfast table, Brittany said looking up from her bowl of cereal, "Mom, you have to go tell Lucille what happened and that you're not going to Memphis."

I was sitting directly across from her but didn't feel like eating. My whole internal clock was off from being inside the hospital for so many days. "I know. It's just that . . ."

The clock on the wall began to play. It played a new tune every hour, on the hour. This hour it was playing the theme from Titanic. I loved that clock. Each hour the face of the clock came apart like puzzle pieces, exposing motion inside, while a carousel of Swarovski crystals turned around at the bottom. Over the years it's been quite the conversation piece. I bought the clock for Walter years ago as an anniversary present. The very sound of it was always a comforting reminder that we were home, safe and sound.

"He's fine. I'm here. Go," she said in an almost paternalistic tone. She was right.

My body felt tense as I drove to Lucille's place. I hadn't

spoken to her in a few days, and she was expecting to leave for Memphis the next day. I dreaded letting her down like this.

"Hello! Hello?" I said into her empty apartment, having let myself in. *That's strange*, I thought. *I don't remember seeing her in the dining room.*

I went back down to the dining room, where just a few scattered stragglers remained from lunch. Most of the tables were littered with the morning's dirty dishes that still needed to be bussed. You could hear the cleanup commotion going on behind the kitchen doors. I asked around, "Has anyone seen Lucille? She's not in her room."

"Oh, I think she's up on the first floor getting her nails done. She's got some big trip coming up," said an elderly lady, barely looking up from her half-eaten plate of eggs.

I swallowed hard as I entered the makeshift salon. I could see Lucille, but she couldn't see me yet. I knew she was going to be so disappointed about canceling our trip.

The stylist was holding her hand and painting her fingernails a light pink. Lucille was going on and on about the book tour and how she was going to be on television again. Suddenly, the stylist looked up and said, "Is this who you're going with?

"Judy!" Lucille yelled as she ripped her hands out of the beauticians', smearing the polish. Her eyelashes seemed a mile long as she batted them at me. "Do you like . . ." She stopped mid-sentence. "What's wrong? Something's wrong. Oh my gosh, what is it?" Her half-painted nails were now at her face, covering her mouth.

The nice lady who had been painting her nails jumped up to grab a chair for me to sit on. We were a little crowded in there because it wasn't meant to be a salon at all, it was just an oversized bathroom with a mechanical lift so those in wheelchairs could take baths.

"Walter just got out of the hospital. He had a heart attack." I said, my eyes welling up. I could hear the echo of those words as they bounced off the tiled floor and walls.

"Oh, no!" She shook her head in disbelief and dismay.

I went on to tell her the whole thing, including the emergency room, stress test, cocky doctor, and how frightening the whole ordeal was. Then I sorrowfully ended with, "I'm sorry, but we have to postpone our Memphis trip." I felt so bad, but I knew it was the right thing to do. There was no way I would have ever left Walter home without me.

"Who cares about Memphis? We'll go later," she said, looking to the stylist for an agreeing nod. "You need to get back home to Walter. I love you."

I reached over and gave her a hug and a kiss on the check. "I love you too."

"Tell him I love him too. Now, go," she said as gave me a hug and practically shoved me out the door.

As I drove home, my mind drifted back over the events of the past week. I was so glad that Walter was able to make his own decision about the open-heart surgery and was now home safe and sound. What if I had made it and made the wrong one?

In life, we're faced with so many choices, and some have lasting consequences. I'd learned a great deal from Walter that week. He'd followed his gut instinct, but then checked it with someone he trusted and respected. I also learned something new about Lucille. As much as she wanted to go on this trip, as much as she had prepared mentally and physically, she never lost track of what true priorities should be.

Chapter Nineteen

⚜

Memphis

Over a month had passed, and things were mostly back to normal. Walter and I were cuddling up on the couch in the great room on a Saturday afternoon. I loved sitting in the great room because it had soaring ceilings and a wall of windows that overlooked the backyard. There were two couches separated by a coffee table, but we always sat together on one. I guess we reserved the other for company.

Walter looked me straight in the eye and said, "You can go, you know. You should reschedule that trip to Memphis. I'm fine." He slapped my knee softly and added, "I'm more than fine. I feel like I'm thirty again, not sixty-three."

I had to think about that for a moment. I wanted to go, but what if he was just saying he was fine. "Are you sure? I mean—"

"Yes, I'm sure," he replied confidently. "Get out on that tour, before it's too late and the book is old news."

Less than two weeks after that, Lucille and I were pulling up at the airport. "Get me one of those red wheelchairs and a man to push it," she said in a bit of a bossy tone.

I couldn't believe what I was hearing. "Really? I thought you hated wheelchairs."

"Oh, you'll see," she said with a wink, "sometimes a girl's gotta have one of those."

I took her to a special counter, one I didn't even know existed. They came right around with a chair and a helper, and they even checked us in. It was a breeze, perhaps the fastest I had ever checked in at any airport.

Lucille in her wheelchair, the airport helper, and I approached security through a separate, special line. She gave me a wink, pulled out her ID, and handed it to the TSA agent. I was still astounded, looking back at the line, thinking, *how did we just bypass all those people?*

"1912, huh?" asked the large, muscular black man. He had to be at least 6' 2" and pushing three hundred pounds.

"Yes, sir," she said with a big smile.

"Well, you just come right through here, young lady, and have a nice time in Memphis," he said in a voice that was way too sweet and sappy for a man of his stature. It was like that big, tough TSA agent melted right in front of my eyes. Lucille waved to me as she passed without being scanned. I, on the other hand, was directed to cut in line for the body scan so I could meet her on the other side.

"See?" she said once we cleared security, looking at me with that I-told-you-so face. "*And*, we'll get on and off the plane first, too. It pays to be my age, you know."

It was Mother's Day, and I felt mildly guilty for spending it away from my own mom and possibly taking Lucille away from a chance to see her own family. "Isn't this great?" I asked, looking around the Peabody Hotel lobby, trying to be cheerful. The lobby was absolutely stunning, with large granite columns that lined the room, reaching two stories high, to sections of stained glass that filled the ceiling. The blues, browns, and yellows of the stained glass looked much like a fine oriental rug with its unique design. It was surrounded by thick and stately dark inlaid wood. Large metal and crystal chandeliers hung down to light the cozy sofas and chairs that filled the room below. In the center of the lobby floor stood the fountain, known for being carved out of a single piece of travertine and for being home to the famous Peabody Ducks.

"It's like I'm in a dream. I love it! Absolutely love it," She replied with wide eyes and raised eyebrows.

We were both starving, so getting a bite to eat was our top priority. In the hotel restaurant, Lucille reached for the vase in the center of the table that held a small bouquet of flowers. "Take a picture of this," she said as she placed one of the flowers between her teeth and smiled. "Send that picture back home. They'll think we're really living it up."

"This is a different Mother's Day, isn't it?" She asked as she looked around and back at me. "I usually spend it thinking about those two boys of mine. And . . ." she paused, and her faced turned serious, "the other one."

"The other one?" I asked, a bit confused.

"The one I miscarried," she said, tears welling up suddenly in her eyes.

I had to swallow hard. I too, had miscarried a pregnancy, in between my two girls. It wasn't something I liked to talk about. "That's hard. I know from personal experience," I said quickly, hoping she wouldn't want to discuss the details.

There was a reflective pause and then she said, "I always wondered . . ." She shook her head as if to shake off the thought.

"Wondered?" I said in a low voice. Fighting against my urge to shut the conversation down before we got in too deep, I leaned in and took her hand.

"I never had a daughter . . . and I always wondered if that was going to be my daughter. That baby." A single tear fell from her eye. "We didn't talk about things like that back then. They were so common that you just kept quiet about it. Joe and I never really discussed it. I just spent a few days resting and that was it. Things just went back to normal." With that being said, she picked up her fork and sniffed loudly. And as quickly as she had saddened, her demeanor became conversational again, subdued, and through the rest of our dinner we kept to cheery topics, more lighthearted ones. But still, I never forgot that look of sadness on her face when she spoke about the daughter that never was, and it made me profoundly grateful for my own children, the babies I *had* managed to bring into the world.

I was tired and not feeling all that great, so after we ate, I felt like we couldn't get to our room fast enough. Lucille looked over at me standing by the bathroom door in our hotel room. "Are you sick?" she asked, clearly concerned.

I didn't want to ruin our trip, and I especially didn't want to see her worry. After all, she was ready to live it up. "I'll be okay," I said, heading toward the door. "I just have a little headache." That was certainly an understatement. I had a massive headache, the kind where light hurts your eyes, and, as we say in Texas, you just want to throw your toenails up. "I'm going to check the gift shop and see if they have something I could take. Will you be okay here for a minute?"

"Why, of course. What a silly question," she said plopping down on the bed and sliding her hands across the white down comforter in an effort to smooth it back out.

When I got back to the room, she patted my bed. "Take your Advil and lie down for a while. You're tired, and you should get some rest. I don't know how you do it. You do too much."

I lay across the bed diagonally and tried to relax, but my head was pounding. There I was, lying face-up with my feet together and arms straight by my side. *If I die from this headache, at least I've already assumed the position*, I thought ruefully.

A few minutes later, Lucille got up from her own bed and went to the bathroom. She was fidgeting around in there and running the water. The next thing I knew, she had sat down alongside me, holding a cool cloth. "Here, this will help," she said as she gently placed it across my forehead. Then she looked down and said, "Look at those feet. They are so cute," She said with a giggle as she ran her aged hands down my ankles and gently rubbed my feet. Tears streamed from my eyes, but I didn't move or make a sound.

I didn't want her to see my tears, but they just kept flowing. I wasn't sure if I was crying from the headache or from the fact that my friend was rubbing my feet—feet that had been in sweaty shoes and on airport floors and were swollen from travel.

After about an hour, I got up to take a warm bath. As I looked around at the eclectic items gathered in our bathroom—clothes hanging up, our make-up side by side on the sink, and a shower chair perched in the corner—a smile came to my face. Lucille had hidden a couple of those pink pads out of sight, as if she didn't want me to see them. As if I didn't know that getting older came with some challenges.

I should have known that Lucille would be busy on the other side of the door. When I came back out in my pajamas, all freshly bathed and feeling much more like a human being, she motioned to my bed and proudly said, "There. I've fixed the pillows just right, just like how they taught us in nursing school: one this way, one that way, and then a third across the top. But before you lie back down, let me rub your shoulders. I think this is a tension headache."

They say, "Once a nurse, always a nurse," and Lucille was definitely in nurse mode. The strength of her hands was amazing. Her fingers creaked like old wooden boards in a turn-of-the-century home—noisy but strong.

I closed my eyes and started to imagine all the things Lucille's hands must have touched over the past century. I imagined her harvesting potatoes as a little girl and taking care of patients in the hospital. I thought about how much she must miss holding hands with her late husband, Joe.

That night, it was as if her hands had healing powers. My very own Saint Lucille tucked me into bed, and I fell into a deep, peaceful sleep, my headache gone.

The next morning, I awoke to the sound of her singing in the bathroom. With my headache gone, I could finally notice the room we were staying in. It was painted a Tiffany blue, which went quite well with the two-tone brown carpet that looked as though it had vines running through it. The floor to ceiling blue and brown silk drapery finished the classic look. The air was filled with the powdery scent of Chanel No. 5, and all was right with the world. "You're up?" I yelled toward the bathroom door.

"Up and ready," she said, opening the door, grabbing the side of her dress, and making a grand entrance into the bedroom.

"Wow!" I cried out in reference to her large patterned, multicolored dress that looked like something straight out of the 60s. It was sleeveless, so she coupled it with a long sleeve lime undershirt and matching lime green ribbons, one in her hair and one around her neck. "Okay, let's do this."

The Peabody is a great hotel, full of history, class, and its own little quirks. As we exited the elevator, I said, "See that fountain over there? It's going to be filled with ducks later, so we can't miss that."

"With what?" she asked, a funny look on her face.

"Ducks."

"That's what I thought you said." She shook her head slightly, as if in disbelief.

The car service my agent set up took us to the television station for the morning show. I probably should have requested an actual car, because the big red Cadillac SUV was a bit of a challenge to get in and out of. Of course, Lucille never complained one bit.

Lucille was a huge hit, as always. She embraced the book's ethos and was living proof of the title, *Age to Perfection*. The female host, Marybeth Conley, loved her so much that she invited us to go on her radio show next. "Of course. We'd love to. Right, Judy?" The invitation was directed at me, but Lucille decided to answer for us. I knew she wasn't really asking for my formal approval. She would take any opportunity that she could get to be in the spotlight.

The radio studio was on the second floor of an old office building. It was very different from the studio we record my show in. When we walked through the front door, I saw the building's narrow, steep staircase and turned back to the host with wide eyes. I had never seen Lucille climb stairs that steep or that many all at once. What if she fell? I stood there in hesitation, still looking at the host, "I don't know—"

"Nonsense," Lucille said, nearly pushing me over. She grabbed the handrail and said plainly, "You just put one foot in front of the other." Before we knew it, she was at the top of the stairs. "There!" she let out with a huff.

For the next hour, she sat perched up on a bar stool with her mic and surprised us all. Not only was she full of spunk, she nearly took over the show. I guess her past appearances as a longevity expert on our show had turned her into a pro. She was hysterical as she flirted with the male co-host, even telling the audience that he had proposed to her during the break.

When we got back to the hotel lobby, I said, "Lucille, it's been a long day. I think we should go rest."

"Not before those ducks you promised me. Where are they?"

As if on cue, the elevator opened and the Duck Master appeared. The ducks emerged, waddling single file from the elevator to the fountain. Lucille started clapping and bouncing in her seat on a nearby bench. "Look at that! Will you just look at that," she repeated, shaking her head in disbelief. Lucille was just like a little child, completely mesmerized by the well-disciplined ducks that waddled one by one into the fountain.

That evening, Lucille slipped into her red satin pajamas. She looked over from her bed to mine and said, "Do you know how to do bicycles? Bicycles in bed?"

"What are you talking about?" I asked a little confused. *Surely she's not talking about the exercise!* I thought.

"Like this," she said as she put her hands under her hips and lifted her legs high in the air. Her red silk pajama legs slid down, exposing her thin, white legs. She was doing it, bicycle exercises in bed. It wasn't long before I was doing them in my bed, too. "I do this every night so I can keep myself looking good," she said through huffs.

About thirty minutes later, she was snoring away, lying flat on her back with her hands folded upon her chest and her wig half off her little head. After a long and eventful day, Lucille had finally run out of steam. I stared at her for a moment, wondering how I was so lucky to have such a great friend. She really was the best friend a girl could ask for.

The next morning, I woke up to Lucille singing in the bathroom again. It was a song I had never heard before, but a sweet sound that I could get used to hearing morning after morning. She was up and at 'em at the crack of dawn, complete with the scent of her freshly sprayed perfume. I sat up, stretched, and yelled toward the bathroom door, "So are you ready for another big day?"

"This will be the best day of all," she said with a smile as I opened the hotel door and she passed through. "Thank you for planning this part. It really means so much to me." She was referring to our little side trip to St. Jude's Children's Research Hospital. She was solemn and sincere, as if she were on a mission.

"Sorry I couldn't get you a full tour of the place. I guess they have to be very careful with visitors."

"I understand. Just going there and seeing it in person will be enough. And they have that museum. We can do that," she said, buttoning the last button on her blouse.

Most of the ride, she was quiet, and just looked out the window of our chauffeured red SUV. When we arrived, Lucille seemed somber. I knew that she had donated to St. Jude's every month for years. Now she was standing on the grounds of a place she was so very passionate about. It was almost surreal as she stood there, soaking it all up. "Here, take my picture. Right here, right next to the statue." It was a marble statue of St. Jude that was especially tall since it was atop a large block that had "St. Jude Hospital Danny Thomas Founder 1960" chiseled into it. Judas Thaddaeus was one of the twelve apostles of Christ and was later known as St. Jude, the patron saint of hope. I thought about how fitting it was to name a children's hospital after him.

A few minutes later, a little girl came outside with someone who appeared to be her mother pushing her wheelchair. Lucille looked over at her, scanning her round, pale face and bald head.

She looked at me as if to get permission, and I nodded the go-ahead. As she stepped toward the little girl, she bent over a bit and said, "Hello, there."

The little girl smiled at Lucille, a sweet little innocent smile. "Hello," she replied faintly. The girl, who seemed to be somewhere between eight and ten years old, looked tired. Her grayish skin was pale and lacked any pink whatsoever. Her eyes were sunken and dark. She looked tired and exhausted. I felt like she should be at school running around with her friends, not sitting outside a hospital in a wheelchair.

"Do you know how old I am?" Lucille asked her.

"No," replied the girl, shaking her head ever so slightly.

"Well, I'll give you a hint. I'm over one hundred years old," Lucille said with a wink.

The little girl's face lit up, and she looked back at her mom to be sure she had heard, too.

"Have you ever met anyone over one hundred?" Lucille asked her.

"No," she said with a shy smile.

"You know what else?"

The little girl shook her bald head ever so slightly.

"You're going to be okay. I'm old, and I know a lot of things."

I stood as still as could be, listening intently. Their conversation took place in the shadows of St. Jude and there Lucille was, doing his work, offering hope. I found myself wondering which of them would make it to Heaven first. I even imagined them meeting and remembering each other, reminiscing over this sweet moment.

The little girl and her mother both smiled at Lucille, and then the mother wheeled her daughter back inside. It took all the effort she could muster, but the little girl lifted her arm and waved goodbye to Lucille.

As we walked toward the Danny Thomas/ALSAC Pavilion, a museum that shows the history of St. Jude's, I caught a glimpse of a tear falling from the corner of Lucille's eye. "Yep, best part of the whole trip," she said under her breath.

I loved everything about that trip, but that moment stood out. Past the fake eyelashes, the fancy clothes, and all the need for love and attention, Lucille had the warmest heart a person could imagine. I thought back to every person we had met along our path together: the waiters, drivers, people in stores, and even that little girl. Lucille taught me something that I will forever cherish: everyone needs to feel noticed, loved, and encouraged, and we should never be too distracted to make that a top priority, no matter how busy we might think we are.

Chapter Twenty

The Sky's the Limit

After our trip to Memphis, I couldn't get that image of Lucille and the little girl out of my mind. I know Lucille had made an impression on her, and the entire experience made me think about the people who made impressions on me at about that same tender age. My family's move to the small town of Cleburne, Texas from Michigan when I was a kid meant new schools and new friends for both Jennifer and me. I was in the fifth grade and she was in the ninth.

Fifth grade is already an awkward time. The summer after fourth grade, the girls start liking boys, and the boys start liking sports, cars, and anything fast. The boys either like girls or they don't, but the girls know which ones have come to their senses and which ones still haven't. In my case, the awkwardness of fifth grade was coupled with a case of total culture shock.

Everything about my new classroom was different. The kids dressed differently, in old jeans and worn shoes. There was little color, and no dresses on the girls. The posters on the classroom walls were maps instead of inspirational sayings, and the windows were wide open. I never did learn whether they didn't have air conditioning in that old school or if the principal was just cheap.

I once overheard Mom on the phone saying that people from Michigan had thick blood, which was great for cold winters up north, but wasn't well-suited for hot Texas summers. I felt like I didn't have the right blood to sit in that classroom, because just doing so made me feel hot, sticky and sick.

I also learned that people from the North were not exactly welcome in the South, a lesson my new teacher taught me on the first day of school. She was old, probably around seventy-something. Her hair was white, and she wore those old-lady glasses, the kind with the pointy black frames. She was overweight and liked to wear what I referred to as "grandma clothes." Her crumpled toes overlapped each other inside her thick-strapped dress shoes that looked like they were made of fake leather or some kind of soft plastic. She had a pair of those shoes in every color, and apparently nobody had ever told her that open-toed shoes did not go with pantyhose, especially the kind with a reinforced toe.

On that first day, my new teacher looked over the class and then said, with her big Texas accent, "Judy and Virgil, come up to the front." I figured her red face and sour expression were just due to the heat. "Hurry it up, let's go. I don't reckon' I have all day," she insisted as she motioned for us to move faster.

Virgil was taller than me. Of course, everyone was taller than me, but he was tall and lean with very dark skin. He looked over at me with his big brown eyes and long black eyelashes. He seemed afraid, and as he reached the front of the classroom, he dropped his head, refusing to make eye contact with our classmates. I wasn't afraid, so I put on my biggest, cheesiest, dimpled smiling face. I was certain that both Virgil and I were new students and that the teacher was going to introduce me to all my new friends. I couldn't wait to make a good impression.

"Class, this is today's lesson," the teacher said as she stood between us, placing one hand on Virgil's shoulder and the other on mine. "The only thing worse than a N— with a knife is a Yankee with a U-Haul." The class giggled and pointed at the two of us.

What's a Yankee? I thought.

Virgil jerked his shoulder away, walked back toward the class, and threw his dark body back into his seat, putting his head down on his desk.

I just walked back to my seat slowly, confused. Why was everyone looking at me like that? Should I be laughing too? I didn't feel like laughing. I felt my dimples melt back into my face.

Virgil didn't smile much after that, but he and I played together on the playground quite a bit. We had an unspoken bond that year, perhaps because we both were feeling the sting of small-town Texas.

It wasn't until a few weeks later that I finally got a moment alone with Mom. Ever since the move, she had been really busy with work, so we didn't see her much. "What's a Yankee?" I asked curiously. "Are we Yankees?"

"I suppose we are," she replied dismissively, without even looking up. She was clearly too busy to talk about it, so I never brought it up again. I don't think she was ignoring the question, she was just caught up in some work she was doing. Mom was always busy working on something. I wished Dad were there with us; he would have explained this Yankee thing.

I stopped in to see Lucille one day, bearing a gift. At this point in our friendship, I didn't bother to knock, I just walked right in without thinking. She opened the bathroom door, surprised to see me standing in her living room. "Look what I have for you!" I said, waving around a white satin pilot's hat trimmed in soft white fur.

"It's beautiful," she said as she pulled it onto her head, squishing her wig up into it. "I'm going to be the best-looking girl there."

Eden Estates had arranged for her and some others to go up in a Boeing Stearman biplane, the same kind of plane used for training in World War II. It was close to Veteran's Day, and the air was crisp, but nothing was going to keep her from taking to the skies.

"It's hard for my family to believe I'm going up in a plane like this," she said with a devilish grin. "I never liked to fly. Actually, I *hate* flying."

"Really?" I was shocked, because she had flown to Memphis without a hitch.

"Really," she replied emphatically. I figure this is the best way to get over my fear for good. Open cockpit. Besides, Judy, you told me that I can do anything. I *feel* like I can do anything," she added with great enthusiasm. Those words made me so happy inside. I felt as though I had encouraged her, much like how she continued to encourage me time and time again. It felt good to have a symbiotic relationship. Too many friendships these days are all one-sided.

I was so proud of her, and the smile on my face showed it as I hugged her goodbye. "See you tomorrow! Big day!"

The next morning was quite chilly, and I was worried about the wind, but I didn't dare mention it. I figured that the pilot would know best.

Alyssa, a thin blonde who couldn't have been more than twenty who worked for me for a short time, and I pulled into Alliance Airport. There was hangar after hangar, but we were in no danger of getting lost; it was clear which one was our destination. A crowd of seniors was gathered inside with tables, chairs, and red, white, and blue balloons. Just outside the hangar sat the white biplane and countless people taking photos. Of course, I brought my own photographer. That's what Alyssa was for.

"Look at me," Lucille said, patting her white-gloved hand atop her new hat when we approached. She had ridden over with all the other seniors, and she was right: she was the best dressed one there. It was the first time I had ever seen Lucille in slacks, but she made those black-and-white plaid pants look so stylish with her black leather jacket and white scarf.

"You look marvelous, darling," I said in my best Australian accent, trying to say it just the way Doreen would.

"What? I can't hear you," she yelled back.

Of course she can't, I thought. The hat covered her ears and was strapped on tightly just below her chin. She had it on so tight that that thing wasn't going anywhere.

I looked down at her feet and pointed, shaking my head in disbelief. "Seriously, Lucille, heels?" Her cute little toes were peeking through the front of her black leather high heels.

She didn't need to hear me; she knew exactly what I was saying by the roll of my eyes. She replied loudly, "Hey, a girl's gotta look good for her big moment. Besides, you hired someone to photograph me and another to video this. Heels make your legs look longer." She pressed her tongue to her upper lip and smiled a big smile.

Lucille was the life of the party, waving to the other seniors patiently waiting their turn to go up, and smiling and clapping as she bounced around like a cheerleader.

Finally, her big moment came, and it was her turn to climb into the plane. My heart was beating a million miles an hour as I pictured her sliding off that wing in those high heels.

"Piece of cake," she called loudly as she settled into her seat. "Hang on, I want Judy to come get a picture with me," she told the pilot. She waved vigorously and yelled, "Judy, get up here."

I climbed up onto the cold, slick wing, bent down next to her, and smiled with her for the camera that Alyssa was holding. Then I reached in for a strong embrace. "You've got this," I yelled against her cap-covered ear.

As I climbed back down, I heard the pilot say, "Sorry, but we're going to have to replace that sweet white hat with this one," strapping her into an old leather cap.

"Okay, as long as I can change it back when we land," she said, sounding a bit demanding. "I like the white one." Then she slid on her red-rimmed sunglasses. The rhinestones across the top of the frames made her look like a celebrity.

She waved from the plane as it taxied to the runway, and in a matter of minutes, she was up there among the clouds. I felt my heart swell with pride, realizing that it's never too late to look fear in the eye and laugh. I stood there, windblown, looking up at Lucille in that plane with pure admiration.

When they taxied back in, the expression on her face was pure joy, without an ounce of fear or regret.

There she was, climbing back down in those heels. As a nurse, she had taken care of her fair share of wounded soldiers, and now she was the face of bravery itself. She stood tall, looked at me, and with a big smile blurted out in excitement, "I didn't want to come down. That was incredible. Oh, the view! I wish I could do it again, Judy."

Every time I think of Lucille up in the sky, flying close to the heavens, a smile comes across my face. She was ageless, without a care in the world, simply enjoying life to its fullest. And I was there to bear witness to it all.

Things seemed to be back to normal and I was looking forward to the months that lay ahead. Unfortunately, little did I know that I was just on the incline of a large roller coaster ride, about to take the freefall.

Chapter Twenty-One

Star-Struck

The thing about roller-coaster rides is that the view at the top seems so clear, so freeing. You feel like you're on top of the world and you often can't see how far you're about to drop.

It was early one morning, and Judy 2 and I were the first ones at the office. She was wearing a pair of black slacks, an off-white blouse and a pair of very high heels. "Can you believe it's already time for the holidays again?" She asked as I followed her to the breakroom.

"Not really." I said as I grabbed a green tea bag and added it to a cup of hot water. "It seems like this year was a whirlwind. I'm ready to say goodbye to it and start a new one," I replied, thinking back to Walter's heart attack.

"So, what do you have planned?" she asked, sipping her coffee.

"Planned?" I asked, a little curious as to what she was referring to. "Nothing, really, why?"

"You should always have something planned. I think that's what keeps Lucille going. It helps when you have something to look forward to."

She was right, but I couldn't think of anything I wanted to

do, at least not yet. If I knew God, He'd think of something and let me know, usually when I least expected it. I changed the subject. "Today's going to be a great show. Guess who's coming on?" I asked, knowing she would be impressed.

"Who?"

"Suzanne Somers. She's always a great guest. I just love her! If only all our guests could be as spot-on as she is," I said with a smile.

She smiled a big smile back, raised her eyebrows, and offered a faint, "Yay," as she took another sip of her coffee.

Suzanne is great every time, and this time was no different. The hour seemed to fly by as we talked about staying young and staying healthy. She's done so much research of her own on longevity that you can basically ask her anything and she can quote a reputable research study. True to form, Suzanne gave a polished and personable interview. The funny thing about radio is that guests can sound great wherever they happen to be, and regardless of what they're wearing. She could have been sitting on her sofa in pajamas for all we knew, but she sounded like a million bucks.

"Thanks for coming on the show again," I said as we wrapped things up off the air. "Man, we could talk to you for hours. Do you ever get to Texas?"

"Not really, but I could." There was a slight pause and she added with real interest, "Why don't we plan something? I'll put you in touch with my staff, and let's see if we can work out an event there in Dallas."

Both doctors gave me a thumbs-up.

In the weeks that followed, I worked with Suzanne's people to plan some kind of event in Texas. Of course, any event in Texas has to be big. That's just the way we roll. So the planning took quite a while. I searched out venues, researched ticket prices, and even organized a silent auction for Wounded Warriors to go along with our event. During that time, Lucille and I enjoyed many Friday outings, but I didn't dare let on. One Friday, I finally decided that I could tell her. The planning was far enough along that I knew it was going to happen.

We were sitting in her living room making small talk about Halloween. She was wearing an orange and brown outfit, fitting for the fall weather we were having. "Lucille, how would you like to meet Suzanne Somers?"

"What?" she screeched in that funny voice she used when she was caught by surprise. "Meet her on the phone?"

"Nope, meet her in person," I said quite proudly.

"Oh, boy!" she cried out. "I love her. Wasn't she on your show recently?"

"She sure was, and we planned for her to come to Texas. I was waiting to tell you until it was a done deal."

"Terrif—"

"But *wait*, there's more," I interrupted her midsentence. "Doesn't that make me sound like a used-car salesman?" I giggled slightly under my breath. "Anyway, I'm working with her people and the people at the Bass Hall in Fort Worth. We're planning an event: 'Stay Young at the Bass: An Evening with Suzanne Somers.'"

"'Stay Young'? Does that mean you and the docs will be on stage, too?"

"Yep! And do you remember Suzie Humphreys, the one that interviewed you on the Broadcast?"

"Yes," she replied fondly.

"Well, it's going to be all three of us; a three-part show."

"Oh, my gosh!" she squealed as she shook her head back and forth and bounced a bit with excitement in her chair.

"But wait!" I said putting my first finger up in the air as if to quiet her down for the big reveal.

"There's more?" she asked surprised.

"Yes. How would you like to be part of the show? How would you like to come onstage with me?"

"Me? Little old me?" she asked humbly, with one hand across her chest.

"Yes, you."

She never actually answered; she just hopped out of her chair and started going on and on about what she should wear. She was pushing the hangers over quickly one by one as she dug through her closet. "I think red. Definitely red," she said as she grabbed her long, red velvet dress. "Oh, and maybe with some white," she said, pulling out a white fox stole. "And a hint of black, perhaps." While it sounded like a Santa suit, no Santa or Mrs. Claus ever looked as stylish or was in such good shape, either.

It seemed as though the weeks flew by. There was lots of planning and organizing, and before we knew it, it was February, and it was show time.

The Bass Hall had a nice, fitting room for us. It had one large mirror above the long counter, several adjustable seats perfect for hair and makeup, and a few comfortable chairs to relax in. There was also a rack to hang our clothes on. "This is a fantastic greenroom," Lucille said to the makeup artist. "It's better than most of the others we've been in." Her tone was a bit snobbish, as though she were in and out of greenrooms on a weekly basis.

Walter popped his head in the dressing room and motioned for me to come into the hall. "Are you nervous?" he asked. He was looking good since his heart attack. His blue suit fit him just right and his black shoes were polished. I have always had a thing for polished shoes on a man, but rarely does Walter give them a second look.

"Actually, I am," I replied shaking my arms by my side as if to shake the nervousness right out of them. "I don't know why."

"Just think about all those performances in high school," he said with a smile as he grabbed my arm to stop it from shaking. He was referring to my years in theater.

That didn't help. The stage of Cleburne High School was a far cry from Bass Hall in Fort Worth—even if I had a small part, like the time I played a maid in *You Can't Take it With You* (I don't know if that play even called for a maid, but my freshman year the theater teacher wrote one in). I was Rheba, the best maid that had ever graced the stage of Cleburne High. But, the Bass Hall was much larger and the stakes were much higher. This was my career, my reputation, and I was going to be part of a show with a celebrity. I felt sick to my stomach. Showtime was only an hour away, and we still had a dinner reception with Suzanne and a few of our honored guests.

Mary, the personal assistant I had hired after Alyssa left, was a huge help. She was much older than Alyssa, not just in years, but in life skills. This was a perfect job for her because she was working on her PhD in Psychology and needed a Monday through Friday job that gave her relief from the monotony of school life. She was crazy thin, model thin, and she always wore her hair in a tight bun atop her head, almost like a unicorn. I had put her in charge of the silent auction that benefited the Wounded Warrior Foundation. Being true to her fashionista self, she arrived in a burnt orange and gold flecked vintage Chanel tulle skirt with a crisp white button down shirt, and black pointed Christian Louboutin heels. Like any great assistant, she had volunteered Mark, her longtime boyfriend, to be in charge of Suzanne. I love someone that can delegate, and delegate well. Mark spoiled Suzanne all night by opening doors, bringing bottled water, of course only in glass, and making sure she stayed completely on schedule.

Just as we were finished getting ready, Mark popped his head in and announced with a big grin, "It's time!" Mark had Hispanic roots and his thick frame was balanced by his large head and bouncy curly hair. His smile was so big that it was infectious. He was the kind of guy you just felt the need to hug.

"Are you ready to get a bite to eat and meet Suzanne?" I asked.

"Sure," Lucille replied, batting her false eyelashes at me. There was a glow about her that night; she was truly in her element, and she was rocking that long red gown.

No sooner had we entered the reception room than their eyes met. Suzanne came right over and said, "Well, hello. You must be Lucille."

Lucille's face lit up, and she looked as though she could hardly contain herself. "Hello, and yes, I am Lucille." She paused for a moment, studying Suzanne's face and then looking her up and down. Looking surprised, she said, "You look just as good in person."

The two laughed and then embraced for a photo.

After Suzanne walked away, Lucille leaned over and whispered to me, "You know, they don't all look that good in person."

I had to laugh. How many celebrities had Lucille actually met to be able to make a statement like that?

As the time for the show grew closer, I felt butterflies in my stomach. I could hardly eat. Instead, I walked around with Walter and Lucille, shaking hands and welcoming people. It was all I could do not to think about going up on stage. I could hear my own voice in my head trying to talk sense into myself: *This is so stupid; you are on the radio every week talking to more people than this.* They say you know you're crazy when you answer yourself, which is exactly what was going on in my head: *Yeah, but that's radio; they can't see you. Besides, what if you trip, just like that time you tripped going onstage for the Golden Girl pageant?*

"Judy. Judy?" Walter said in a hushed tone, trying to get my attention. He stood right beside me, but I was paying him no mind. "Did you hear me?"

"Uh, sure. Well, no," I replied, shaking myself out of my trance.

"We have about fifteen minutes left. Are you sure Lucille is up for the trick?" He asked with a bit of concern. He was referring to a magic trick we had planned. Lucille was going to climb into a dark box—the Staying Young Machine—and out would climb a young, beautiful girl draped in a Ms. Staying Young sash. Lucille had only practiced it once, but she didn't seem to have any trouble. Besides, I had all the faith in the world in Raymond King, the professional magician, who was also our entertainment attorney. Raymond is one of those guys who was a professional student for years: he was an attorney, a physician, and a magician. If he couldn't pull this off, nobody could.

"Are you kidding me?" I said, waiving my hand dismissively. "Lucille will be fine. She's loving all this. I'm not worried about her one iota."

Nodding, Walter said, "Just think, Judy, we've been coming here for years. Now we'll get to see the theater from a whole different perspective."

As we sat in the green room, I could hear Suzie Humphreys onstage over the speaker. The crowd was loving her. I glanced at the clock and knew we were up in a few minutes.

My stomach turned, and my hands grew sweaty as we walked to the wings of the stage. "You stay right here until I welcome you on. It'll be about five minutes," I instructed Lucille.

I was pretty sure that Lucille could sense my hesitation about going on stage. She grabbed my hand, looked me in the eye, and said, "You got this."

As I prepared to walk out onstage, I turned one last time to blow her a kiss. At that moment, I remembered Lucille up in that airplane, laughing in the face of fear. Suddenly, all my anxiety melted away. I walked out onstage with the doctors, waiving at the crowd and smiling. I looked down, and there was my mom, my dad with his wife, Dana, and my sister, Terri, all looking back at me with big smiles. The view of the theater from the stage was breathtaking, with the soaring, hand-painted ceiling. Walter was right: the view *was* different from up there. I looked up at box M, where we held season tickets. It was empty. For a moment, I imagined that we were sitting up there, watching ourselves.

Dr. Anderson, Walter, and I performed a stage version of our radio show, complete with the vignettes from the show: Dementia Defender, Doc Shock, and the Immortal Minute. But perhaps the most impressive part of our show was our guest. She came out in that red dress with a white collar, looking like a million bucks and decades younger than she really was. After our uproarious interview with her, she pulled off that magic trick like it was nothing.

"Looks like Lucille stole the show," Walter said with a smile, putting his hand on my back as we walked offstage.

Suzanne came on after us and the crowd cheered with excitement. Her dress was fitted, dark metallic, and showed every curve as the lights hit it. She had insisted on having a clear lectern and now I know why. Her level of fitness and beauty is that of a woman half her age and she needed to show it off. After all, she is her brand, living proof that her advice works and that's what keeps people listening to her and buying her books. We all knew that the crowd was really there to see her, not us, and true to form, she gave them exactly what they came for.

After the show, we all went back to the dressing rooms. Lucille was already there, asleep in a recliner, having passed out from all the excitement. Her body was lifeless, and her hair was slightly off center as she snored ever so slightly. "I better get her home," my dad said. He was wearing a black suit and a collared shirt. He even had on those black dress shoes that look so good but kill his feet. He was there as her official chauffer for the night and he looked the part.

I gently shook her arm, and she sprang back to life. "Just resting, that's all," she assured me, all bright-eyed with a smile on her tired face.

"It's okay. Dad went to get the car for you." I said as I reached over and straightened her wig.

She wrapped herself in her pink wool coat in preparation for the cold and windy November air. As Lucille and I exited our greenroom, Suzanne exited hers, and the two of them came face to face again. They embraced for a hug and one last photo. Suzanne turned to Lucille and, with a big smile, said, "You inspire me."

We waited for the car just inside the glass backstage door, trying to stay warm. People were streaming out of the theater and passing the stage door, but not one made it by without a big smile and wave to Lucille. One lady actually stopped at the door, the cold wind blowing through her blonde hair, and with a girlfriend on either side, she yelled and pointed at Lucille, "Can I hug her?"

Lucille looked up at me with a smile. "Sure, let her in."

I gave the guard a nod, and he buzzed them through. Tears filled the lady's eyes as she embraced Lucille tightly. "I can't explain it, but I just love you. Thank you for letting me touch you."

"Yep, it's official: you're a star," I declared proudly as the ladies departed.

My dad pulled the car up to the curb, and we headed out into the cold. "Oh, Judy, this has been one of the best nights of my life," she said reflectively with a tear in her eye. After a moment she perked up and added, "And Suzanne, oh, Suzanne is just wonderful! Did you hear her? She said I inspire her. Can you believe that?"

"Yes, I can believe that," I said, giving her a hug and a kiss goodbye.

That night, Dad, Dana, Walter, and I sat in the kitchen for hours, rehashing each moment in a four-way play-by-play.

"It wasn't a sellout, but for being the coldest night of the year, and a weeknight to boot, I think we did pretty well," I said as I gave Dad a kiss goodnight.

"I think it was great, and I know this will be a night you'll never forget," he said, giving me a kiss on the cheek and a tight dad-hug, the kind where you get a squeeze and a rub on the back at the same time.

I climbed into bed, rolled over, looked at Walter, and thought, *Yep, it was a night I'll never forget.* Everything in the world seemed right. I knew I had made my parents proud that night; I could see it on their faces, and I could feel it in the way my dad had hugged me.

Chapter Twenty-Two

In Search of Home

It was another Friday and we were sitting tucked in a booth at a local seafood restaurant. Since we were early, we beat the crowd. I love being the first ones there, you get to pick your table and there are less distractions. "Judy, I think it's time for me to move," Lucille said as she took a bite of her salmon.

"Move?" I asked as I cracked a crab leg over my plate. "Move where? And why?" I was shocked. I couldn't imagine packing up and moving if I were her. For heaven's sake, she was 103 years old! What could possibly make her want to move at that age?

"The people there are old. Have you seen them?" she asked, completely seriously.

I had to smile, though I tried desperately to keep a straight face. *Did she really just say that? She's the oldest person at Eden Estates*, I thought. I knew that many of her friends had left. Some had died, and some had moved. As I thought about it, I realized that all the new people seemed to have memory problems or other significant health issues. I could tell this change had been difficult for her, but I never thought it would drive her to move.

Lucille was used to being the queen of the royal table. The dining room used to be filled with laughter, mostly coming from her table. She and her friends were like the characters on that show, *The Golden Girls.* They would exchange great stories, gossip about people moving in or out, discuss who the most eligible bachelor was, and talk about their future plans. Friday dinners were always Lucille's opportunity to report on our lunch outing from earlier that day. I got the sense that many of her friends were living vicariously through her little escapades. It had been a table full of friends and full of life, a table where there was always room for one more. Now, her table was down to three people, one of who was on hospice.

"Besides, I don't like the new owners," she said, making a face of disgust.

"Really? Why not?

"They took away the Lazy Susans from our tables. Now I have to get up and reach way over peoples' plates for the salt and pepper. How rude is that?"

I found this to be a completely ridiculous excuse to not like someone. Plus, thinking back over all the meals we had shared, I realized that I had never once seen her put salt or pepper on her food.

"I wrote a letter to the new owner. I told him to put our Lazy Susans back. I also told him that the food has gone downhill. Way downhill."

Listening to her talk, I knew the truth: if all her friends were still there, she probably wouldn't have noticed any of this, wouldn't have cared about it at all. Nonetheless, nothing meant more to me than her happiness. "If you really want to find a new home, we're going to find you one," I said, reaching across to squeeze her hand.

She smiled a huge smile, slapped me on the knee, and said, "Terrific! I knew I could count on you."

About three days later, she called me. With some excitement

in her voice she said, "Judy, I would like to go see the place where Vel lives. She says it's great and has arranged a tour for us next Friday. They will even feed us so I can taste the food."

"Okay, sounds great." I was happy that she found a place to look at. "See you Friday." I was especially glad they were going to feed her. *That woman knows her food, and God save the queen if it's not good.*

Something was different when I picked up Lucille that Friday. Not in her, but in me. Normally, I would be excited about a new adventure, but this time, nothing seemed to excite me. If I didn't know better, I would've said I felt depressed. I was feeling kind of melancholy and extremely fatigued. It was like being numb. I didn't have anything to feel sad about, and sad wasn't the right adjective to describe my sense of nothingness. It was more like I had no feelings, no energy, no excitement, no nothing.

Lucille jumped into the front seat as if she were the forty-something, while I walked back to my side feeling like I was the one who was over a hundred. I climbed in, trying desperately to hide my exhaustion. I was forcing every smile, every sentence, every step.

"I bet this place is going to be great," she said with a smile and lots of enthusiasm. The kind of enthusiasm you have when you're expecting something wonderful to happen. "I can't wait to see Vel. Wouldn't it be great if I—"

"Lived in the same place as her again?" I asked, knowing it was a rhetorical question. I didn't mean to interrupt, but I knew exactly what she was thinking.

"Yes. I miss her so *much*."

Bingo. That was it. This desire to move wasn't about those Lazy Susans, the worn carpet, or the fingerprints on the walls; it was about her entourage leaving her.

* * *

We drove up to Vel's place. From the outside, it looked fairly new, almost like an apartment complex. It was tan, two stories tall, and filled with windows. It had a large entrance at the front and a few "future resident" parking spaces off to the side. We parked in one of those spaces, but I wasn't feeling as if that sentiment was going to come to fruition. Not sure why, call it intuition.

"Here goes nothing," Lucille said with a smile as we walked up to the front door.

Unfortunately, from the moment we entered, we knew it wasn't right. The colors were all wrong. It was pink and tan with the occasional turquoise. I'm sure that the Southwest décor was great for some, but not right for a Broadway star. We gave each other a look, the kind of look that best friends give each other, that "Yes, I'm thinking what you're thinking" look. We both knew this was not the place for Lucille, but at least we would get to see Vel.

We stood there for a moment and waited for someone to come greet us. "Sorry, we're short-staffed," a woman said, approaching us. "Come this way. You can eat and then go on the tour. Just come back up here when you're ready."

"At least we'll get a meal out of this," Lucille whispered a little too loudly for my liking as she made a face of obvious disappointment.

The lady guided us through a crowded dining area. It felt like we were in Florida, not Texas, with all the pinks and greens in the carpet, walls, and drapes.

"Hi! Come join us. We're ambassadors here," said a friendly lady in a cotton printed shirt, the kind they actually wear in Florida. She looked almost too young to be there. Her hair was thinning and red, but dyed to cover up the gray, I'm sure. "It's part of our job."

Her husband, a charming silver-haired gentleman who seemed awfully fit for his age, chimed in, "That's right. We get credit for being friendly to visitors and answering their questions." The two of them looked like the quintessential retired couple, the type that one would see on cruises or in senior resorts. They appeared as though they had come from a history of financial success, but weren't willing to give up making an occasional buck or two, as evidenced by his comment.

I couldn't help but think that this was too much information. Nobody should ever say that they benefit from being nice to you. How could we trust what they were going to say?

"Thank you," I said with a smile. "Lucille here is 103, and she decided that she wants to move."

"Where are you now?" asked the man.

"Eden Estates," Lucille replied giving a thumbs-down.

"Can't say we know that one," he said as he looked to his wife for a nod of agreement.

"It used to be great there, but it's changed. New owners," Lucille informed them.

"Oh, these places all turn over. The owners keep them long enough to make a profit and then sell them off. Usually, that's right when repairs need to be made," the lady said. I looked around and saw that there were many others just like her: older, but highly functional. The crowd was definitely an improvement upon Eden.

A large, dark-haired lady came by to take our order. She was dressed like a waitress from an old diner, and she had the abrupt attitude to match. Not knowing the system, we felt a bit out of place, and the waitress snapped at us, "What'll it be today?"

Just then, Vel entered the dining room, and Lucille gave her a big floppy wave. I could tell that Lucille just wanted to visit with her, but unfortunately, there wasn't much catching up that could take place between the hustle and bustle of the lunch crowd squeezing between tables and our conversations with the chatty ambassadors.

"What would you say is the best part about this place?" I asked, looking at both the husband and wife.

"The people," she said very unconvincingly. If she liked the people, I would think that comment would have come with a smile rather than a straight face.

"Definitely the people," he added with a smile. It appeared he was the charismatic one.

I smiled back at him and then asked, "What's the worst? I mean, are they good at repairs, administrative stuff, and—"

"Oh, repairs!" She rolled her eyes, nudging her husband. "Tell them about the mold issue, honey."

Mold, I thought, *yikes! That could literally kill these people.* "What mold?" I asked with a grimace. "That doesn't sound good at all."

"Oh, it was everywhere," he said, spreading his arms out to invade the personal space of the people next to him.

Before he could say more, the wife interrupted in a gossipy tone, "Yes, everywhere. They kept telling everyone that it was all taken care of. We knew better, though. We all talk, you know." Her face squinted a bit in suspicion.

Lucille glanced over at me. I could tell that she hadn't heard all of the conversation, but she got the gist that it wasn't good news.

Just as we finished up, the lady pulled out a bag. I noticed that everyone started pulling out tote bags. Lucille and I looked at each other, totally confused.

"Oh, we always over-order here. They only serve breakfast and lunch, so we pack up the extras, and that's our dinner. We all eat dinner back in our rooms," the man explained.

"What did he say?" asked Lucille.

"They only serve two meals. Those bags are for what they take back for dinner," I said loudly, talking over all the clacking of people spooning food into containers.

Lucille squeezed her face into a look of disgust. "Leftovers every night? Well, I don't like that." She sat up straight in her chair, as if to show that she was above that sort of thing.

"See you later, darling. Stop by my apartment after the tour," Vel said as she made her way through the crowd.

We managed to get back to the front desk and stood waiting around again for someone to help us. The front-office lady that we had seen before zipped in and out again, not stopping long enough to make eye contact.

"Here she comes again. I'll ask her," I said to Lucille as we saw her coming back. Just as she started to brush past us again, I stopped her. "Miss? We're the ones here for the tour."

She looked up just long enough to say, "Bob will be here to take you on the tour in just a minute," she said quickly, and without making eye contact as she scurried around us.

"'Bob,'" Lucille mused. "It's interesting that we're going to get a tour from a man." She was right—stylish and personable saleswomen had performed all the other tours we had been on.

"Hi, I'm Bob," said a man in khaki pants and a colored, short-sleeved shirt. A large ring of keys hung from his belt, and his shoes looked as though he was in construction, not marketing.

"What exactly do you do here?" Lucille asked as we entered the elevator.

"I'm the maintenance man," he replied as he pushed the button for the second floor. "We're short staffed today, so they asked me to show you around."

Lucille rolled her eyes. I saw her roll them, but that wasn't enough for her. She reached over to whisper in my ear, in the loudest whisper possible, "The maintenance man, huh? That's the best they have to offer me?"

I didn't know what to say. He was literally standing right next to us. I was embarrassed, but laughing a bit inside my head. Not at him, but at her. That was such a Lucille thing to say.

As we walked down the hall, I noticed that it smelled of mildew. "What's that smell?" I asked.

"What smell?" he said.

"I swear it smells like mold in here. Have you ever had a mold issue?"

"We did have a small bit of mold a few months back, but it has all been resolved," he said with an unconvincing smile. "We were even inspected afterwards. It was due to a drainage issue we had from those heavy rains. Do you remember the downpour we had?"

"Yep, I remember it well," I replied, unconvinced by his answer. You didn't need to be a bloodhound to know there was still mold in that building.

"It's all good now. We got a clean bill of health during the inspection."

Nothing he could say would make me believe him.

He showed us the chapel, which also doubled as the activity room. Then we were off to see an apartment. "Now the one that's coming available is not exactly like this, but it's close. You can get a feel for how great they are."

"Great" was not the adjective I would've used. The appliances and countertops were dated. It had light wood cabinets with white laminate counter tops. It was plain and boring, like a dorm room.

"Can you take us to Vel's room?" Lucille asked. "I think I've seen enough."

"Sure. She's actually a bit far from where we are now, though," he said as if to get approval for the long journey. Lucille nodded him forward.

The long walk to Vel's was silent until just before we got to her door, when he said rather loudly, "Do you have any more questions for me?"

"Nope, not a one," Lucille said rather sharply.

As soon as we entered Vel's apartment, Lucille lit up. The two of them had plenty to catch up on. I had always been fond of Vel. She was a smart lady, full of great stories from her interesting life.

"What are those men doing on your porch?" I asked, noticing workers outside.

"Oh, they're trying to get rid of some mold in my outside closet," she answered.

"*Really?*" I said sarcastically, turning to look at the maintenance man. He had quickly shown himself to the door, moving too fast for me to make eye contact or question him about it.

"Let me show you around!" Vel said proudly. "I have a two-bedroom apartment and I love it here. I have lots of room for my things."

I could tell that Lucille was impressed with Vel's place as she looked around. "Look at this, Judy. Did you know that Vel is an artist?" she asked, admiring Vel's colorful paintings of different sizes on the wall.

"I didn't. Wow! I love your place and your art, Vel." I said, a little shocked. I knew she had written a book once, but I had no idea she could paint, too.

"Thank you," she replied with a sweet nod. Her voice was so unique, deep, and sounded like a cross between the Deep South and California. She tended to drag out certain letters just long enough to sound a bit snobbish.

"Come in and sit down."

I was grateful for the invitation since my legs were feeling weak and achy. "Your furniture is great," I said, forcing a smile through the pain.

"Her husband was a doctor, too, you know," Lucille informed me.

"Yes, that's true. My dear, late husband was a very well-respected psychiatrist." There it was, that accent. I love the way she drew out the I in "psychiatrist."

The furniture in her apartment looked like it was the remains of downsizing from what must have been a grand home and an even grander life.

My mind wandered as the two of them went back and forth, catching up on all the latest gossip. Looking around, I wondered, *What if? What if something were to happen to Walter and I had to downsize? What would I take, and what would I leave behind?* I went through my house, room by room, in my mind. I would take the family photos, the personalized Christmas ornaments, and the art that Walter and I had collected together. I'm sure I would leave the stuff that was just stuff—things that don't have a memory or a story associated with them.

Sitting there in deep thought, I also wondered about my mom. At some point, she would have to downsize from her home, too. What if she waited too long? What if she couldn't tell me where she wanted to go or what she wanted to take with her?

As I thought about all this, the conversation between Vel and Lucille played softly in the background like music. Suddenly, Vel spoke directly to me: "Well, have you given it any thought?"

"I'm sorry. Given what any thought?" I asked, embarrassed that I had drifted out of the conversation.

"What would you do if something happened to Walter?" She asked matter-of-factly. "We both lost our husbands, and honestly, you never know what could happen or when."

Had this woman just climbed inside my head?

Suddenly, I felt as if my entire body had caught on fire, and I sat there paralyzed with fear. I didn't dare mention that I had just been thinking about that very same question. Sitting there between two widows, I gave the most honest answer I could: "I would have to be locked up. I think I would go crazy. Walter and I do everything together; we even work together." I could hear myself being a little defensive. After all, why did she have to bring this up? "A life without him is beyond my imagination. Yes, I'm certain I would need a straitjacket."

Lucille gave me a kind, loving, and comforting look. I knew that she understood, more than anyone, the deep, complex, and loving marriage Walter and I have—a marriage beyond most people's ability to grasp. She also knew what I had recently been through and how lucky I was not to be the third widow in the room.

"No. No, you wouldn't," said Vel, shaking her head. "You'd move on." Her tone was very matter-of-fact.

I quickly changed the subject to hold back my tears. Pointing across the room at a rather large antique wooden chest, I said, "That's a great piece. I love the detail. I can see why you kept it all these years." It was funny that I saw it as an antique, but she probably thought it looked as new as the day she bought it.

Vel walked over to it, removed a fox stole from the bottom compartment, and wrapped it around her neck. Then she sashayed across the living room, telling us the story of when her husband gave it to her. "I used to love to wear this," she said with a big, bright smile. "That's one of the benefits of being married to an intelligent and successful man." As she danced around the room, I could see myself in her position, trying to keep appreciation for a great husband and all the memories alive.

Hours went by, and I grew excessively tired. I didn't want to break up the party, but I desperately needed to go home and rest. "I hate for us to run out, but I still need to drive Lucille to her place before I can go home." I didn't want to tell them I wasn't feeling well. The attention needed to stay where it belonged: on them.

Vel walked us to the door and hugged and kissed us both goodbye.

As Lucille and I got in the car, we looked at the building and back at each other. "Nope," we said almost in unison.

"But I think I know just where to take you next. There's a great place close to my house, where Walter and I once took dancing lessons. I was so impressed with them, and I think you will be, too."

"Okay," she said in a hopeful tone. "Next Friday?"

"Next Friday."

After I dropped her off and started heading to my place, I thought about her need for a new home. We all wanted to belong, to find that sweet spot in life. We're all looking for the place where things seem just right, where we like the people next to us—and we like ourselves. And liking the food and the décor doesn't hurt either. . . . As I pulled up my driveway and into my garage, I thought, *Lucille has lost her sense of home,* and I knew that, in order for her to thrive, I needed to help her find it again.

Chapter Twenty-Three

Winds of Change

It was a long week, and it felt like a lifetime between Fridays. If it weren't for my promise to take Lucille to see the next contender for her new home, a place called The Conservatory, I would probably have canceled our next outing. As tired as I was and as unwell as I felt, I am always true to my word, so I knew I needed to suck it up and keep my promise.

I could feel that change was in the air; it's something you can sense, much like the when the smell of spring fills the air, or the first snow of the winter season is about to fall. I knew that Lucille was desperate for a new and exciting place to live, one where she could flourish. She needed it, and, come hell or high water, I was going to make it happen no matter how badly I felt.

On Wednesday, I had a bad night and couldn't get out of bed come Thursday morning. Something was wrong, terribly wrong. My entire body was in pain, and I couldn't get my legs to move, not even to get up to go to the bathroom. Walter had already left for work. Thinking I was just tired, he let me sleep in, which was a rarity.

From the phone by my bed, I called our office. "Can you

ask the nurse to make a house call? I think my arthritis is acting up. Tell her to bring a steroid shot with her." I had previously had arthritis pain, but never like this, and usually only when it rains.

I lay in bed in agony, crying, but trying my hardest not to cry too hard so my bladder wouldn't explode. I had to go, but my body couldn't take me there. At that moment, I developed a new respect for the bedridden.

"Thank God you're here," I said to the nurse when she arrived. She'd been to my house before, but never my bedroom. Luckily, she found it without any trouble.

"What happened?" she asked a bit shocked to see me in my pajamas with my hair a mess from a restless night's sleep.

"I don't know. I guess it's some kind of flare." My voice was low and each word took effort to say. "Perhaps my arthritis is getting pretty bad. Is it supposed to rain or storm or something?"

"No, I don't think so. This is the worst I've ever seen you. This doesn't look like a flare from rain, besides there isn't even any in the forecast."

She gave me the shot, wished me well, and left. I lay there another few hours. Eventually I rose, but the rest of the day was tough, and I barely made it through. She was right: this was more than arthritis, more than something caused by the weather.

Friday came, and I was grateful that my body was in a vertical position and ready to meet the day. As always, Lucille came out dressed to the nines, complete with the ribbon in her hair and the flower on her lapel. We parked in the "Future Resident" parking space at The Conservatory.

"I remember telling Walter to park in this spot when we would come here for dancing lessons," I said.

"What did he say to that?" she asked.

"'Okay, but remember, I am *never* getting old!'"

Walter always had a thing about the word "old." On his sixtieth birthday, I even put "The 21st Anniversary of his 39th Birthday" on the invitations.

As the automatic doors slid open, Lucille caught her first glimpse of the interior. The place was filled with hard woods, fine fabrics, and an entire front-office staff to greet and welcome her. I could hear her sigh of relief. She turned and gave me a smile, wink, and nod of approval. We knew, we both knew: this was it.

"Karen, the salesgirl, was kind enough to come in on her day off to give us a tour," I told Lucille. Karen had worked many days straight, but she didn't want to just pass us off to someone else. Honestly, I think she just wanted to meet someone who was so spunky at 103.

We had lunch with Karen, a boisterous blonde who actually looked a lot like Kasey, in the beautiful dining room with soaring ceilings, floor-to-ceiling drapery, beautiful lights, and staff that was dressed like we were in a fine restaurant, not some roadside diner.

"I can't wait to show you the gym and the theater," Karen said in her sweet, Southern accent.

Resident after resident was more than happy to greet Lucille with a warm introduction, some even with a hug. Lucille pranced through the halls like a prize horse after a winning race, leaving behind only the scent of her Chanel No. 5.

"This place doesn't have much turnover, so pay attention to what Karen says so you can make a decision," I whispered into Lucille's ear.

At the end of the tour and the gourmet lunch, Lucille decided to put down a deposit. She was so happy and giddy. I was happy, too, but I was just so exhausted, and my legs hurt so much that it was hard to be enthusiastic.

On the ride home, Lucille was so excited. It was as if someone had injected her with 200 mg of pure life. "Oh, I need a new bed for when I have company. Now that I have a second bedroom, I can have guests whenever I want." Lucille continued to ramble on and on about all the things she was going to need. Going from a studio apartment to a two-bedroom, two-bath place meant reinventing her space. Being able to decorate again, now with a fresh color palette, seemed to light up a different part of her brain. She had a new life and a new purpose. I hadn't seen her smile that big and for that long in at least a few months.

This move also meant a day of shopping. I knew we couldn't do the in-and-out-of-the-car routine, at least not with my enduring exhaustion, her age, and the Texas summer heat. "How about we plan a trip to Nebraska Furniture Mart? They have acres and acres of furniture, all in one location," I suggested.

As soon as I said it, I realized it was a terrible idea. The Mart was about an hour away, and for some strange reason, road trips were becoming really difficult for me.

"That's a great idea!" she said.

I smiled back, but it was a weak and faint smile. It was all I had to give. As soon as I had suggested the Mart, I knew it was anything but a great idea.

The weekend was eventful, more eventful that I would have liked. My illness hit a new high that resulted in a trip to the emergency room. At some point, I knew I needed to tell Lucille my diagnosis, but somehow, some way, regardless of my circumstances, I picked Lucille up for her big shopping trip on Friday. She climbed into the car, while I made my way to the back and opened the hatch. I looked down at the turquoise walker she was using more and more often and said a short prayer that I would be able to lift it into the back of the car. This was Lucille's day, and I was determined not to ruin it.

"This is so exciting." She was bubbling over with enthusiasm. "I've been laying it all out in my head," she said, using her hands to outline the apartment she was imagining in the air. "I go over it again and again every night." She looked over at me with a big smile. As we drove down the highway, passing so many familiar sights, she mentally walked through it again. "My old place had built-ins, so I'll definitely need a new dresser. And I don't like having the TV up on the wall; perhaps I should have a nice stand or cabinet for it to sit on? Oh, there's so much to think about! I'm so excited about this furniture place . . . where is it again?"

I had both hands on the wheel, staring forward to concentrate on the road. I could feel my arms pulling me forward toward the wheel, trying to get comfortable, but it was no use. *Breathe in, breathe out. Smile, turn, and speak.* "It's pretty far, but you're going to love it." I was working hard to keep it together. I was already fatigued, and my legs hurt—sharp pains ran from the middle of my thighs down through my knees, just from the short twenty-minute drive from my house to her place—and we still had about forty minutes to go. Most of the time was spent listening to Lucille bubble over with joy about her new place, a sound that was music to my ears. Her happiness was a great distraction from the pain.

"Are you hungry?" she asked at one point. By the way she asked, I could tell she was hungry and hoping we would stop.

"Actually, I am," I replied, suddenly remembering that I had forgotten to eat. All of my focus had been on mustering enough energy to make this shopping trip happen. "Well, we could eat before or after we shop. Which would you prefer?"

"How about right now?" She asked. I was right, she was hungry. "There's a hamburger place right there. Burgers sound good," she said pointing to an In-N-Out. "Let's just go through the drive-through and eat in the car."

In the car? This was a far cry from our usual outings. Things like paper napkins, plastic utensils, and straws had never been a part of our lunch festivities in the past. It was all too reminiscent of my rushed childhood, where too many evening meals turning spent at a drive-through, rather than at a family dinner table. Many people who grew up during my era experienced this. Somewhere along the line, convenience became the new norm, especially for parents that worked long hours. For those of us being raised by a single parent who worked one or two jobs, drive-through meals were not just expected, they were a necessity.

As Lucille and I sat there eating, my leg and back pain became excruciating. Sitting had become the hardest thing for me to do. I knew then that regardless of how this might change our day, I had to tell her.

"Lucille, there's something I need to tell you. I don't want this to upset you, but I figure you'll find out sooner or later." As soon as I said it, I knew there was no going back. I didn't want to worry her, but I knew she needed to know.

"What is it?" she said quietly concerned as she took my hand, reassuring me that I had her full and undivided attention. There was a long pause and she added, "Tell me." Her eyes began to tear up, a mirror image of my own. Tears began to drip from both our faces and down to our paper napkins.

"Last Sunday, I was in the emergency room. I've been pretty sick for a while," I said, frustrated and tearful. I was afraid to tell her, not because she wouldn't understand, but because I wanted to be the one person she could always count on. Always, no excuses.

"Oh, Judy. I knew something was wrong. You haven't been yourself, and you've seemed sad lately. I knew it; I just knew it." She rubbed my arm in long up-and-down motions while holding my hand tightly. I could see the wheels of her mind turning, and she flipped from best friend to nurse. After all, why not? She had played that role well into her eighties, and it was a role she felt comfortable in. She needed to know everything. She needed to understand. "What is it? Will you get better? How can I help you?"

I told her everything. I told her how they thought I was having a heart attack at the emergency room and pumped me full of nitroglycerine and morphine, but heart attack didn't fully fit my symptoms. My mind went back, revisiting the whole ordeal.

"Sunday morning, around three a.m., I woke up with crushing chest pain, and I felt like I couldn't breathe. I was convinced it wasn't going to pass quickly, so I woke Walter up. We started getting ready to go to the hospital, but then it passed. My legs were still weak like they've been for weeks, but at least the chest pain was gone. I was so tired, I begged Walter to just let me go back to bed. He agreed, under the condition that if it came back, we would go, no questions asked. I agreed."

"Judy, you know you should never ignore chest pain," Lucille said in her best nurse voice.

I knew she was right. After all, Walter's heart attack had come out of the blue. He didn't have any risk factors and had received a clean heart scan just two years prior. Had it not been for a highly inflammatory infection he caught from a patient, which caused the inflammation that led to the blockages, he never would have been in that situation, proving you can never be too careful.

"A few hours later, we got up and got ready for church, but it seemed like so much effort just to take a shower. Raising my arms to shampoo my hair was a monumental task. Everything took effort, and everything took too much time. We were late, so we sat in the back of the church. When the first hymn came up, we stood up and opened the hymnal, but as I started to sing, nothing would come out. I got this terrible feeling and was weak and afraid. 'It's coming back,' I told Walter.

"'Let's go,' were the last words I remember him saying as we rushed to the car.

"The ride to the hospital seemed to last forever. It was strange, but I could clearly hear this faint whistling. The band The Scorpions had a song, 'Winds of Change,' which became synonymous with the fall of the USSR; Klaus Meine wrote it after a trip to Russia a year before the big fall. It starts with this eerie whistling, which for some reason I was definitely hearing. I'm not sure why, but this song has played in my mind more than once during a life-changing event. Not the whole song, just the whistling.

"The second we entered the emergency room, I could tell they were taking my case seriously. They didn't even ask for my insurance card before I was in a room and getting all sorts of tests: an EKG to check my heart rhythm, a chest x-ray to look at my lungs, and a CAT scan of my chest just to be sure they weren't missing anything."

"They knew it was bad," she said as she listened intently.

"I remember them giving me nitroglycerine, and I was thinking, *you don't have a heart attack in your knees! Whatever is happening in my chest is also happening in my knees!* But I was too weak, tired, and breathless to argue.

"'Are you a vegan?' the emergency-room doctor asked.

"'No,' I answered. I'm about as far from a vegan as one could get.

"'Vegetarian?'

"'Not even close. Why?'

"The doctor told me that my protein was very low, as was my calcium. They were going to check my calcium again with a different type of test, just to be sure. The doctor was clearly perplexed.

"Later, she sent me home, told me to see a cardiologist, eat red meat, and take calcium supplements. It was a rather anti-climactic ending to a terrifying day."

"That's it? Didn't she figure it out?" Lucille looked perplexed herself.

"They didn't figure it out, but Walter did. It pays to be married to a genius. Though if you ask him, he'll tell you that it was an unlikely diagnosis. He chalked it up to divine inspiration." *A genius who's also spiritual; I'm so lucky to be married to him,* I thought. "He tested me for Lyme disease, and it was positive, both types of tests. He said he had never had a test so positive in all his years of practice."

"You'll get better?" she asked tilting her head down and looking at me, half asking, half requesting.

"I hope, but it will take lots of prayers." I replied with a faint smile.

"I'm going to go home tonight and say the rosary. I'm going to pray on my knees for you every night until you get better. You have to get better. You have to!" Lucille said with such pleading passion. "Perhaps we should skip our shopping trip?"

"Not on your life. I could use a little fun," I said, knowing darn well that all I really wanted to do was skip the trip. I was already so tired, and my legs hurt so much. I couldn't possibly cancel because I didn't know what tomorrow would bring. What if I never felt well enough to take her? I guess I was thinking it was now or never.

In the end, I'm glad we went. Lucille picked out the perfect TV stand, bedroom dresser, and guest bed. She did it all in what seemed like record time.

"Are you okay?" she asked as we drove home.

"Yep," I replied, lying through my teeth. I wasn't okay. My legs were cramping, and I had to use cruise control half the way. If she could drive, I would have asked her to.

The rest of the ride back was nearly silent. I tried to stare out my window, keeping my head at an angle so Lucille couldn't see the pain on my face. I gripped the steering wheel with my left hand and held onto her hand with my right. "Winds of Change" whistled through my mind, and I feared the future. They say that people get a diagnosis they don't want to hear, and they either scream that it's not fair or embrace it with all they have. I never thought I would be the former kind of person, but I was. *Why is this happening to me?* I thought over and over. That question would soon be answered—and in a way I never saw coming . . .

Chapter Twenty-Four

The Long Ride

Just as with life, it isn't the destination, but the journey that manages to take it all out of you. For me, life seemed to be becoming one long ride after another. I somehow managed to get to Lucille's place, get her walker out of the back, kiss her goodbye, and wait for her to clear the door. After she was inside, I felt a wave of pain wash over my body. Tears started to fall at a record pace. I just needed to get home. If I could get home, I could rest.

Pulling out of her driveway, I decided to take the back roads home instead of the highway, not realizing that it would take even more time. I drove through residential streets, but before I could get home, pain came over me like an exploding volcano, suffocating all my senses.

I hit the last number I had called from my cell phone, ringing my office. "Judy," I gasped when she answered, "I'm driving and I'm in so much pain and I don't know what to do."

"Pull over!" Judy 2 commanded in her best motherly voice.

"No, I can't. I just need to get home. Talk me through this," I managed to argue through my tears.

"Okay . . . breathe . . . in . . . out. Try to stay focused. You can do this. In and out. Judy, I'm going to pray for you. Would that be okay? Can we pray together?"

"Sure," I said, barely able to get the single word out. I groaned, as the pain seemed to sear through my back. I hoped that God would listen, but in that moment the pain was so consuming that I doubted it. I wasn't sure when my faith had become so weak, but it apparently had.

"Lord Jesus, please help Judy. Please help her focus and relieve her pain . . ."

The prayer seemed to go on for several minutes, with Judy 2 occasionally stopping briefly to make sure I was okay. She prayed all the way until my front tires reached my driveway.

"Thank you so much," I squeaked. "I'm home."

"Okay, go inside and lie down. I'll call Dr. Gaman and tell him what happened, but I'll let him know that you're home safe now. Love you. Bye," she said before she hung up.

It was a sad reality, but I knew then that I would no longer be able to drive, at least not for a while. How could I be such a strong person and not be able to fight this? I lay on the couch in my living room, crying tears of desperation. I had to lie on my side since my back felt like it had electric shocks going through it. I could feel the warm tears rolling out of my eyes, across my face, and down to the seat cushion. Never before had I felt so alone and afraid. The pain was swirling around by body like a spring Texas tornado. After a couple hours, the storm had been calmed.

For the first time in my adult life, I wasn't worried about work. I didn't care about anything on my desk, upcoming meetings, or deadlines. It wasn't just because of the pain. For months, I had felt my workaholism melting away. Lucille and her unconditional love had given me a sense of purpose and a new sense of self-worth.

It took everything I had to pick up the phone and call my father. "Dad, I just can't do it." I explained, deflated with nothing left. I knew I needed help. "I'm so exhausted, and the pain is incredible. It really scared me. I have so much to do. How am I going to get it all done?" I'm not sure why I called my dad; maybe I was looking for strength, and he was the strongest person I knew.

"You have to slow down. You have to give yourself time to heal," he counseled me quietly in a parental tone. They were reasonable words, but I am not always a reasonable person. "Slowing down" is not in my vocabulary or my genetic code. He, of all people, should've known that.

"I'll try, Dad. I love you," I said as I pulled the phone from my ear to hang up.

The next evening the phone rang, and Walter answered it. I couldn't make out what was said, but from Walter's tone, I could tell it was serious. "Who was that?" I asked.

"Your dad. He'll be here in a week. He insisted on coming down and being your driver, so you wouldn't be tempted to get behind the wheel of a car again."

I was both shocked and happy. I knew my stepmom, Dana, was the one behind his decision. She and my dad had married a couple years after Mom had moved us to Texas. Over the years, she and I had become very close. She was twenty years my dad's junior, so oddly, Walter was older than her.

Dad had so much to do, even though he was retired. In fact, it often seemed that he was even busier now than he had been when he was working. Simply living on acres and acres of land was a job in itself. Not many seventy-six-year-old men spend their days riding a four-wheeler, chopping down trees, and clearing paths that were destroyed by storms, but my dad could run circles around most people half his age. I guess he's so healthy because he's always been active, never shying away from physical labor.

As the days passed, I looked forward to his arrival with ever-greater anticipation. In my opinion, he couldn't get here fast enough. I was going crazy, the pain was incredible, and my mind was starting to fail, rendering my memory non-existent and sentence structure a forgotten art. I have never felt so incompetent, helpless, and hopeless in all my life. I wondered if this was God's way of offering up a cure for my workaholism. Sometimes the best medicine is the hardest to swallow. Giving up control of my life, my work, and my destiny was not only hard to swallow, it was choking the life right out of me.

When it was time for Lucille to move into her new home, I so desperately wanted to be able to help her. I told her as much over the phone, grasping it tightly at each fresh wave of pain.

"No way! You're going to rest," she informed me in her best nurse's voice. Luckily, she had arranged for a full-service mover to pack and unpack for her. I paced around my bedroom, feeling useless and aggravated. She was going to move and make this big change without me by her side, on a date that I had picked based on my schedule. I felt like I had let her down. I felt like a failure.

The days were dark and dreary, not outside my windows, but within my own head. Not only was I unable to help Lucille, but I also knew I couldn't make the upcoming trip to see our new grandson in New Jersey. I could hardly walk across a room, let alone an airport or two. It simply wasn't going to happen.

Mom called at one point, and I filled her in: "I told Walter to go by himself. The baby is only young once, but Walter is very apprehensive about leaving me here. Dad is coming down, but not for another week."

Mom was in Michigan with her husband, Louie, where they were handling the sale of his old property, something they had long awaited. "I can stay with you," she offered in a firm but gentle voice. "We should be back just as Walter is leaving. That way, you won't have to be alone at all. I can stay with you for a few days, and then Walter will be back, and your dad will be there." Mom sounded so sure of herself. She was happy to help, and I knew she wanted to do whatever she could. I was happy, too—happy and comforted by the fact that she cared and that she would be there to ease my rapidly multiplying and consuming fears. I was so consumed by the thoughts of never getting back to a normal life, that for a moment, I completely forgot about her Alzheimer's diagnosis.

Something happens to you when you're sick. I'm not sure why, but no matter how old you are, how educated you are, or how happily married you are, we all still want our mom and dad when our bodies fail us. I was lucky. For the first time in many, many years, I was going to have both. "Winds of Change" whistled through my mind again, only this time with a sense of hope.

When the time came, Walter said his goodbyes, and against my better judgment, I drove him to the airport. I was used to navigating the DFW airport, even through the years of never-ending construction. What I wasn't used to doing was navigating it with Lyme disease. After I dropped Walter off, it took me ten minutes to exit the parking garage. There were countless arrows labeled "Exit," but they all seemed to send me around in circles. I looped around the parking garage for what felt like an eternity. My hands were sweating, and my heart was pounding. I felt panicked. *What if I never get out of the airport?* I thought. *What if I run out of gas trying?* I was afraid and not my usual rational self. I was so focused on figuring it out, that my eyes burned from not blinking.

I eventually made it home, drained by my airport ordeal. I was so tired and weary that I got confused just trying to find the right key for the door. Finally, I got in and was able to crash on the couch.

The first thing I did was pick up the phone and call Mom. "Are you almost here?" I asked, anticipating an affirmative answer.

"No, we've been delayed," she said pragmatically and without remorse. "I'll probably be there tomorrow." My heart sank, but I tried to convince myself that I could handle one night alone. After all, there was no alternative. Besides, one night alone was not the end of the world.

But as I lay there, frightened and crying, all my efforts to rally myself failed. I felt alone and terrified. Nothing was working—not my brain, not my limbs, not even my faith. I was on all-systems failure.

The next morning, I woke up feeling pretty good. I knew help was going to be there soon and I had made it through the night without a major flare. My mom called and by the tone of her voice I could tell it wasn't going to be positive news. "We've just now left Michigan," she said. I felt my heart sink. I had gotten through the night by envisioning my mom driving all through the night and anticipating her knock on my door when I awoke in the morning. "I'm so sorry, but things took longer than we expected. We're heading out in the next few minutes."

I sat on the bed and sobbed. I felt completely alone. I didn't dare tell Walter how things had turned out or how I felt because he would be so guilt-ridden for leaving. So I did what I had to do: I climbed into my car and drove to see Lucille in her new place. I knew I wasn't supposed to be behind the wheel of a car, but this was an emergency. I needed refuge from my own thoughts, fears, and incredible sense of disappointment. Luckily, Lucille's new place was only about seven minutes away, or two-and-a-half songs on the radio, depending on how you looked at it.

Lucille opened the door and greeted me with, "What are you doing here? You're supposed to be resting! Are you okay?" She was half happy to see me, and half upset that I had driven there. She put her arms around me and hugged me tight, so tight that I crushed the pink silk flower on her lapel.

She took me by both shoulders and looked me square in the eye. "I'm fine, or I will be fine. I'm just tired," I said in an unconvincing tone. I left out the part about being depressed, frustrated, and angry. I looked around at her apartment. Her things looked as though they had always been there. This place suited her quite well. I could tell she was happy from the beaming smile on her face. She was like a queen in her castle.

"Come, come in here and lie down." She directed me toward her bedroom, and I obeyed, lying down diagonally across her pale peach silk duvet that covered her bed. She sat facing me, propped up on a few of her coordinating silk throw pillows, her hand stroking my hair as she started to sing. Her voice sounded like an angel's. It was old and crackly, but it was an angel's voice nonetheless. Although I've never heard an angel sing, I'm pretty sure it's more about the feeling they emit, rather than their perfect pitch. Her touch reminded me of my Grandma Grieve, my dad's mom, who would stroke my hair and sing to me when I was little. I turned my head away from her, and tears filled my eyes, falling one by one onto her beautiful silky pillow sham. I was so grateful to have Lucille in my life. She was truly a gift from above. I thought to myself, *I have to get better. I have to. But what if I don't?* The dialogue within my mind was a constant battle between good and bad, hope and despair. But through it all, Lucille just kept singing, running her hand over my weary head.

I stayed with Lucille all day, but before heading home, I called my mom to see how things were going. Almost afraid of the answer, I managed to ask, "Where are you?"

"In Indiana."

"Indiana?!" I blurted out, stomping my foot. "But you've been driving all day!" I knew I had just yelled at my own mother, but I didn't seem to care. I was flabbergasted, not just by their complete disregard for the urgency, but the fact that she didn't offer an explanation for her delay.

It took my mom and stepdad two more days to make it to my house. I never found out why it took that long. Maybe they got lost. Maybe they didn't really leave when they said they did. I never asked; I guess I just didn't want to know the answer. In the meantime, I felt as though I had gone into survival mode, just taking each hour as it came. I struggled to fight back my feelings of disappointment, frustration, and despair and to muster the strength to do simple, everyday tasks. I did at least keep my promise not to drive again, after I had barely made it to Lucille's and back. I didn't want to tempt fate.

Finally, I heard their knock at my door. Louie, tall with gray hair and a large belly, walked in and declared, with a big, cheesy grin, "Sorry! We got behind some slow drivers." He laughed at that, but I was far from amused. Mom stood there in his shadow. Luckily, she didn't seem amused either. Her clothes were wrinkled, and her short gray hair was a mess. By the sigh she let out, it sounded like she was glad it was over.

It was late, and they were obviously exhausted, so Louie stayed that first night. The next morning, he left Mom alone with me.

It was a tough day and night that followed. Lyme disease is like having shingles, Alzheimer's, and mono all at the same time. The nerve pain was unbearable, I couldn't remember anything, and the fatigue made even the smallest task seem insurmountable.

The next afternoon, I had an incredibly bad attack in the

nerves in my back. It came on suddenly, and the shriek of pain that came from my lips would have sent even the most experienced nurse into panic mode.

"It's okay. Here, let me help," my mom said in a comforting tone as she jumped up, grabbed my arm, and guided me toward the bedroom. She was able to get me to the bed one slow step at a time as I bent over and twisted around in agony. Then she lay beside me as I screamed in pain. The tears fell from my face like a running faucet.

After what felt like an eternity, the pain finally began to subside, and I was left exhausted. Mom's soft hand draped over my forearm. She'd always had such soft hands.

"Heavenly Father, please help my daughter." Her voice was trembling, and I could tell she was trying to hide the fact she was crying. "Please take away her pain. Please comfort her," she prayed under her breath with the occasional sniffle. She prayed and prayed.

At first, I didn't have any interest in her prayers. I doubted He would listen anyway. I had been so mad at Him because I prayed that Mom would hurry up and get here, and that took forever. Obviously, He wasn't interested in my timeline or my needs. But as she prayed, something changed. I could feel a glimmer of hope come back into my body. Like a spark of positive energy and a belief that God might be listening. He was listening to the pleadings of a mother for her child, and somehow that seemed different. As she tightened her grip around me, I heard her sniffles and felt her wet tears. It was as if I were a little girl again and she was cradling me in her arms. I felt her fear, pain, and frustration, and it made me forget about mine.

At that moment, I was no longer mad about the long trip. I wasn't frustrated by my pain and by the disease. I was grateful. I was grateful for my mother. I was grateful for her love. I was grateful for her faith. I was grateful that her diagnosis was progressing very slowly and that she still knew who I was. I decided that I loved her just the way she was. Even if that meant she was late, occasionally dismissive, and at times unavailable. And I decided that I would always love her from that point forward. Unconditionally.

Chapter Twenty-Five

Mission Accomplished

Thirty days. That's what they say. After thirty days of treatment, one of three things will happen: one, you get better and are completely cured; two, you *think* you are better, but then you experience residual symptoms and relapses; or three, you don't get better and just continue to get worse. I was only a little over a week in, but with no relief in sight, I had succumbed to defeat.

"I've decided that the treatment probably won't work, so I began researching physicians who specialize in failed treatments. There's one in New York that sounds promising," I said to Walter as he sat on the edge of the bed, stroking the hair on my head. I was too tired to get up. He was fully clothed in a suit and tie and ready for a full day of work, and there I was in pajamas, hoping just to make it to the kitchen for some breakfast.

"Give it time. You're not done with the treatment yet. I think you'll get better. I really do," he said, patting my shoulder and leaning in to give me a kiss on the forehead.

Seeing the glass half-empty is not my style, but I just couldn't seem to snap out of it. That is, until my next trip to the airport. Yes, I drove to the airport again, against my better judgment.

Dad walked purposefully toward the car with a single tote bag, and a determined look on his face. As I looked at him, so strong and ready to help, I thought that I had nothing to offer him. I couldn't possibly be good company. I looked bad and felt worse. I was still struggling with the reality that, after spending years trying to ensure that my parents always saw me at my best, they were now seeing me at my worst: little, if any, makeup; no desire to dress up; and no energy to do anything that required effort.

I noticed that something about Dad was different. His step was determined, and his face was serious. He embraced me in a tight hug, saying, "I'm here now, and we're going to get you better!" He held my shoulders and looked me right in the eye. "I can't have my baby girl sick." They were words that brought such comfort to my heart, words that I needed to hear. To this day, I'm not sure what was more comforting: his declaration of healing, or the words "my baby girl." I don't think he had ever called me that before, and if he had, it would have been before my parents' divorce.

The days that followed were a blur. I remember starting sentences and not being able to finish them and having thoughts that were as fleeting as a shooting star.

"Eat this," Dad would say, offering me a piece of beef jerky. "Gotta get your protein higher."

"Did she take her meds today?" Walter asked each day as he came in through the back door carrying his briefcase.

"She sure did. I made sure," Dad would reply looking up from the evening news. He had made it his mission to ensure that I followed the doctor's orders.

He also had an uncanny understanding of my need to get

out of the house or stay busy when I had even the smallest bit of energy.

At about week two-and-a-half, I had a rough day. A *really* rough day. The pain in my legs was severe, and my mind wouldn't work at all. My thoughts were all jumbled, and I suddenly realized that I couldn't type. Not because my hands didn't work, but because my sentences were gibberish. I looked at my dad with complete despair in my eyes, as though all hope and faith had vanished from my world. I realized then that the things I loved to do might not exist in my future. As tears fell down my cheeks and red blotches formed around my eyes, I asked, "What if I never write again?"

He looked at me, grabbed both my arms and his eyes commanded that I look right at him, and said, in the sternest voice I had ever heard from him, "You are *not* going to talk like that! If I hear you speak like that again, I'm going to whoop you." Then he dropped his hands from my arms and let out a huff. He was serious, and I believe he meant it.

The next day, I couldn't find him and ended up looking all over the house. I finally spotted him through the window. He was lying in the hammock by the pool, shaded only by the tree branches above him. He seemed relaxed. I watched him for a moment, feeling lucky to have a father that would drop everything and travel twelve hundred miles to take care of his baby girl.

A couple of hours later, he came inside, entering the kitchen and said, "I just spent two hours praying you would get better."

Praying? My dad had never spoken to me about prayer. My mom once told us as kids that he didn't even believe in God, though I never fully believed her.

I doubt he realized it at the time, but the simple act of him praying for me, and even taking the time to let me know he had, was the turning point that brought my faith back. It was the moment when I first started to believe that I was actually going to get better. Lucille, my mom, and now my dad had all petitioned God for my healing. I now knew in my heart of hearts that there was hope.

Every day, Dad continued to speak positive words to me: "You're getting stronger. You're getting better. You're getting over this bit by bit. You can do this."

At one point, we even made a trip to the local hobby store and purchased some green beads, one bead for each day of treatment I had left. I decided that I would drop a bead in the trash and say aloud, "Goodbye, Lyme disease," each day. I was convinced that when the beads were gone, the disease would be, too. I was no longer going to let it control my life. Dad's words gave me strength, and the beads disappearing from the jar offered me hope. Each day I felt a little better and a little stronger. Bead by bead the attacks were fewer and further between.

It was a bittersweet reality that I *was* indeed getting better, because time was flying by, and my dad would soon have to go back home. During those two weeks together, he was my cheerleader, chauffeur, and, above all, my hero. I had nothing to offer but a broken body and a crushed spirit, but he took it all in and gave me back my faith and my health, helping me heal from all the scars of the past.

Lyme disease was a bit of a gift. In some ways the pain and suffering were worth how it changed my relationships with both of my parents. Four decades into my life, I finally realized that my parents love me and have always loved me. I had made the mistake of defining their love on my terms, not theirs. I think many of us fall into that perfect-parent trap, where we have to check all the boxes: picture-perfect relationship—check; family dinners—check; family vacations—check.

Suddenly, none of this mattered. I realized a truth that some people never get the privilege of understanding. I had to love unconditionally in order to accept unconditional love.

I knew that this lesson could not have penetrated my heart and mind had it not been for my amazing friendship with Lucille. Over many lunches she reassured me that my parents loved me and that I was worth being loved. She wore so many hats for me: confidante, best friend, and now, angel with a mission. At this point, I would've said her mission was accomplished, but that's because I hadn't yet fully grasped her mission . . . not by a long shot.

Chapter Twenty-Six

⌐✑∿✑⌐

Play Ball!

Lucille loved the Texas Rangers about as much as she loved God and her family. She never missed watching a game in all the years she followed them. She knew all the players' names and stats, just like Little Walter. The two of them even talked about who should be traded, which player wasn't worth his salary, and who didn't get the appreciation he deserved. It was funny how she acted like she was their secret manager, a manager they didn't even know they had.

When she signed the papers to officially move into The Conservatory, Karen seemed happy. She liked Lucille from the moment she met her. She took interest in Lucille, which gave me comfort. She even asked her, "Well, having lived this long, I bet you've done just about everything."

"Not everything," Lucille replied. "I haven't thrown out the first pitch for the Rangers."

"Oh my, are you a Rangers fan? Me, too!" Karen squealed as she grabbed her hand to hold it for a moment. "As a matter of fact, one of our residents' sons works for them. I'll see what I can do." She saw Lucille's eyes get wide with excitement, so she added, "No promises, though."

"Wouldn't that be great!" Lucille leaned over to me and winked, saying, "Told you I was going to like it here."

Lucille brought that conversation up a few times over the following weeks and then seemingly gave up on the idea when it didn't materialize. So, of course I was thrilled when Karen called me at work and announced, "Judy, I did it! Lucille's going to throw out the first pitch at a Rangers game!" Karen was so excited that I could picture her jumping up and down as she told me. "I want to tell her, but we need to make it good, *real* good. She's going to be so surprised." She let out a squeal. "Why don't you plan to come over here sometime this week for lunch, and we'll do it then?"

I could hardly contain my excitement for Lucille, but I somehow managed to keep it a secret. I was trying to catch up on all the work I had missed while I was out, so I rarely called Lucille during the week. The day of our planned lunch, I sat down with Lucille in the dining room at her assisted living place, acting as if everything were normal. Then Karen and several staff members came in with balloons and a red box.

"What's all this?" Lucille asked as she looked around the room and over both shoulders. She was confused by all the commotion.

"Open it," Karen said, as she knelt down and handed her the box.

Lucille opened the box, which was filled with red shredded crinkle paper. In the center of all that padding sat an official Texas Rangers baseball. Lucille seemed excited just to get an official Ranger's baseball.

"You're going to do it," Karen informed her, her eyes filling with tears. "You get to throw out the first pitch!"

Lucille bounced up and down with joy, and then proceeded to spend the next hour making sure that everyone in the dining room saw the ball and knew that she was going to be throwing it out at a coming Rangers game.

"What are you going to wear?" I asked her amid all her bubbling joy. "You'll have to wear pants, you know," I asked in a confirming tone as I looked at her long black skirt, high collar cream silk blouse and pearl necklace.

"Oh, I need white pants. White pants and a jersey. And a red ribbon for my hair." She was definitely going into panic wardrobe mode. "Oh, I have to call Walter and Little Walter. They aren't going to believe this!" She was talking so fast with excitement. "Do you think Little Walter will give me pitching lessons?"

"You bet." I assured her with a smile. "I know he would get a kick out of that."

With each passing day, the anticipation grew. "I just need to get it over the plate," she would say with determination as she practiced her pitch for her big day again and again. I had to laugh at her persistence. "I don't want to look like a wimp out there."

The Friday before the game, we were in the car, heading to lunch. Lucille was wearing a green and yellow skirt with a yellow blouse and a green flower. She had several dangle bracelets around her left arm that chimed together when she moved her arm. Lucille looked over at me, raising her arm and chiming her bracelets and asked with a pointed first finger, "Can you call Walter? I need to ask him something."

"Sure," I said, dialing him on speakerphone.

"Walter!" she yelled, clearly excited. I had to laugh because she always assumed that since it was a speakerphone, she needed to talk really loudly. "I would like you to walk me out to the mound. Would you do that?"

"Of course. I'd love to." I could sense the excitement in Walter's voice. This was just as much a treat for him as it was for her.

"I started thinking about it. It's going to be a big day, and I really should have my doctor right there with me. I may get nervous or weak or something."

Walter chuckled. "You'll be fine, but I see your point." I could tell that he was thrilled by her request; after all, he was a huge Rangers fan too.

We smiled all through lunch, and just about every conversation was about the Rangers: "I don't think anyone has ever been a bigger fan. . . . Do you think I can get it over the plate. . . . Who's your favorite player?" It went on and on. It was so cute the way she was so consumed with her upcoming big day.

Finally, the day had come.

"I'm so tired, honey," I said to Walter mournfully as we drove to The Conservatory. I had been feeling much better since Dad left, but I still had days where the pain and fatigue washed back over me in waves. Those days were a little depressing, but I was determined not to let them destroy my spirit.

"I know, but you can do it."

He was right. I just had to focus all my energy on getting through the day and forget about the pain in my legs, the fogginess in my brain, and my need to lie down. It was Lucille's day, and of all the days we had shared together, this one was very special. I wasn't going to let Lyme ruin it, so I put on a big smile, stood tall, and walked up to the door.

"Wow, they went all out," Walter smiled, and his voice changed to a higher pitch as we walked through the sliding doors at The Conservatory. A red carpet, flanked by balloons, ran from inside out to the van parked just outside.

Lots of people were gathered for the big send-off, and Lucille was playing the part of celebrity in full force. She waved, shook hands, and kissed cheeks as she walked the red carpet and climbed into the van wearing white pants, a blue Rangers jersey, a red ribbon in her hair, and another around her neck. She pulled me toward her and whispered, "I put a belt on," pointing to a red braided belt that cinched in her jersey. "A girl's gotta have a waist, you know," She said with a smile and a wink.

It seemed like a dream. There we all were in the van with Lucille: some of her friends, Karen, several other Conservatory staff members, and Walter and me. She was beaming and filled with pure joy as we all sang "Take Me Out to the Ball Game." The moment seemed magical—so magical, in fact, that I completely forgot about my pain.

At the stadium, Walter and Lucille parted from the group so they could walk out on field. As the rest of us headed toward the stands, Karen held up several big posters, each with a single letter that spelled L-U-C-I-L-L-E. I looked back over my shoulder, and there was Lucille's son, Jim, who's strong with broad shoulders and receding salt and pepper hair, and looks half his age. Beside him was his wife, Carrie, who is shapely and fit with long brown hair and *was* actually half his age, and all their friends. He had a big smile, as if to say, "That's my mom!"

We each grabbed one of the signs and stood in the stands a couple rows behind home plate. Walter and Lucille walked out to the plate, and then it was Lucille's moment to shine. Her right arm went up and back as her tongue stuck out slightly and touched the top of her lip, proving she was concentrating as hard as she could. She stepped forward and followed through with her arm, releasing the ball at just the right time. Just like she had practiced. She kept her eye on the ball long enough to watch it make it right over the plate, or at least get close.

Her throw would be replayed over and over again online,

becoming a YouTube sensation. That throw also made the Rangers' year-end highlight reel. But perhaps the most impressive part was when Doreen called me all the way from Australia, "Judy, I can't believe it. I just saw Lucille on TMZ. Her and Walter!"

Lucille taught us all that we should dream and dream big. There she was, 103 years young, and by sharing her dream with others, she was able to make it come true. "Next year, I'll do even better!" she crowed as we all climbed back on the bus to head home. "They said I should come back next year, and I told them I would!"

I smiled at her with no doubt in my mind that she would.

Chapter Twenty-Seven

❧

The Prayer
of Saint Lucille

My Lyme disease had gotten better, to the point that I was back to work, full time and full speed ahead again. I felt as though I had missed out on so much while I was sick. It wasn't just the pain, it was also the brain fog. Now that I was feeling half-normal again, work was back on my mind. Not only did I have new deadlines to meet, but I also thought I ought to review the things I had tackled while I wasn't at my best. Perhaps I had made some mistakes?

Still, I felt different. I was busy, but not consumed with my job. I was at peace and ready to tackle all my tasks, but I didn't feel as though my job defined who I was or my worth anymore. I was so grateful that things were starting to seem normal that I started to write again. It was a huge relief that I could write, and then read what I wrote. It confirmed that my mind was clear, and I hadn't lost my ability to communicate in black and white.

* * *

I had just settled in at my desk for the morning when a call was transferred to me. I was surprised that Jim, Lucille's son, was calling me at work. "Judy? I'm guessing nobody called you."

"Called me about what?" I was almost afraid to ask.

"Something is terribly wrong with Mom." By this time, I had stood up and grabbed my purse with my free hand. "She's so confused. She doesn't know who anyone is. We're at the hospital."

"I'm on my way," I said without even considering that my desk was piled with work and that I had meetings that would need to be canceled. I just left.

As I drove to the hospital, I tried to imagine what it would feel like for Lucille to not know me. It was a stark reminder that someday my own mother might not recognize me—a thought I always tried to bury whenever it crept up. Since Lucille had always been as sharp as a tack, I had never even considered the possibility that she might lose her wits.

As I walked down the cold hospital hallway toward her room, I took a deep breath. Though I had been in the ER prior to Walter's diagnosing me with Lyme disease, this was the first time I had been in a hospital ward since Walter's heart attack. Taking another deep breath, I entered the room and forced a smile. I could actually feel the muscles of my face pushing the worry away to disguise my fear.

"Judy!" Lucille hollered with a big smile the moment she saw me walk through the door. She was in the bed, wearing a hospital gown, and covered with a thin white sheet. I was so relieved. For a moment, I wondered what all the fuss was about. She seemed fine to me, minus her less than stylish outfit. Then she motioned for me to come closer. She glanced over at Jim in the corner of the room and then quickly looked back at me. "Who is that man in the corner?" she asked.

Oh no. How can she not know who Jim is? I felt frightened and a bit confused. *What is going on in that head of hers?* I thought. I looked over at Jim, who was red in the face, clearly hurt that his own mother didn't recognize him. Worse yet, she knew who I was, but not him.

"I know the numbers: 973462. No, no. 97234623. Wait, I am going to get it. 9273462." She went on like this, speaking gibberish. It was like that game she and I used to play in the grocery store aisles, where she would rattle off everyone's phone numbers to prove to me, and mostly to herself, that her memory was still as sharp as ever. She would go through ten or twelve memorized phone numbers, getting them all correct. Unfortunately, this time was different. None of these numbers were even close to any of the numbers she previously knew. I knew it, and I had to believe she knew it, too, judging by the frustrated face she made each time she tried again.

Jim and I made small talk, but I could tell he was very uncomfortable in that hospital room. His arms were crossed, and his legs were planted in a wide stance. His blue collared dress shirt was untucked, and the arms were rolled up, exposing his muscular forearms. He hated hospitals in general, and I'm sure he was doubly uncomfortable with the situation. He tried to distract himself with calls from the office. "Jim, why don't you go back to work?" I suggested, deciding to put an end to his discomfort. "I can handle this tonight. I'll keep you posted." Jim always seemed to be a workaholic. I remember Lucille telling me stories about Jim working long hours and rarely taking vacation. Besides, I never saw him relaxed, although I'd only seen him a handful of times before this. I guess it takes one to know one. For people like us, work is sometimes the best place to be during stressful times.

"Thanks, Judy," he replied with what seemed to be a sigh of relief.

"I have a son," Lucille said suddenly with big eyes as if the light bulb in her head just went off.

"Yes, you have two sons," I said, looking at Jim and then back at Lucille.

"Of course. I have two." Lucille looked Jim right in the eyes and said, "Goodbye, Brody."

The room suddenly felt so heavy, and I could feel Jim's sorrow compound. I just wanted to reach over, hug him, and say, "She didn't mean it! She just isn't right, right now, that's all."

Jim's wife once told me that he doesn't like hospitals because they bring back so much pain from when his son, Brody, died. Brody's death at age twenty-four was completely unexpected. He was a seemingly healthy, strong firefighter who died of a sudden stroke while he was off duty. I can't even begin to understand what Jim must have felt at that moment when his mother called him Brody. He didn't say a word, simply turned and left, but Lucille was none the wiser about the mistake she had just made, the wound she had just reopened. And not just opened but poured salt right into.

The numbers thing went on and on for hours. Finally, I just decided to give in and tell her she was right. She smiled and asked about another set of numbers, and I said, "Correct!" We did this over and over again. She was obsessed with the numbers and wouldn't stop talking about them.

"I'm going to stay the night," I said to Walter as my cell phone glowed in the now-dark room. "I just can't leave her here alone and so vulnerable. That's not what friends do." I shivered from the air blowing from the vent above. I could only imagine the germs that were coming through that vent, infecting us both. I've always been a bit germaphobic but having a fragile immune system after my Lyme disease took my fears to a whole new level.

I looked over at the chair that reclined into a makeshift bed. It was covered in that plastic material that hospitals are known for. It was hard and cold, but I didn't care. I just pulled my new bed as close to hers as I could, wondering if either of us would get any sleep that night.

Soon after that, the doctor entered her room and announced, "Hyponatremia," as he tossed his hands in the air as if to say, "that was easy." I was relieved. I knew what that was, and I knew she would get better. "Hyponatremia is when the body's electrolytes get off-balance and the sodium concentration goes too low. It can be very dangerous, but it can also be temporary and quite correctable," he reassured us.

That whole night, Lucille never once forgot who I was. I seemed to be the only thing she could keep straight. Even when she had spoken to her son Joe earlier on the phone, she was confused and incessantly asking about those random numbers.

After hours of numerical rambling, she finally gave up and there was silence. Just as I was drifting off to sleep around midnight, I heard her praying: "Dear God, please look after Joe and Jim. Please be with them all the time. Please forgive me for all the bad things I've done. I'm not perfect. I've done so many wrong things in my life. Please forgive me for not being a better person, a better mother. Hail Mary, full of Grace. Joe, Jim. The Lord is with thee. Blessed are Joe and Jim. Blessed is the fruit of thy womb, Jesus. Please forgive me. Please forgive me. Our Father, full of grace. Holy Mary, who art in Heaven. Jim. Joe."

It went on like that all night long: God, Jesus, Saint Mary, Joe, Jim, and begging for forgiveness, as if this was going to be her last night on this earth. The only break in the prayers was the occasional snap back into reality and a glance over at me in the bed next to her, followed by the words, "Hey, Judy, why aren't you asleep? Go to sleep. Oh, Judy, bless you for being with me."

Then she would drift back into prayers, forgetting I was even there. It was those moments of clarity that gave me hope that it would pass quickly. I would have been frightened, but I had seen patients with this condition before and I knew it was only temporary.

By morning, the numbers had stopped, the prayers were over, and the treatment had started working. It was unfortunate that she could remember so much of her ordeal. Ignorance is bliss, but she was not ignorant of it, and she definitely was not blissful.

I'll never forget the sound of her prayers that night. Prayer is sacred, and it's especially sacred to hear the prayers of another when they think they're alone with God. I was honored to bear witness to her faith and her deep love for her sons. It was like getting a glimpse into her heart, mind, and soul. I also knew those boys were lucky, very lucky, because I understood the power of a praying mother. Many nights I had prayed over my children as they slept. I prayed when they were little when they were ill, and especially when they were teenagers. My own mother had prayed over me when I was lying in the bed crying out in pain just a few months earlier. I have no doubt that God moves prayers from mothers to the front of the line, giving them priority.

"I knew I was saying it, I knew it was happening, but it was like watching someone else saying and doing it all, and I couldn't stop. I'm so embarrassed," she said in a remorseful, quiet tone. After a moment, another thought occurred to her and she yelled out. "Oh, no! I called Jim 'Brody.'" She placed her hand over her mouth for a moment and then added, "I can't believe I did that. I feel terrible." A tear ran down her cheek. "I wish I could fix that." She sat quietly in deep regret. I sat by her side, feeling her pain.

A bit later, she looked around the room and then back at me. "I have to tell you something else. This is so embarrassing." She motioned me closer so she wouldn't have to say it too loudly. It didn't matter that nobody else was around to hear her big secret. I indulged her by getting as close as I could. "The maintenance man," she whispered.

"What about him?" I whispered back, a little puzzled and hoping she wasn't confused again.

"He saw me nearly naked." Her eyes were big as saucers, and the volume and pitch of her voice went up. She wasn't confused this time, though—she was spot-on. The maintenance man at The Conservatory had been the one who found her in her silky slip, all confused and nearly unconscious. My chuckling seemed to tame her embarrassment and eventually we were both laughing together.

The next day she was back to normal. Completely normal. I knew she was herself again when she started complaining about the food. I was glad she didn't like the food; that meant she would work harder to get out and back home.

The aide helped her into a wheelchair, the required throne for exiting any hospital, and we traveled back down those hospital halls. As I helped her into the car, I leaned in as if to tell her my own little secret. "Lucille, there's only one thing left to do."

"What's that?" she asked.

"When we get back, I want you to look that maintenance man right in the eye, wink, and smile."

We laughed all the way back to her place. She was definitely my sweet, mischievous Lucille again.

Chapter Twenty-Eight

❦

The Bumpy Road

Life can take a dramatic turn at any time, usually when we least expect it. If I had learned nothing else in the past year or so, I had learned that. But how we handle the bumps in the road will dictate whether we sit down in self-pity or get up and keep moving. I think Dory said it best in *Finding Nemo*: "Just keep swimming!" Even so, I've always thought that it's best to swim with someone, rather than alone, and Lucille was definitely my swimming partner.

It was early spring, and I pulled up to The Conservatory right on cue. It had only been a few weeks since the incident, but I was glad Lucille was back home, and we had gotten back into our routine. I sat and waited for a moment, admiring the freshly planted flowers at the entrance, but there was no Lucille. Concerned, I went in. This was the first time Lucille hadn't been right there waiting for me.

"Hey, have you girls seen Lucille?" I asked the dark-haired lady at the front desk.

"No, I haven't seen her all day," she replied.

I could feel all the hairs on my body stand up. Almost immediately, I did an about-face and went back out to my car, which was still running under the overhang. I found a permanent parking space and walked back through the sliding doors and right past the lady at the front desk, quickly and with purpose.

For four years, she's been right there when I pulled up. Something must be terribly wrong, I thought. The worst possible scenarios played through my mind as the soles of my shoes hit the thick carpet that ran through the long halls of The Conservatory. I found myself trying, unsuccessfully, to think good thoughts and consider simple explanations. I passed door after door, not seeing a single soul. Everyone was at lunch, just like they were supposed to be. The place felt empty and lonely, the halls, longer than they ever had. I thought to myself, *Why does she always pick the apartment farthest away from the front door?*

The Conservatory felt different this time, abandoned. Usually when I visited, people would be going up and down the halls, passing with a warm smile. Where the halls meet, two or three people were almost always gathered at the hall table, working on a puzzle. It was always the same puzzle, but each time, a few more pieces had been added.

Thoughts of my recent visits flooded my mind. I would sit in "the Judy chair," a white, high-backed chair with blue and green tassels, open my laptop, and write. I was with Lucille the day she bought that chair. It was the last thing she'd purchased to make her home complete. At the store, she had looked at it, walked around it a few times, then came back and said to the saleslady, "That's it. I'll take it." A few minutes later, she announced to me, "That's the Judy chair. It suits you." So, there we would sit, me in my chair and Lucille across from me, all dressed up, quiet, but ready to answer any questions I may have. I often needed her to clarify my scribbled notes. She wanted to hold the finished book about her life in her hands so badly. Our working together gave her hope that it would be finished sooner rather than later and that her wish would come true.

She'd become obsessed with the book in recent months, and even had a running list of people who wanted to buy it. Just the idea of someone wanting to spend money to hear about her life was part of the thrill. These writing days were any day but Fridays, because Fridays were just for fun outings.

I finally reached Lucille's door, and since I never knocked anymore, I went right in. "Are you okay?" I said loudly, almost out of breath from the anticipation.

She was sitting in her favorite chair, facing the window that overlooked the pool. All I could see was the top of her head, but then she turned around to face me. "Well, I'm feeling a bit tired today," she said quietly and without much expression. "I thought maybe we could just stay in." She was still in her pink silky pajamas and matching pink and white robe with no makeup.

"Of course we can. Not a problem at all," I responded with a smile, trying not to sound worried or disappointed. "Do you want me to go grab us a bite from the dining room?"

I could tell she was thinking as she tilted her head and looked up at a spot on the wall. "Well," she said pausing for a moment, "I wish I had some cottage cheese."

"Cottage cheese it is," I replied with a smile. "I'll be right back." As I walked back down the halls, they seemed less daunting. I was worried, but I tried to push those negative thoughts aside. Instead of going to the dining hall, I made a quick trip to the store.

"Bottled water, Boost for energy and calories, cottage cheese, peaches, cinnamon rolls, and Greek yogurt," I announced as I unpacked the bags back in her room. Something deep inside me had told me to grab a few extra items because if she didn't feel like going down to the dining room today, she might not want to go tomorrow, either.

"You were fast! Look at that. You really did a big shopping trip, didn't you?" she said, shaking her head in disbelief. "Oh, Boost, I love that! I think I'll have that with my cottage cheese."

"You got it," I said as I poured it into a wine glass. I wanted to give her something a little fancy since we were just staying in.

We sat and visited for a while, I in the white Judy chair and she in her favorite reclining rocker. "I think we should do this more often," she said, pulling the lever to recline back. "Just stay here," she said as she closed her eyes for a moment.

She was quiet and reserved and her movements were slower than usual. Her get-up-and-go had gotten up and left. "Absolutely," I replied matching her quiet tone.

After about an hour of chitchat and a plate of cottage cheese and peaches, she said, "I think I need to take a little nappy-poo."

A *nap?* I thought, she hasn't even gotten out of her pajamas from the morning. "Let me check your blood pressure first, just to make sure you're okay," I said, grabbing the cuff from the couch and placing it around her arm.

"Nurse Judy. My own personal nurse," she said, shaking her head sweetly.

If there was one thing Lucille obsessed over, it was her blood pressure. I once took her to Dr. Rothkoft, the cardiologist, for her check-up, and he told her to stop worrying about her blood pressure. I remember his exact words: "Lucille, your blood pressure is fine. You have the heart of a twenty-nine-year-old. I promise you will not die of a heart attack or stroke, so stop stressing about it. That stress will kill you before your heart will."

"Looks okay," I told her. "So, I'll see you in a couple days?"

"Yep, couple of days," she replied. I knew a couple meant two to her, so I may as well have said, "See you on Sunday."

I leaned over and kissed her cheek. I always loved the feel of her cheek on mine. Her skin was so soft, and her body was always a degree or two warmer than mine.

I left that day with a funny feeling. Something was different about her, but I couldn't quite put my finger on what it was. Maybe it was that she was simply slowing down. I didn't want to believe it. I wanted her to stay vibrant and full of life, but I was willing to take her any way she came.

That night, Walter and I went out to the movies. I don't remember what we saw, but as usual, I put my phone on silent in the theater. When we got back home, I pulled it out and noticed that I had two missed calls from Lucille.

I put the phone on speaker and played her first voicemail so Walter could hear it too. "Judy, my blood pressure is up. I took my blood-pressure medicine earlier, but I don't know if I should take another one."

"Call her back and tell her 'no.' She should not take another one," he said emphatically.

"Okay," I said, pressing the button for the next voicemail.

"Judy, since I didn't hear from you, I took another one. Call me back and let me know that I did the right thing."

"No!" Walter yelled in frustration. "Call her right now!" His face turned red as he walked quickly toward me.

He sounded angry, so I obliged as quickly as I could. Walter stayed close to listen in on the conversation. His head bent down close to the phone. She sounded normal, even better than she had that afternoon, in fact. She assured me that her blood pressure was stable.

"Let me talk to her," Walter said, leaning in to speak directly into the phone. "Lucille, do *not* take extra blood-pressure medication. Let me be the doctor, not you."

"Okay," she replied sheepishly. "I've done that before, you know, and I've always been fine."

"Lucille—" Walter began sternly.

"But I won't do it again," she replied quickly, cutting off his lecture before he really got started. "I'm fine. I promise I'll call you if my blood pressure goes too low, but right now it's fine: 150/82."

Walter and I went to bed and slept soundly that night, but I kept my phone nearby with the ringer on, just in case.

It was silent all night, but sure as the morning sun, Lucille called around nine a.m. the next day. "Hey there, girl. What're you up to today?" I greeted her.

"Judy. I'm calling because Lucille fell." It was the lady from The Conservatory calling on Lucille's phone.

I motioned for Walter to turn the television down. He could tell from my face that something was very wrong.

"Fell? Is she okay?" I asked.

At that, Walter turned the television off completely. He watched me as he listened carefully.

"She has a huge bump on her head, but she's talking and everything. I think she tripped. They're going to take her to the hospital now."

"Did they take her blood pressure?" I asked, assuming it had to be that extra pill.

"They said it was fine. She seems fine, except for that nasty bump."

"Okay, where should we go?"

"HEB. That's where she told them to take her." Hurst-Eu-less-Bedford is a good hospital, and she was familiar with it since it was so close to her old place. Plus, Emily's mom was an emergency room physician there, so I knew Lucille would get extra-special attention.

"Thank you. Please tell her we'll meet her there."

I hung up, looking pale as a ghost. Walter got up from the couch and walked over to where I was standing in the entry way that separates the dining room from the front living room. "Walter, she fell," I said as I stared forward. I was shocked and sad. *How could she be heading back to the hospital again so soon?*

"I heard," he replied, stroking my arm to comfort me.

"They say she has a really nasty bump on her head." I turned to grab my shoes. "We need to get to the hospital."

At that, Walter sat back down and flipped the television back on. My whole body ran hot with anger and disbelief. *What is he doing? Why isn't he putting his shoes on? Why aren't we running out the door?*

He could tell I was irritated because I looked at him, threw my arms up and let out a huff. "Relax," he said calmly. I was actually annoyed at how calm he was. Then he added, "It's going to take them a while. They need to check her in and get her stable. Then we can see her. I know how this works, and we need to give them some time to do their thing."

I knew he was right, but I didn't understand how he could watch television at a time like this. "Well, when are we leaving?"

"In an hour or two. Remember, she's not even there yet."

I walked around the house, trying to find something to do, searching for anything to keep me busy. I loaded the washing machine, folded the clothes in the dryer, put the clean dishes away, and wiped the counters clean. Thirty minutes down, only an hour and a half to go.

"We're looking for Lucille, Lucille Fleming," I said to the gentleman at the emergency room front desk two hours later. He looked down at his computer screen, not answering, but I assumed he had heard, based on his typing away.

After a few moments, he looked at the lady sitting next to him. "Do you have a Fleming?"

The lady looked at some list on her desk and said, "Nope."

"Well, she's here," I retorted pointedly, looking at each of them in turn.

"Maybe she just hasn't gotten here yet," the man suggested.

Frustrated, I grabbed Walter's hand and went over to a large police officer standing at a desk just to the left of the door. He was twice my size, and my pale skin looked almost translucent in comparison to his deep black arms. I don't know why, but I trusted him to solve this mystery and give us answers.

"They lost her," I addressed him with tears in my eyes. "The ambulance picked her up and said they were taking her here. How could you lose a 103-year-old lady?"

He squinted at me and asked in a very deep voice, "Did you say 103?"

"Yes, and she's with it. Really smart; you can't miss her. She's a hoot. No matter where she goes, people love her. Somebody has to—"

"Hang on, I heard that come across dispatch," he interrupted. He disappeared behind the desk and did that thing police officers do: he found the answer. He helped me.

"North Hills. They took her to North Hills," he said. "You go out here and—"

"I know how to get there. Thanks," I replied, scurrying to the car, pulling Walter along in my wake.

It didn't take but maybe ten minutes to get there, but it seemed like an eternity. "Is a Lucille Fleming here?" I asked the lady at the front desk of the North Hills emergency room.

"Yes, go through these doors, and it's the first room on your left." She said it extremely calmly and slowly, the way hospital clerks so often do. I suppose they see people in a panic all day long and feel they need to balance it out.

As Walter and I entered Lucille's room, we both let out an

audible gasp. She was in a hospital gown that was hanging half off one shoulder, and something was missing, something very important. Her hair. The bump on her head was huge and sticking out like a unicorn's horn. Her forehead was covered in dried blood, and some had even gathered in the corners of her mouth. She looked frightening, but not frightened, and I really didn't know what to say. Fortunately, Walter did.

"Look at that. That's some bump!" he said, smiling at her.

She smiled back. She seemed to be in great spirits given the circumstance. "I bet! You know, I have a bit of a headache," she said, squinting her eyes.

Walter and I both laughed at the idea that she only had "a bit" of a headache. Then Walter stepped out to talk to the emergency room physician.

"Judy, come here. I need to ask you something very important," Lucille said seriously.

I bent down close to her, held her hand, and looked her in the eye. "What is it, Lucille?"

"Judy, is my hair on my head?" she asked in a whisper.

"Nope," I replied as I shook my head and smiled.

"Oh dear," she said with a frown. "Can you look around and see where it is? Maybe they have a bag with my things." She was far more worried about her wig than the ever-growing protrusion in the center of her forehead.

"Sorry, it's not here," I informed her after looking through the single bag of clothes, twice.

"Brother," she said with a sigh.

Walter came back in. "I asked, and her blood pressure is stable. I was really expecting it to be low."

"Low? I checked it this morning, and it was fine." Lucille laughed, "I told you I've done that before. That extra pill didn't do this."

"Well, what happened? Did you trip?" I asked.

"No. I was standing one minute and was down the next. There's no way to explain it. It just happened," she replied very matter-of-factly.

"Walter, look at her hand. Something's wrong with it," I said, taking her left hand in mine. "I think it's broken."

"Ouch. That hand's tender," Lucille said, squinting her eyes in pain.

Walter came over to take a look, seeming unimpressed with my assessment. "It's probably just bruised. The doctor will look her over. Lucille, if you haven't already, ask him about your hand. They can snap a quick x-ray if he feels the need."

"Okay, will do," Lucille replied dutifully.

"Walter, that hand is broken," I insisted. "I know her hands. I would know them anywhere, and that hand doesn't look the same to me."

"Judy, I really don't think it's broken. It's just bruised. It looks fine to me. I'm sure she hit it on the way down."

Lucille suddenly broke in, "Hey, it hasn't been a couple days yet. I just saw you yesterday. You need to go home and spend time with your family. I'm sure they'd like to see you, too." She started to shoo us away with her good hand, brushing it back and forth toward the door. "I'm fine here, really. Go home, you two."

"You heard the woman," Walter said in an upbeat, loud voice.

I gave him the evil eye. I knew he really just wanted to go home and kick back but I was worried, really worried. "Should I come back tonight when you get settled in your room?" I asked as I sat down on the edge of her bed and held her good hand, stroking the top of her wigless head.

"Heavens, no. Go home and get some rest. The two of you work too much."

I reached over and kissed her bloody forehead. "Okay. I'll leave my number with the nurse. I love you."

"I love you too, Judy," she said with a smile, "and you too, Walter!"

The next day was Sunday, and I was anxious to see Lucille again after church. Mom and Louie came over for dinner, but I couldn't tell you what we ate or what we talked about. My mind was on Lucille.

"Mom, do you want to run up to the hospital with me?" I asked as we carried the dirty dishes from the dining room to the sink.

"Sure. When do you want to go? How long will it take?" she asked as we entered the dining room for the next load.

"Let's go right now," I said, turning to Walter and Louie and setting the dirty plates back on the table. "We'll be back within a couple hours." I didn't know how long we'd be, but I didn't want to be rushed because I had committed to a certain time.

On the way there, something occurred to me. I turned to Mom and said, "I hope you don't mind, but I have to stop by her place first. It's really important."

The lady at The Conservatory's front desk was nice enough to give me a key to Lucille's apartment. She knew that Lucille and I were inseparable, so she didn't even think twice.

"Oh, no!" I yelled as we walked into her kitchen. It looked like the paramedics had pushed things all over the place when they had loaded her up.

Suddenly, my eyes landed on something. "See this?" I asked, holding up a handful of red Boost bottle caps that I had gathered off the kitchen floor.

"I sure do," Mom replied as if she knew what I was getting at, though she probably didn't. Those red caps were from the Boost drinks I bought Lucille just the day before.

"Ugh," I sighed. "Well, let me run and grab what I came here for."

It wasn't long before we arrived at the hospital. We entered Lucille's room, and she was sitting in bed, with the covers pulled up over her chest. She looked very alert and smiled when she saw us come through the door. I proudly pulled something from my purse, raising it high in the air. "Look what I have!"

"My hair!" she yelled joyfully. "Judy, you're a life-saver." She fitted it on her head.

"Now, this isn't going to fit the way it normally does, not with that big bump. Here, keep it off the bump, it needs to heal."

"Okay," she said, straightening it with one arm. "Like this?" Her hair was on, but mostly on the back of her head.

"Beautiful. Yes, just like that."

I noticed that her hand was badly bruised now. "What did the doctor in the ER say about that?"

"Not much. Oh, is that your mom over there?"

"Yep," I replied as Mom and Lucille made small talk. It was the first time I remembered them actually meeting. I'm sure they felt like they already knew each other.

"Lucille, we need to have an intervention," I said sternly during a lull in the conversation, holding up one of those red bottle caps I had found in her apartment. "You are a Boostaholic!"

"What?" she said with a guilty look.

"I have proof, you know. I counted all the caps. You drank six of those in less than twenty-four hours."

She looked over at Mom, and Mom shook her head in disapproval, though she did so with a half-grin.

"This is serious!" I exclaimed, annoyed at their levity.

The two of them burst into laughter.

"Well, I'm going to talk to the nurse about that hand. I still think it's broken. I know your hands. That's not just bruised; it looks different to me."

"Okay. It does hurt pretty bad. Maybe they can x-ray it."

I looked at her, a bit puzzled. "They didn't do an x-ray in the ER?"

"No. He just looked at it and said it was bruised."

"Doctors," I muttered with frustration as I glanced back at Mom and rolled my eyes.

It was a bit weird being there with both my mom and Lucille. For a moment, I found myself wishing that Mom and I could be as close as Lucille and I were. It's not that I wanted Mom to be Lucille, or Lucille to be my mom. I loved them both, but in different ways. I wondered if they could sense that.

A few days later, I had to break the bad news to Lucille. "I hate to tell you this, but you can't go right back home. You've had a terrible concussion, and with that broken hand—" I looked down at her hand, which was now in a brace.

"I really want to go home," she argued with a pouty face. "I want to go back to The Conservatory. I miss my apartment, I miss my friends, I miss playing duplicate bridge, and I miss the food," she pleaded and whined.

"I know, but you can't just yet. I'm going to look at a place tomorrow near my house called The Carlyle." I was relieved that my Lyme disease seemed to be in remission and that I actually had the energy to do so. "It's supposed to be beautiful, and they have a whole rehabilitation unit. Two weeks to a month, tops."

"Okay, Judy, whatever you say. I'll do it," she grumbled.

I knew she wasn't happy with the arrangement, but there was no way she could be fully independent again just yet. Not after that nasty bump and losing the use of one hand.

"Have you seen yourself?" I asked with a slight chuckle.

"No. Do I want to?"

"Probably not."

She pointed to my purse and commanded, "Grab your phone and take a picture of me. I want to see how bad it looks."

I took a couple different shots of her, being sure to capture images that showed how the blood had drained from the big bump, down under her skin, and into both eyes. "Are you ready for this?"

"Oh, my!" she gasped as she looked at each photo. Suddenly, an idea seemed to occur to her. "Hey, I want to send a video to Walter, Joe, and Jim. Can you make a video of me?"

"Okay, go," I said, holding my phone directly in front of her.

"Hey, Walter, look at me! You should see the other guy!" She grinned for a moment. "Okay, now let's make the rest of them," she said.

I was thrilled to see that she had kept her spirits high, and it was good to see her filled with that spunk that she had been missing lately. I knew this was going to be hard. People don't take falls like that and bounce right back, especially people who are 103. I knew she wanted to go home, but that was a really bad fall and she suffered a concussion, so that meant serious rest and rehabilitation to ensure she was stable enough. The last thing anyone wanted was to have her fall again. If anyone could pull through this, though, it was Lucille. Attitude is everything when we face trials, and she always had the best attitude.

Chapter Twenty-Nine

More Bumps in the Road

"The Carlyle's not bad. It's actually quite pretty. They have a chapel, full physical therapy, and it smells good, too. She's only going to the rehabilitation side, so it shouldn't freak her out too much," I said to Mary, my personal assistant. She was in the kitchen wearing a blue and green vintage Chanel blazer over another designer t-shirt, jeans, and standing perched upon a pair of nude Dior pointed toe heels while reviewing my weekly schedule.

"Well, the sooner she gets back to The Conservatory, the better. I know how much she misses that place." She looked back at the schedule and reminded me, "You have a 9:00 a.m. meeting that you can't be late for."

"Oh, that's right. That's an important one." I took a sip of my morning tea, then packed up my computer. As I headed out the door, I looked at Mary and said, "Concussions are nothing to mess around with. Besides, we need time to get her place cleaned up. If she saw it now, she'd freak out."

Mary probably never dreamed that part of her job would be to help me look after Lucille. She never complained about it, and honestly, I think she actually liked it. It gave a whole new dimension to her day, a break from the hustle and bustle of keeping me on task, managing my schedule and taking on the role of being our house manager. Lucille liked it too, because she knew that if I couldn't be there, Mary would be. Besides, they were both huge fans of Chanel.

It only took Lucille a few days to make some new friends at The Carlyle. She loved the physical therapists, and they seemed to love her, too, judging from the way they always gave her a little extra attention. Anything they asked, she did it, making her a dream patient. She even took it upon herself to work on rehab alone in her room, constantly doing leg and arm exercises.

"It won't be long 'til I'm out of here," she said with determination as she sat up straight in bed, fully clothed in a gold skirt and cream-colored blouse. "I love the exercise people who give me therapy, and the nurses are okay, but the food is terrible." She stuck her tongue out and made a sour face, "I wouldn't feed it to my dog."

"Lucille, you don't have a dog," I pointed out. Besides, nobody was as picky about food as Lucille. Perhaps she should have been a food critic.

"Well, I wouldn't feed it to yours or anyone else's," she said with a pouty face.

I sat on the end of her bed and put one hand on her leg. "I want to remind you that Walter and I are going to California in a few weeks. I met with your care team, and as long as you heal properly, you can get out of here the day or so after we get back."

"You know me. I will do everything, *everything*, to get back to my home at The Conservatory." Her pouty lip grew even bigger. "I want to go home."

"I know," I assured her as I patted her leg, then quickly changed the subject to the Texas Rangers.

Her pout turned to a smile at that. "I'm going back, you know. They said I could," she said as her voice grew louder, "and I'm going to throw that first pitch out again. Can you call them? Tell them I'll be ready."

"I'll see what I can do, but that's a great attitude. Don't lose that." I reached over and kissed her on the forehead. "See you tomorrow."

The next morning, Mary and I went over to see Lucille. On the way, we stopped at a sweet little teashop, All About Cha, located around the corner from The Carlyle. It was a favorite hangout of local writers and students. They were playing jazz, but not too loud and the sound of the barista making lattes drowned it out a bit. They had every kind of tea imaginable and a small menu for breakfast and lunch. We would've liked to have stayed and enjoyed breakfast, but we were on a mission.

"Here you go," I said as we entered Lucille's room, placing a square to-go box in front of her.

"What's this?" she asked as her eyes grew big. She opened it slowly and peeked inside. "A waffle?! With chocolate sauce?! And whipped cream?" Lucille licked her lips and then gave me a smile that stretched from ear to ear.

"That, my dear, is not whipped cream; it's vanilla ice cream. Belgian waffle a la mode!" Lucille loved everything a la mode. Every desert she ordered she always asked for some ice cream on top. "After all, waffles make everything better," I said with a wink and a kiss to her head.

Mary and I took turns talking, but Lucille never looked up from her waffle. I'm not even sure she was listening. She savored every bite, as she slowly slid the fork out of her mouth to be sure she wasn't missing a single morsel.

"You know what? I think I'm going to live now," she said with a smile when she finished, dabbing the chocolate sauce off the corners of her mouth.

"Good," Mary replied, clapping her hands together. Mary looked especially fashionable that day, wearing a leather coat over her pink silk Gucci blouse. Instead of heels, she was sporting a pair of Marant western boots.

"Oh, I have an idea!" I walked over and pointed to the hook on the back of the door. "I'm going to bring your Rangers jersey over here and hang it right here. You can look at it all day long and be inspired," I exclaimed as I held out my arms in Vanna White style.

"Her Rangers jersey?" Mary asked quizzically. Raising one eyebrow. She didn't know about Lucille's desire to throw another first pitch.

"Yes, she's going to get better and throw that first pitch again," I replied nodding my head up and down to get Mary to understand how important this goal was.

"Yes. Yes, I am. Judy, if you can't get ahold of them, ask Karen. I'm serious about this." Lucille handed the empty waffle box to Mary to throw away and then leaned back and closed her eyes. "This time, it's going to be even faster, and right over that plate."

The weeks went by quickly, and Lucille took her rehabilitation very seriously, even asking for a special exception when she found out that the therapists don't work weekends.

"Glad you guys are here," she said with a big smile to Walter and me when we dropped by just before our trip. "I have something to show you." She swung her feet to the side of the bed and started to get up. I noticed she had managed to get her panty hose on. By her outfit, I could tell she was dressed up to see us. She was wearing a coral-colored skirt, a white blouse, and even took the time to put a white ribbon in her hair, and another around her neck. I'm sure she would have added the flower if she'd had the right color with her.

"Lucille, you are on a fall hazard. They aren't going to let you go for a walk without the physical therapist," I pointed out sternly.

"Oh, forget them," she said with a dismissive flip of the wrist. "I can walk just fine. Besides, my doctor is here and that is far better than a physical therapist."

With that, she hopped up, just like old times. "Look, I'm not dizzy, and I feel terrific." She stood tall and proud, giving me a big smile of self-approval. "Let's go."

Lucille walked to the end of the hall quickly and with a spring in her step. "Wow. I think you walk faster now than you did before," Walter said, praising her for her efforts. We were both truly impressed.

"I told you so." She said as we entered the room and she sat on the edge of the bed. "Now, you two lovebirds go have a great time in California, and I will see you when you get back. Conservatory, here I come! I'm going home!" she said joyfully, with a big smile. She gave a hug and a kiss goodbye to each of us.

"Mary will be here every day to check on you, bring you anything you need, and grab your laundry. Love you," I said, blowing her one last kiss as we walked out the door.

Calistoga Ranch, just outside of Napa Valley, was the perfect getaway. I wasn't surprised, since Walter is the best vacation planner, always finding just the right place at just the right time. It was a good time for a vacation. My Lyme disease seemed to be in remission, I had been looking forward to some quiet time to write, and for the most part, work had been steady but manageable. The towering oak trees hid the upscale cabins just enough to make every couple feel secluded. The cabin's hardwoods, the sound of the trickling creek that was just a stone's throw away, and the wooden deck, complete with a hot tub, all made it feel like this place was as far away from the realities of work and life as one could get. Our particular cabin even had a giant oak tree sticking up through the deck and reaching for the sky, extending far past the roof.

"Where do you think you're going?" Walter asked on our second day there.

"Up there," I said, pointing to the tree. I tossed a pillow, with a book tucked into its case over the first large branch, then grabbed the base of the tree branch with both arms and scaled the trunk with my feet until I could pull my body up onto the thick branch. "Look, I've still got it. Once a tree climber, always a tree climber." Then I sat back against the pillow and read in the solitude of nature.

When he saw me climb back down a few hours later, he teased me. "You had enough, huh?"

We enjoyed our little cabin in the woods for several days. Perhaps the best part was the outdoor shower for two. There's nothing like a brisk shower in the early morning and then a dip in the hot tub, situated just below my favorite tree, by the light of the moon. We were like two newlyweds, only at our age, we had more appreciation for every moment we had together. There were days that we never once turned on the television or checked our email.

Twice a day, we trekked up the hill to The Lakehouse, a five-star restaurant on the property. It was well worth the uphill climb to this jewel in the woods that was only available to guests. Just as the name implied, it looked much like a lakehouse with its log cabin feel and fireplace to warm the cool, California evening air.

I had no sooner finished my appetizer of foie gras with black-berry, hazelnut, and hibiscus syrup that they brought out the main course, lamb with perfectly spiced carrots and braised fennel. "You know, if we keep eating like this, we're going to blow up," I said to Walter half joking as I rolled my eyes. "It's too bad Lucille will never get a chance to eat here. She would love this food."

"Who wouldn't love this food?" Walter said with a smile as he took a bite of halibut. Perhaps the food tasted so good because they sourced it from local farmers in Napa Valley and from their own on-site garden.

When it was time to head back home, I reluctantly climbed into the backseat of the car that would take us to the airport, sad to be leaving our little sanctuary in the woods. We couldn't have been halfway to the airport when my phone rang. "Right on cue," I said, showing Walter the screen.

"Hello, Lucille. Are you chomping at the bit to get out of there?" I asked jovially.

"This is the paramedics," said a young male voice. "Lucille took a bad fall in the bathroom. We're in here with her. She asked me to call you before we did anything else."

My heart started pounding, feeling like it was going to lob itself right out of my chest. It was like being zapped back into reality through a wormhole. Even my vision started to tunnel as I gathered the strength to ask, "Is she okay? What was she doing in the bathroom alone?"

"Well, she has a really bad bang on the head, and we're pretty sure her right shoulder is broken or dislocated," he replied.

"What? What?" Walter kept asking, knowing that something was very wrong.

"Lucille fell and it's pretty bad," I told him then fell silent in disbelief.

"Hello?" the paramedic called nervously, breaking my reverie.

"Sorry. Okay, where are you taking her? Tell her I love her and that I'll get there as soon as I can. Our flight arrives later this afternoon."

He gave me the name of the hospital, and that was that. For the rest of the ride to the airport, I sat there with my phone in my lap as tears streaked down my face. I had a bad feeling, the kind you have when you know life is changing fast, and you can't do anything about it. My stomach ached, and my head felt hot. Walter reached over, grabbed my hand, and gave it a squeeze. The rest of the car ride passed in strained silence.

As soon as we landed, we headed to Baylor Grapevine, a hospital that is close to home. It's the same hospital where Little Walter was born. "Well, at least she'll be close," Walter said, breaking the silence as we entered the sliding glass doors. The sound of those doors pierced my ears, not because they were loud, but because they were becoming too familiar. It was a sound I had come to associate with stress and anxiety.

As we walked into her small, dreary hospital room, I noticed she didn't look so good. She was wigless and her hospital gown was two sizes too big, leaving it to hang off both her shoulders. I took one look at the goose egg on her head and said, "Oh, boy, that's a really big one." There was already so much bruising that I knew it was bad.

"Oh Judy, I'm so sorry you have to come home to this. I can't believe it. I was up," she said lifting one arm, "and then I was down," she added as she lowered it back down. It was just like last time." She shook her head as if she herself couldn't believe it had happened again.

"You shouldn't have been in there alone. What were you doing in the bathroom alone?" asked Walter.

She avoided the question, but I knew she had heard him loud and clear by the way she looked at him and then changed the subject. "They say it's broken and displaced," she said as I pulled back the blue sling to get a better look at her shoulder. She moaned in pain at the slight jostling. It was bruised all right and looked completely out of place, bizarre, like it was going the opposite direction from the rest of her body.

"I'm so sorry! Oh my gosh, I barely touched you. Walter, look at that! It's totally displaced. It looks really bad." I could feel my face contorting in appreciation for her pain.

"Well, at her age, they aren't going to operate, that's for sure," he said in his serious doctor voice.

"Will it heal?" I asked, knowing it wouldn't.

"Not normally, no," he said sympathetically as he looked at me and then at Lucille.

"What?!" she screeched. "That's my pitching arm!"

I didn't know what to say, so I gave a faint smile and went to the window to open the blinds. Things had definitely gotten too dark for my liking.

The days went by, and Lucille's new bump slowly went down. The blood from the bruise drained into her face again, and she looked simply terrifying. Her whole face was a mixture of blues, reds, yellows and greens. I assured her that the worse she looked, the faster she was healing. Things always get worse before they get better.

"I know you want to go home. I don't want you to lose that passion, so I bought you something," I said to Lucille as I entered her room one day.

"What? What is it? Oh, I can't wait to see what's in that pretty bag," she exclaimed as she took the gift bag from me. She started pulling out the tissue paper until she reached a pair of ruby-red sequined slippers. "I love them! Put them on my feet," she requested, using her good arm to pull the covers up.

"There's no place like home. These are just bumps in the road," I said as I placed the slippers on her feet.

"Yes, bumps in the road," she said with a smile and a faint grin. "I will be back at The Conservatory in no time." Her voice didn't have the usual determination, but I wasn't sure if that was because she was tired, or because she didn't really believe her own words.

"Lucille, I need to talk to you about something." I motioned for her to move her hips over and then I sat down on the bed facing her.

"Okay. What is it?" She seemed intrigued and nervous at the same time as she tilted her head down and looked at me.

"I need to find a new place for you to rehab. You can't go home just yet. You've had two concussions in a short period of time, and your brain has been jiggled way too much." I paused for a moment, looked down at my hands and then back at her. "I'm really mad at The Carlyle for not taking better care of you, so I'd prefer that you don't go back there. I mean, look at you."

"They weren't *that* bad." She reflected for a moment and then added, "Well, the *food* was bad."

I giggled under my breath. It was just like her to remember the food. "Give me time. I'll find some other options."

"Okay, but I don't want to die in a hospital or a nursing home," she said emphatically.

"Lucille," I said, my hand on her face and our eyes no more than ten inches apart, "I promise you that you will not die in a nursing home or a hospital." I could feel my eyes starting to water and the blood rushing through my body at the very thought of Lucille dying. "You will die a sweet old lady tucked into your own sweet bed." Luckily, I was able to choke back the tears and give her a smile to seal the promise I had just made.

She looked at me, smiled back, and drifted off to sleep. I am not sure what made me make that promise, but it was one I intended to keep. The only problem was, I had no idea how hard that would be to do.

Chapter Thirty

Out of Options

Even the most comforting routines change over time. I don't even remember when we stopped getting the print edition of the newspaper delivered and Walter started reading the news on his phone. Phones are a little much for me first thing in the morning, so I developed the habit of thumbing through the numerous gift and clothing catalogs that had arrived the day before, bending the tops of the pages and marking things I would never actually order. I'm not sure how I made all their mailing lists, but mail order catalog people really love me for some reason. Somewhere along my journey, I had lost my obsession with the obituaries. Maybe it was because Lucille had taught me the art of legacy living. Not one of the legacy type obituaries seemed to impress me anymore. Lucille had them all beat. As for the resume obituaries—I just felt sorry for them. I was glad that I wasn't going to be one of them, not anymore.

"What's on tap for today? Are you going to try to look at places on your lunch break?" Walter asked almost apologetically as he placed his cup of green tea on the dining table.

"I made a few appointments," I said a bit nervous about what the day would bring. Out of all the things I could be doing, looking at rehab facilities was not something I could possibly be looking forward to doing. "The social worker at the hospital gave me some names."

"Good luck. I just wish someone had been there. Even if they couldn't catch her, we still need to understand why she's falling." Walter's voice sounded a bit frustrated. He took one final sip of his tea and then said, "Is she tripping, or bending over and blacking out? It's such a mystery. There wasn't anything unusual in her blood work; it's not like she has hyponatremia again or something." He pushed away from the table and kissed my head. We were off to work and then I needed to find a place for Lucille.

My first workday after our vacation started with a desk piled high with papers and messages, an email inbox filled almost to capacity, and a request from Little Walter to pick him up from the high school at three thirty. He was at that awkward age, fifteen, where he was too young to drive and it wasn't cool for your parents to drive you. Usually Mary picked him up, but she had to leave early. It was back to the pressures of life, almost a kind of culture shock. Somehow, I needed to fit in looking for a place for Lucille. I wanted to run back to California, climb that oak tree again and never come down.

The first place I looked at came highly recommended by the hospital and was only a block or two away. It looked okay from the outside: it was a fairly new brick building, all one-story and spread out. The exterior was quiet and calm, but as soon as I opened the door, I was assaulted by those all-too-familiar sounds: the beeps of call buttons; the nurses scurrying around, pushing metal drug carts; people in wheelchairs hollering for help. It felt like hell. It even smelled like hell, a cross between body odor and urine, mixed with the antiseptic smell of pine cleaner. If I had to imagine hell, this is what it would be.

"I can show you around," said the dark haired, middle-aged lady at the front desk who didn't bother to stand when she greeted me. "Our director isn't quite ready for you."

I decided to be polite and let her take me down each hall, passing door after door of despair. It felt heavy and sad. I looked at her with lowered eyebrows and said, "I thought this was a rehabilitation facility."

"Oh, yes ma'am," she quickly replied. "Rehabilitation is right over here." She led me to an empty room with a few pieces of equipment that looked as though they hadn't been used in years. She smiled like she was proud of her rehabilitation room, but quite frankly, it was nothing to be proud of.

"Where are the therapists?" I asked somewhat accusing her without coming right out and calling it a fake rehab room.

"Oh, they only come in part-time," she explained in a bit of a nervous tone. I think she realized I wasn't impressed.

"I see. Well, I think I've seen enough," I said with a polite, but unenthusiastic smile.

"Don't leave just yet. Let me walk you to the director's office. She should be ready for you by now." It was as if she didn't want to be blamed for blowing the appointment.

I didn't want to go. I already knew it would be pointless. There was no way I would put Lucille in this hellhole. "Okay," I said, not knowing why on earth I had agreed.

The director was a plump lady whose office looked like a tornado had just hit it. I wanted to tell her that she was breaking all kinds of fire codes, but something told me she wouldn't care. "I noticed a lot of call lights on," I said after our brief introductions. "What's your response time?"

"Response time? I'd say its average. About ten to fifteen minutes."

I gave her a look of shock, pushing my head forward and dropping my mouth open just a bit. *Ten to fifteen minutes? Are you kidding me? Someone could be dead by the time they got to them.* I thought of my mom; she would never have stood for that.

"Well, I don't think this is what I'm looking for," I said as I reached to grab my purse from the chair next to me. "Besides, Lucille would want a private room."

"We don't have private rooms, but since we have some vacancies, I could put her in a room that doesn't have a roommate. I can't guarantee that it will stay that way, though. I mean, if we get more admissions—" She was rambling and so matter-of-fact that I couldn't tell if she wanted our business or not.

"I know what you mean. I can just show myself out. Thank you for your time," I said, pushing my chair back and hitting a giant pile of binders on the floor behind me.

As I left the building, I looked back at the bustling nurses' station. There was a big plastic banner hanging above it that read: "Voted #1."

I felt sick to my stomach as I looked down at my list. I had time for one more tour, so I put the car in gear and headed to the next facility. It was only about two miles away and was situated at the back of a residential neighborhood—not exactly where you would expect to find a business. It was an older building that didn't look at all well maintained.

As I walked up to the door, two nurses' aides stopped me. They were hanging out on the side rails of the ramp, smoking. One blew smoke in my face and said, "That's not the front door. It's over there," pointing with her cigarette. Both girls looked like complete hoodlums. Their scrubs were wrinkled, they smelled like old tobacco, and their hair was a mess, like they'd just rolled out of bed. Maybe they didn't have time to get ready, or the money to afford extra pairs of clean scrubs, but my mom always said, "Cleanliness and pride in your appearance doesn't cost more than a bar of soap and a hairbrush, and an iron can make anything look better."

I immediately headed back to my car.

"Wait, where are you going?" called the other girl as she flung her cigarette butt into the parking lot. "The front door's over there if you want to take a look around."

"No, thank you. I've seen enough," I said as I climbed into my SUV and drove away.

Angry tears streamed down my face. I was angry that my efforts were proving to be useless. I was angry that our country doesn't take better care of our elderly. I was angry that all of this was happening and there was nothing I could do to stop it. I just wanted to wake up from this nightmare and have everything back to normal.

I drove up in the hospital parking lot and had a good cry. I only had one tissue left and it was soaked and falling apart in my hand, so I decided the tears had to stop. Once I was able to pull myself together, I called Walter. "It was terrible, honey," I said as my tears started to flow again. "I made Lucille a promise, and I intend to keep it. There is no way I am going to let her go to one of those places. She would die. For sure, she would die." Walter calmed me down in a way that only Walter can, and we talked until I stopped crying. Then I sat another twenty minutes or so, until the redness left my blotchy face.

"You're back," Lucille said when I dropped by to visit her in the hospital that afternoon. "Hey, the food's not too bad here. They even have gluten-free stuff on the menu. You should order something." She was sitting up, eating a scoop of ice cream, and wiggling her shiny red feet back and forth, just like Dorothy. Her face was discolored by the blood that had drained under her skin. The bruising looked like someone had beaten her with a base-ball bat. Both eyes were black and blue, and her checks were a purplish color. The ice cream had dribbled onto her gown, a side effect of having to eat left-handed.

"Lucille, I don't have good news." I said as I sat next to her and wiped the ice cream from her face and gown.

"Oh?" She placed her ice cream cup on the tray to the side of her bed.

"They say you need to go to rehab within a day or two, and I didn't like anything I saw today. As a matter of fact, I hated it. No way, no how," I said, shaking my head from side to side.

"Well, I'll just go back to The Carlyle, then. I mean, the food's terrible, but it's only for a little while until I can go back home to The Conservatory. Maybe a week or two." She took my hand as if to reassure me everything was going to be okay.

I didn't have the heart to tell that her she might never go back to The Conservatory, no matter how much she knocked those slippers together. It was her favorite place, a place where she had friends and an apartment she adored, and . . . good food. "Well, they—" I started to argue.

"Look, I didn't want to tell Walter this, but I was taken off the fall-risk list that morning," she admitted a little sheepishly. "I talked to the doctor on-call and convinced him that it was non-sense. After all, I was going home the next day, anyway. That's why I got up to go to the bathroom by myself. Now, I know I lay there for a long time—"

I quickly and abruptly interrupted her, "Thirty minutes! You could have died!"

"But I didn't," she said calmly as she touched my arm. "Look, I won't get up by myself again. I'll be more careful. Don't look at any more places. It's settled; I'll go back there." She sat up straight and looked at me with a determined expression.

I stood up and nervously started straightening her hospital room, straightening her sheets, and folding towels on the sink. When I got to her bedside tray, I pointed to her ice cream cup and asked, "How many of those have you had today?"

"We're not going to talk about that," she said raising a finger and pointing at me while giving me a wink. "Sit down and tell me about your day. Busy day at work?"

That was just like Lucille. She always had a way of stifling a conversation by making a decision. One thing I had learned over the years was that when her mind was made up, it was made up. And I knew that even if I didn't like The Carlyle, I was out of options.

Chapter Thirty-One

❦

Revolving Doors

There's something to be said for second chances, but it's not always something good.

After speaking at length with the social worker, Joe, Walter, and, most importantly, Lucille herself, it was decided that she would indeed go back to The Carlyle for another round of rehabilitation. Before she went back, Mary and I wanted to make The Carlyle feel as much like her apartment as possible, so we stopped by The Conservatory to pick up a few of her things.

"Do you want this, too?" asked Mary, holding up an arrangement of fake blue flowers and greenery. The porcelain bowl it sat in was one of Lucille's favorites. She once picked it out to match her living-room furniture.

"That should be good. Okay, do you think we have everything?" I asked, looking worriedly around the room.

"As much as will fit in that small room and not feel crowded." Mary said as she grabbed the last bag. "Remember: it's about giving her a taste of home, not giving her the whole thing." Mary was right. That's why she was my sense of reason at times like this. It's what made her a great assistant.

"I just hope I don't live to regret this decision to go back there," I said, making eye contact that lasted a little longer than usual. I guess I was looking for a sign of reassurance of approval. Mary didn't offer it, she just broke eye contact and held the door open so we could leave.

Somewhere along the way, Joe and Lucille had given me co-medical power of attorney along with Joe, since I was close and always on call for her. Joe and I spoke often, and he and Lucille trusted me, but I was still afraid of making a bad decision on her behalf. Like this one, what if sending her back to the Carlyle wasn't the right choice? Then again, what other choice did I have?

Lucille's room was looking more like home. Her bedside table had a few photos of Joe and Jim on it and her dresser had her favorite blue vase that was filled with fake blue and purple hydrangeas. I also stuffed a few of her ribbons and flowers in the top drawer next to some make-up. "Look at my room! Oh, and my favorite flowers, too!" Lucille exclaimed as the transport ambulance crew brought her through the door of her room in The Carlyle strapped to an orange gurney with red straps.

"Your clothes are in the drawers, all washed and ready," Mary reported with a big smile.

"You girls are too much. How will I ever repay you for all you do for me?" Her face had a smile of gratitude and tears filled her eyes.

I looked at her, now situated in her bed and said in a very motherly tone, "Your job, your only job, is to get better. Remember what the hospital said: no getting up by yourself. For some reason, your blood pressure keeps bottoming out."

"I know. Don't worry. No more solo bathroom breaks for me," she said with a sheepish smile.

As Mary and I were walking back out to the car, I turned to her and said, "It really is crazy. She was on blood pressure medication for years, and then it suddenly becomes normal and she goes off them, only to develop postural hypotension. Oh, sorry, that means that when she stands up, her blood pressure just disappears. Poof—nothing!"

Mary opened the passenger door and climbed in. "Is that why she kept falling?" she asked, sounding excited that we finally figured it out.

"Yes. It's also why nobody could understand what had happened, not even her. No warning, just out like a light. Her brain's fine, but I guess her little body is just giving out. At least that long stay in the hospital let someone see what was really going on." I paused. "Oh, crap, did we plug her cell phone in?"

"Sure did," Mary said in a reassuring voice, "and I set it next to her in the bed." I was not surprised; Mary usually thinks of things like that without having to be asked.

"Thank you. Thank you for everything," I said in an exhausted voice as we pulled out of the driveway.

The Carlyle was close enough that I could stop in before and after work. Sometimes I even went by during my lunch break on the days when I actually took one. Walter would come with me on the weekends, and we would wheel Lucille out for some fresh air and sunshine. Just for kicks, we let her stand up a few times, but never for long and always in Walter's arms. Her shoulder was starting to heal, but it was still slightly deformed. It wasn't sticking out quite as far, but it still looked odd.

"Honey, I don't think she'll be walking around again by herself for a while, or possibly ever again, for that matter," Walter told me in private after one of our visits. We were snuggled up on the sofa, and I was happy to be resting in his arms.

"Don't you speak like that!" I said sharply with a frown as I pulled away from him. "She is strong. Don't you ever dare tell *her* that. She needs to hear positive messages, not messages of defeat."

"Judy, I'm just trying to prepare you, so that you can prepare her," he said, tugging me back into the cuddle position. "I think her little body has just had it. As doctors, we're taught that we eventually get old and our bodies fail. Nobody asks why. I just wish I knew what had triggered her blood pressure to short-circuit like this."

"Me, too. She can't handle any more falls. This is ridiculous." I paused, thinking. Then I placed my head back on his chest. "Regardless of what you say, I'm going to keep praying that she makes a full recovery," I said, knowing darn well that those prayers might not be answered.

That night, I wrote in my prayer journal, just as I had so many nights before. I prayed for my children, for my husband, and for Lucille. I prayed that we would have the wisdom to know what to do for her and that her body would get stronger and stronger with each passing moment. Those prayers kept me going and kept me hopeful in what seemed like a hopeless situation.

It couldn't have been much past midnight when my cell phone rang. I sprang from the bed to find Lucille on the other end. In a frail voice, she said, "Judy, help me. They put me on this bedpan hours ago and nobody will come to take me off."

Suddenly, I was filled with anger. As much as I was sound asleep just moments earlier, I was wide awake now and my blood was flowing. I could feel my pulse in my ears. I threw on my clothes and ran out the door. On the way there, I tried to call The Carlyle, but nobody answered. When I arrived, I flung open the doors and strode purposefully down the hall. My red Irish walking cape was flapping behind me as I almost sprinted toward her room. When I got there, she was lying there dressed only in the sweater she had been wearing earlier that day. She looked exhausted and pale, not to mention embarrassed. The covers were at the end of the bed, and the bedpan was half under her, half dripping onto the pad below. With her broken arm in a sling, there wasn't much she could do to help herself.

After cleaning her up, putting her in a nightie, and tucking her in below some clean sheets, I started toward the door. "Where are you going?" she asked in a whimpering, sad voice.

"Oh, you just wait here. I'll be right back." I went to the nurse's station, but there was no nurse. I went up and down the hall until I found someone. Then I kept going until I found another, and then another. I made them all follow me back to Lucille's room. They stood there lined up like rookie soldiers. I was their drill sergeant, and I was about to let them have it for dereliction of duty. "Do you see this woman? Do you think she can help herself?"

They all shook their heads no except for the girl who looked like she was about to cry. "I grew up in nursing homes. My mother was the director of nurses for years, and you wouldn't have lasted one second under her supervision. You can bet that I will be speaking with your director first thing in the morning—"

"I just want to say—" interrupted the aide closest to Lucille. She wanted to argue, but I wasn't having it, any of it.

"Say nothing. There is nothing to say. I was an aide once. I know your job is hard. But there is no excuse. Furthermore, do you see this?" I asked, pointing to her bedside table. "This is her dinner tray. It's still here, where it was left. How in the *hell* do you think she was going to take the lid off and feed herself from across the room? And with a broken arm?" I gazed into their eyes for a moment and then yelled, "Pathetic! This is what you call care?" I stopped to make sure I had their attention. "Why did you decide to go into this field? You—you're an aide!" I said pointing at the aide then pointing to the next one, "And you, you're an LVN. Why are you even here?"

The LVN spoke up. "To help people. I wanted to help people." She said quietly, sounding sincere as she looked right at me.

"Then maybe you need to remember that this is not just a J-O-B, this is a passion. Get your passion back and start helping people. Do I make myself clear?" I yelled, staring just long enough into each of their eyes before saying, "That is all. You may go."

As soon as they were out the door, Lucille's eyes grew wide, she sat up as best she could, and with an energetic voice, she said, "Way to go, girl! You sure told them. I bet they never do that again. You were terrific. Your mom would be so proud. I can't wait to tell her how you told them off like that and then sent them back out the door with their tails between their legs. I'm wide awake now. Doubt I'm gonna get much sleep. Whew!" She looked so empowered and full of energy, a complete change from just moments before. She was sitting straight up, her eyes wide open and a big smile on her face. I, on the other hand, was shaking from the adrenaline of my anger.

I gave her a kiss goodbye and put her phone next to her. I passed back by the empty nurse's station on my way out, looking all official in my red cape. I caught a glimpse of myself in the glass and for a moment, I thought I saw my mom in my reflection. The only difference was that her cape had been blue. I remember it so well: a blue cape with a perfectly white hat and crisp uniform. And at that moment I was proud of myself for doing exactly what my mother would have done.

The days that followed were without incident, and my visits were down to once per day, although we spoke quite frequently on the phone. One day, Lucille didn't call me all day. I was so busy that

I didn't even give it any thought. On my way over to see her, I called her, and she sounded weak. "Judy, I don't feel well."

"How don't you feel well?" I asked feeling a bit panicked. "You sound weak. Why didn't you call me to tell me you weren't feeling well?"

"My phone wasn't by me. The aide left it on the table, out of my reach," she said, sounding a bit tearful.

"Okay, I'll be right there," I assured her. "Let me call Walter. He's on his way home, so I can have him stop in and check on you." Walter had signed up for physician privileges at The Carlyle so he could monitor her progress and give orders, hoping to make the situation better.

As soon as I walked into Lucille's room, I could see she was sick. Her face was red and her body was clammy with a glow of sweat. "Oh, my gosh, you're burning up!" I said, touching her forehead gently.

I ran back out the door to the nurse's station. "What was Lucille's temperature today?" I asked the lady behind the desk.

"Umm, I don't know." She turned to another nurse and asked, "Did we check Lucille's temperature today?"

The second nurse fumbled through some papers and found one that had notes scribbled all over it. "It was normal. Completely normal. Why?" I could tell she wasn't giving me a straight answer.

"Why? Because she's burning up! Anyone can look at her and see that she's sick. Hand me the thermometer. I'll check it myself." The two ladies scrambled around, searching through drawers, and finally passed one to me.

When I put it in Lucille's ear to check her temperature, nothing happened. I looked down and saw the dead battery sign. I marched right back out to the nurses. "Seriously?" I demanded, waving the dead thermometer in the air. "This doesn't even work.

Don't lie to me; I know you didn't check her temperature today."
They looked surprised, like they never expected me to call them
out for their carelessness.

I turned to see Walter coming toward me. "Thank God you're
here. Come quick. She's so sick."

Walter took one look at her and called 911 then called Baylor ER to let them know she would be on her way. He walked out
the door to the nurse's station and said, "When was the last time
you checked on her? Never mind! Don't even answer that. She
is septic and is going back to the hospital." Then he went around
to the computer and started typing. He never told me what he
typed, but I could imagine he put some ominous notes.

The ambulance arrived, the medics strapped her in, and
off they went. Walter and I stayed behind to gather her things.
When we walked out toward the nurse's station, our arms full, the
nurse in charge said, "Can we help you with anything?"

With the blue flower arrangement in one hand and a bag of
clothes in the other, Walter turned toward her and replied very
seriously, "I think you've done enough. She will never be coming
back here."

Walter climbed into his car and rolled the window down. "I
left my stethoscope at the nurse's station."

"Do you want to run in and grab it?" I asked.

"No, I never want to see those sorry excuses for nurses again
in my life," he said in an angry voice as he shifted the car into
reverse.

There I was again, pulling back into the hospital parking lot. It
felt like *Groundhog Day*. Same story, different day. Only this time,
she was sick. Really sick. The kind of sick that requires gloves
and gowns and signs on the door warning of infection. For the
first time in my germophobic life, I didn't even care about what

I might catch by simply walking through the front doors of the hospital. I didn't even think twice.

"It's good to look at someone without a mask," she said with a smile. She was in a hospital gown and the sheet was only draped across her legs, with her toes peeking out at the end of the bed.

Honestly, I didn't even think to grab a mask, which was very unusual for me. "Well, as long as you don't poop on me, we should be fine," I said as I winked at her and kissed her head.

I hated the hospital. It always meant having to start over again and again, especially with hospitalists, the group doctors who only see patients in the hospital. Since they're in a group, the patients get passed back and forth depending on what day it is. Walter and I quickly became quite close to one of the doctors in the group, but then the weekend rolled around and another doctor took over. He stupidly put Lucille on a diuretic, which gave her hyponatremia again, sending her to the ICU.

On Easter Sunday, we decided to visit Lucille after church instead of our usual early morning visit. She was back in a regular room with the nurses' station just outside her door. "I'm so glad you're here," said one of the nurses. "She's been all upset, thinking you forgot to come. I told her you would be here and that you were probably just at church."

As soon as we opened the door to her room, she lit up. She was sitting in the bed in a white hospital gown with blue checks, her wig was on and so was her big smile. "Oh, I'm so glad you're here. It's late, later than you usually come." She pointed over to the shelf where a colorful basket sat, "Carrie came to see me and even brought me an Easter basket. Oh, she looked so cute, too. You know she always looks cute. That girl is so fashionable. I was a little embarrassed, though. I wish I looked a little better today." Lucille always spoke highly of Jim's wife,

Carrie, usually referring to how smart she was or how great her outfit was.

Then it hit me: she wanted me to get her up and dressed for Easter. I felt mildly guilty for not coming sooner, especially since Easter is a very important and dressy holiday for Catholics. I'm sure she felt her hospital attire was somewhat sacrilegious.

"See this little plant?" she said, holding up the sweetest little Easter pot, which contained a tiny green plant. "That nurse gave it to me, the one I told you about yesterday. It was her day off, and she came in super early, just to bring it to me."

Okay, I thought, *you don't have to rub it in.* I smiled at her and said, "That was so thoughtful. And on her day off, too. Impressive."

"I'm so glad to be back here at Baylor," she said, scooping up a bit of ice cream from what was left of her lunch. "They sure know how to feed you."

"And you're getting better at eating left-handed," Walter chimed in.

She raised her spoon at him as if to agree. Then I got her dressed for Easter. The yellow flower matched her green and yellow skirt and lime green top. I even took a moment to fluff up her wig and make it look new again.

The days passed, and Lucille grew stronger. She wasn't well enough to go home yet, and it was still a roller coaster of good and bad days. But her shoulder continued to heal and became stronger each day.

I left the hospital one day after a lunchtime visit and called Walter from the car. "What am I going to do? She can't stay there, she can't go home, and I can't bear the thought of going to look at another place. Besides, look at The Carlyle and how that turned out. It looked great on the surface, but the care was terrible."

"Yeah, that was a bad place. They sure can fool you. No, she can't go back there. No way," he agreed.

"I made that promise to her, and I intend to keep it," I said. "She will not die in the hospital or some nursing home, but I only have one day to come up with a solution."

"Are you asking to bring her home?" He knew me so well. "You have to go to Utah in just over a month. Then what?"

I knew he could hear my voice quiver since I was trying to hold back tears. "Can we?"

"Yes, but we need to talk to Joe. There are a lot of things to consider here. They need to be okay with it. And we need to figure out where she will go when you head to Utah."

A huge feeling of relief washed over me. I didn't even care about the logistics of how; I just knew I was going to keep my promise.

Later that night, after talking to Joe and his wife, Sue, I went back to the hospital to tell Lucille the good news. She was in bed, her little red slippers peeking out at the bottom of the covers. I leaned over, grasped her hand, and said, "Guess what?"

"I know what. Joe just called and told me. I'm going home with you!" she said excitedly. "Thank you so much. You're taking me in." Her happy face turned to tears of gratitude as she grabbed my hand and squeezed it tight. "My dear best friend, I love you so much, and I can't believe it. I'm going to live at my doctor's house. Talk about private home health care! Thank you, Judy. Are you sure Walter is okay with this?"

"I'm sure. Tomorrow. You'll come home with me tomorrow." I gave her a big hug, careful not to put too much pressure on her bad shoulder.

I left the hospital feeling a great sense of peace, knowing that I had a solution. It was as if the weight of the world had suddenly been lifted from my shoulders. For weeks I'd felt like I was drowning in indecision and doubt, but now I could breathe again. I also felt so thankful to be married to Walter. I always knew he was a good man. No—a great man. This was going to be a journey for both of us, and there was a real chance that I was taking Lucille home to die, but I also knew that she had the best chance for life with Walter and me by her side.

Chapter Thirty-Two

❧

Roommates

It was the last day of March, and it was beautiful, a perfect day to leave the hospital. The sun was shining, and the birds were chirping in the distance as we loaded Lucille into the car. It was eerily peaceful.

She was all smiles and told just about everyone that her doctor was taking her home to his place. From the look on several faces, I could tell they didn't understand our relationship. More than once, I heard an almost accusatory tone in someone's voice as they asked, "Wait, she's not your mother? You're not her daughter? But she's going to your place?" I'm not quite sure why they found it so weird, or what they thought I had to gain, but instead of being happy for her, they all seemed suspicious. I guess that says more about society than it does about me.

"Walter, be careful!" I shouted as he tried to wheel Lucille up the front steps backwards. "Oh my gosh, you're going to jiggle her to death. Will you please try not to be so rough? Seriously."

Her face was still bruised, but the bruising was fading. She was wearing a pair of yellow slacks and a deep purple shirt. She lacked the ribbons and flower I brought her to match her outfit,

305

probably because she was in such a hurry to leave. "Now you be quiet," Lucille scolded me. "He's doing just fine. I'm not a china doll, and I'm not going to break. Walter, you're doing fine, honey. Don't listen to her."

"Thank you, Lucille," he said, giving me a pouty look.

I couldn't believe it: they had just put me in my place. I decided to keep my mouth shut and stop watching as he maneuvered her through the front door.

"Here you go," I said, stretching my arm out to show her the twin bed that had been set up next to the Steinway in the great room. All the other bedrooms were upstairs, and by putting her in the great room, she would be close to our bedroom. "I even picked out all your favorite colors. Good, bright, happy colors for your bed."

Lucille's eyes filled with tears, and her gratitude showed through her quivering face. "Oh, Judy. Oh, Walter. This is terrific. A girl couldn't ask for more. Thank you," she said, reaching for my hand. "Thank you two so much."

"How about you climb up here and take a nap? It's almost lunchtime, and I plan on making you something very nutritious," I said with a big smile. "I have you captive, and from now on, only high-nutrient, high-quality, good-tasting food is going in that body."

"Sounds good," she said as she nodded her head in agreement. Then she frantically started looking around. "Oh, where's my phone? I need it handy in case of an emergency."

I handed it to her and smiled, "I'm just in the other room. If you need anything I will hear you, don't worry."

As I was pulling ingredients out of the refrigerator, I could hear Lucille's voice echoing from the other room. "Oh, you should see it. They put me in the best room in the house," she said with excitement. I think she was trying to whisper, but that was the loudest whisper I'd ever heard. "The ceilings, oh, they have to be thirty feet high! And the chandelier, oh the chandelier! Hang on, let me count them—forget it, there are too many lights to count. They even gave me my own piano. A Steinway. And a view of the pool."

This went on and on, not just once, but over and over again. I think she called just about everyone she knew. I was secretly smiling as I plated the food.

"Should I get her?" Walter asked as I started carrying the plates to the dining room.

"Yes, but make her leave the phone on the bed. No phones at the table. Even she has to live by the house rules," I replied with a wink and a smile.

Later that night, I tucked Lucille into bed, pulling the purple and white comforter up to her chest, grateful that I wasn't making another trip to the hospital or sleeping with my phone. "Here you go," I said, handing her a bedazzled round silver bell. "Just ring it if you need me."

"Well, look at that. Jewels and all! I feel like a queen," she said, holding the bell in her good hand. She was wearing the same red silk pajamas that she'd had on in Memphis.

I placed the bell on the bed within reach of her good arm. "Just ring it like this, and I will be here. Ding! Judy appears, just like magic." I removed her wig and kissed her forehead goodnight.

Sometime during the night, I heard the bell's faint ring and rushed to her bedside, only to find her sleeping soundly. She must have shifted, jiggling the bell, or perhaps I just imagined it. I pulled up a chair, grabbed a blanket, and propped my feet up on the edge of her bed. There I sat, vigilantly watching over her as she slept, grateful that she was home and comfortable.

Around four in the morning, she woke up and saw me. She

was surprised, and whispered, "What in the world are you doing out here?"

"I'm watching over you," I explained.

"Nonsense. You get back in bed with Walter, where you belong. Go on," she ordered, shooing me away.

It was a long night, and the morning came all too quickly. By the time I got up, Walter was gone, and Mary had just arrived. She was wearing tennis shoes, cut offs, and what appeared to be a vintage sweater. Mary had agreed to watch Lucille while I was at work each day and she came dressed for the task. This was going to be our first trial run.

Before I left for the day, I helped Lucille to the restroom. "You look tired," I said as I lowered her onto the toilet. I didn't mind taking care of Lucille at this level; it just seemed natural. I guess it was a cross between having spent years in the medical field, and loving Lucille like she was a blood relative.

"Well, someone kept me up all night," she replied with a small laugh and a grin.

I leaned over to pull her red silk pajama pants off, and when I stood back up, I saw the strangest look on her face. She was staring forward blankly, and her face was a grayish-white.

"Lucille?" I said in a panicked voice. "Can you hear me?" *Oh God, help me*, I thought as I caught her just as she slumped over. How could this be happening? She was just laughing with me, and then she was out, just like that. "Mary! Mary!" I screamed.

The bathroom door burst open, and Mary rushed in. She could see that something was terribly wrong by the tone of my scream and the wide-eyed look I gave her. Lucille was slumped into my chest and I was holding her under both arms. "Quick, grab all the pillows you can find and throw them on the floor," I told her. My bedroom was right across from the hall bath, so the floor was lined with pillows in no time.

I tried lifting Lucille up off the toilet, but she was too heavy, a dead weight. Somehow, I was able to hang onto her while still protecting her bad arm. For a split second, I thought back to that moment when I was sixteen, when I was holding that poor old lady and dropped her. Suddenly, I had an incredible burst of strength, hoisting Lucille right off the toilet and lowering her onto the bed of pillows on the floor. It was smooth—no slips, no falls.

"Help me lift her legs up and get blood back to her head," I said to Mary. "Oh and give me one of those Depends. I don't want her to be embarrassed that she was naked like this."

Within a minute or two, Lucille was completely back to normal. "What am I doing down here?" she asked inquisitively as she looked around. "Mary, Judy, what happened? I was up there, talking to you, and now I'm down here. Just like that." She seemed shocked and had no memory at all of passing out.

"I think this is what has been happening to you. Your blood pressure just bottomed out. It was quite frightening. No more trips to the bathroom." I managed to get her out of the bathroom, into the wheel chair, and back to the bed.

"I am not peeing in the bed," she said with as much authority as she could muster.

"No, I'm going to get a bedside commode for you," I said with a huff, releasing some adrenaline as I sat down in the wheelchair beside her bed.

"Oh, boy, Walter's going to love that. 'What's that next to your Steinway piano, sir?'" She asked in a deep voice as she raised her hand up toward the piano. "'Oh, that? That is the finest bedside commode available today,'" she joked.

"Safety first," I reminded her as I shook my first finger. "Look at that, now I get to be the bossy one."

It was in the wake of that moment that I truly realized the enormous undertaking this would be. I knew I was up for the task, but I also sensed that the point of no return was coming. I could no longer imagine her going back to The Conservatory and living life the way she wanted to. My dear, sweet friend's body was simply giving out. Her spirit was strong, but her body just couldn't keep up.

It soon became apparent that Lucille's needs were more than Mary and I could handle. She needed to use the bedside com-mode and I found myself getting up to check on her several times a night. Mary was taking great care of Lucille, but all her regular duties were taking a backseat, so we agreed to have home health come in. A lovely Tongan lady named Atu looked after Lucille while I was at work. I trained her on how to handle her and dress her, and what to do if she passed out.

I kept Joe and Jim updated on her status, but my reports to them didn't show much hope of recovery. After about a week, Joe asked in a concerned way, "Judy, do you think I should come visit Mom? I mean, do you think—"

"Yes, I think that would be a good idea. You and Sue can stay here. You're welcome to come whenever and for as long as you want." We all knew that this might be their last trip to see Lucille, and we wanted to accommodate them any way we could.

Lucille's blood-pressure drops were getting worse. She would be fine one minute, and out like a light the next. Since she couldn't get up and move around, she started becoming frail. Her mind was sharp, but her body was in rapid decline. Frailty is a sign the end is near, something I had learned over all the years I worked in primary care.

I reached out to local hospice, but only under the condition that they would not use the word "hospice" around Lucille. "Look, she's a nurse, and she knows what that word implies. I want her to die happy, not deflated and thinking everyone gave up on her," I explained to the intake nurse. She nodded as if she completely understood.

I made scrambled eggs, avocados, and fresh berries for breakfast. Lucille was next to the table in her wheelchair, dressed in a peach colored skirt, a yellow cotton blouse, with ribbons in her hair and a pink flower on her shoulder. I looked at her and smiled as I said, "I spoke with Joe today. He and Sue are going to fly out to see you. We thought it would be fun. You know, like a sleepover. I told them to stay here at Chateau Gaman." Lucille understood that she wasn't getting better.

Not long after that, they were right there in my living room, holding her hand and making small talk. I had placed the two black chairs from either side of the chess set next to her bed so they could visit with her for as long as they wanted. By the next day, Lucille's conversations with Joe were sweet and very reminiscent. I once heard her say, "I hope I was a good mother, Joe." He of course reassured her that she was the best mother he could ever ask for.

These conversations made me wonder what my final moments with my children would be like. Would I be second-guessing some of my decisions? Would I be left wondering? I thought I had been a good mom. I always told them I loved them and took good care of them. My only regret was spending too much time at work, something I had finally gotten control of.

Sue was so supportive, but she was also very practical. She Skyped each of the grandchildren one by one and let them say their goodbyes. It was unspoken, but the grandchildren knew this could very well be their last conversation. They held back tears and tried to be positive. Each call ended with, "I love you, Grandma." They also called Jim, Lucille's other son, who couldn't make it in person, as he was very busy at work. He didn't say it, but I could tell by his distracted tone that he didn't believe she was going to die that day. With each call, Lucille grew weepier and her "I love you too" was a little softer. She seemed to be fading.

I left the room and called Walter. I couldn't stand it, it was too sad and I felt like I should be doing something, anything but sitting there and watching her die. "Walter, can you come home? I think this is it," I said, my hand sweating against the phone.

Walter, being the great husband that he is, immediately canceled his afternoon patients and rushed home. I was secretly wishing he could turn all this around; I didn't want her to die, not today.

As I entered the kitchen, I overheard the hospice nurse in a firm voice tell Mary, "I've seen a lot of people die. I can tell you one thing: that lady right there is not going to die today. I know it for a fact."

I stood in the doorway between the kitchen and the great room and looked at the nurse, at Lucille, and back at the nurse. I was confused by that comment because by all accounts, and Lucille's and her family's actions, she was definitely ready. I had been watching Lucille speak with Joe and noticed her closing her eyes for a moment between sentences. She sure looked like a dying person to me.

Walter made record time getting home. It felt like he had beamed himself to her bedside. He scooted her over a bit and sat next to her. He was wearing suit pants, a blue dress shirt, and a blue and brown tie. "What's going on here?" he asked Lucille with a smile. It was the loudest anyone had spoken in hours.

"Oh, Walter," she whispered, "you're home early. I think this is it." He sat with her for a while, refusing to give in to her talk of "it," but instead making small talk like it was just another day. She whispered and he spoke back in a regular tone of voice.

Joe and Sue's flight was going to be leaving in a matter of hours. "We really needed to get into Lucille's storage unit to find something. Can you take us there?" Sue asked. At the time, I didn't understand what could be more important than staying by her side, so I hesitated to answer.

"You guys, go. I'm here. She's not going anywhere," Walter urged us as he extended his arm and shooed us off.

"Yes, go," echoed the hospice nurse.

I had to admit, I was irritated that Sue, Joe, and the nurse thought it was a good idea to leave. I hated going to the storage unit. It was a painful reminder of the day I had packed Lucille's things up and moved them out of The Conservatory just a few weeks earlier. I remember standing over the boxes, crying, feeling like a failure, a traitor. All she wanted to do was go back home, and there I was, packing up that home so she could never go back. There was such finality in those moments, such terrible despair. Mary and Katheryn had helped ease the burden as we reduced all of her earthy possessions into a pile of boxes, most of which were stained with my salty tears, then taped, labeled, and their contents entered onto a spreadsheet.

We pulled up at the storage place and parked in the back. I put in my code and we took the elevator to the second floor. It was dark inside and warm. As we walked down the hall toward her unit the lights flickered on. They were on motion sensors, which is great for seeing where you're going, but not so great for seeing much further down the hall. I put in the key, turned the lock. "What are we looking for?" I asked as I rolled up the storage door.

Sue looked at me emotionless and said, "The cremation policy." I looked back at her, stunned. It made perfect sense, but I didn't realize that's what all the urgency was about. "And a few other things," she added.

We stepped into the ten by ten unit and started moving furniture so we could reach the boxes. I felt sick to my stomach. I knew that at any moment, I was going to throw up, or burst into tears, or both. A single tear fell from my right eye and I quickly wiped it away before grabbing another box to look through. It felt weird to be going through her things, especially while she was still alive. I didn't want to be there. I didn't want to be anywhere. I just wanted life to rewind, or to skip forward.

When we returned to the house, Lucille was sitting up on the side of the bed. Walter was sitting right next to her, their hips touching. Lucille's feet were swinging back and forth. It was like stepping into the Twilight Zone. This couldn't be the same person we'd left just over an hour ago. They were sitting there laughing and having a good old time. I looked at them in amazement and asked, "What happened?"

Lucille smiled, looked at Walter and then Walter replied, "She just needed a little ice cream, that's all."

I couldn't believe my eyes. I walked in the kitchen to look for Mary and she stood there with her hands out and shaking her head as if to say, "Don't ask me." The hospice nurse turned to both of us, winked, and waved goodbye.

That evening, after everyone was gone, I looked in on Lucille. She was lying in bed, clutching her crucifix, and begging for forgiveness for all the bad things she had ever done. My heart was heavy, and it was as if I could see a cloud of burden floating above her remorseful body. Without even thinking, I went to her bedside, took her crucifix, and said, "Don't worry.

It's already done. That price has already been paid." I kissed her on the forehead and placed the crucifix on the piano, out of her reach. She let out a sigh of relief and smiled peacefully as she closed her eyes.

The next morning, Lucille woke up, stretched her arms out, and said with a smile, "Look, I'm still alive." She pulled the covers back, exposing her pink and white silk pajamas. "I hope I didn't disappoint anyone," she said as she tried reaching for her wig. I guess we never really know when it will be our time. Well, you best get to work. Hey, hand me my wig before you go."

Atu, the aide that stayed with Lucille became quite fond of her. She had lived in Hawaii and always told Lucille how good she looked as she dressed her in bright colorful outfits. She even started bringing flowers for Lucille to place over her ear. Lucille was looking very happy and very Hawaiian. With each passing day, Lucille grew stronger. During the workday, I would get texts from Atu with photos of Lucille. Lucille was always smiling. Those photos gave me great relief because I knew she was being taken care of and I could do my work without having to worry.

When I got home one day, Lucille was sitting up in yellow pants, a pink shirt, and a flower from Atu in her hair. She looked at me and said, "Guess who came to see me today? Father Dugan. He read me my last rites. Oh, and he gave me this thing." She reached over to the small bedside table I had placed between her bed and the piano, and grabbed a small brochure that included a prayer for the elderly. It even had pictures of old people on the front. She held it out for me to get a closer look.

I thought it was a little depressing, but I didn't want to say so. I smiled and politely said, "That's nice. What do you think?"

"Nice? I can't believe he gave it to me. He thinks I'm *old*," she said, disgusted, as she tossed it back to her bedside table.

* * *

About four or five days later, I walked in the door after work, and Lucille was sitting in a high-backed chair in the front living room watching television. She used to sit in that chair when she would come to visit. She liked the leather seat and the tufted fabric back that was surrounded with carved wood that went nicely with the claw feet. She greeted me with, "Look at this," as she raised her broken arm. "I've secretly been doing my own rehab. Also, I love that new wheelchair you got me. I'm going to start wheeling myself around from now on." She was referring to a chair I'd ordered. It reclined, so if she started feeling faint, I could just lay her back until she came to again.

And she did just what she said she would. She learned how to use both arms to wheel herself from the great room, to the dining room, to the front living room so she could watch the Rangers. During one game, she said all excited, "Grab the phone and take a video of me. I want you to send it to the Rangers. I saw that George Bush Sr. threw a pitch from a wheelchair, so I think there's still hope."

I took the video, but I didn't have the heart to tell her the Rangers weren't going to have her back. Karen had received a letter stating that they simply had too many requests and they couldn't honor hers. We knew that if she found out, that would be the end, so we just stayed quiet about it.

The days were filled with plenty of sunshine; fancy meals at the dining room table, complete with fine china and crystal goblets, and lots of stories. I firmly believe that if you're going to die, you need to at least do it in style. Lucille was taking it all in, every bit of it, as if each day were the last. It's funny how the beauty of this world becomes so much more noticeable when you're about to leave it. It also brought out the best in everyone, including Little Walter, who was always happy to chip in and help.

One morning, I opened the back door and placed her wheelchair in the doorway. It was early, and I wanted to get some good time in before I headed to the office. "Smell this," I said, handing her a bunch of lavender from my garden. It was a mild, yet calming scent, medicinal and herbal.

"Smells good," she said, passing it back to exchange it for the sage, oregano, and then the thyme. She took just a brief moment to smell each one, bending her head over the herbs and breathing deeply.

"I want you to remember how good this earth smelled," I said sincerely with a comforting smile. "You can even taste them if you want, though I don't know how well they'll go with your breakfast."

"Why, what's for breakfast?" She asked in anticipation.

I wheeled her back to the table and told her not to peek. A few minutes later, I came in and plopped down a giant waffle in the shape of Texas covered in blueberries and whipped cream. Her eyes grew big, and a huge smile took over her face. I smiled back at her, proud of my little creation and sat down across from her. She grabbed her fork and knife and didn't even stop for a quick pre-meal prayer. A few minutes later, with blueberries and cream all across her face and her plate nearly empty, she looked at me all satisfied and said, "Blueberries. Isn't this a great last chapter?" I smiled back and nodded in agreement.

Chapter Thirty-Three

❦

The Big Mistake

Lucille grew a little stronger each day, but I knew that was no guarantee that she was going to fully recover. We still had to help her dress, get on the bedside commode, and do most of her daily tasks. At night, I would get up to check on her several times, just to make sure she was still breathing. It was much like how a mother looks over her newborn baby night after night.

One night, I thought I heard a funny sound coming from the great room. I quietly peeked around the column just outside my bedroom door. The location of her bed was perfect, because it sat against the wall that separated my bedroom from the great room. I held the column with both hands and stretched my head out to see if she was asleep. It was hard to tell since she often slept with her eyes slightly open.

"Boo!" she yelled, then giggled. "Look at me, I'm dead!"

I jumped a mile high and nearly had a heart attack. "How could you do that to me?" I panted.

"You have got to stop checking on me like this. I'm fine," she said holding up the bell to remind me that she could call for me if she needed me. "Go back to bed. You've got to get some sleep." There she was scolding me again, right there in my own house.

The next morning in the bathroom, Walter turned to me with his electric razor against his chin, his blue eyes sparkling from the reflection of the lights, "Judy, you're exhausted. I know nobody expected her to rebound like this, but you need to talk to her about that Mustang Creek place. Even Joe agrees that it would be good. Besides, you have to go to Utah soon, and I can't stay up with her every night for those two weeks."

I knew he was right; I just didn't want to think about it. Things were good, the best they had been in weeks. Plus, I had a history of going out of town and then bad things would happen. I couldn't bear the thought of her going backwards, or worse, dying.

"Mary, what should I do?" I whispered across the island in the kitchen. She was folding Lucille's clothes; she always tried to get the laundry out of the way first thing after arriving each morning.

"We can go over there and look at it again," she said, picking up the finished stack of clothes to carry them to the living room. We had previously looked at Mustang Creek when Lucille needed rehabilitation, but we rejected it at the time, as they only offered assisted living, rather than rehab. "I think it will be good. Besides, there's lots of help there at all hours. It would also be good for her to make friends, maybe even play a little bridge." While she would never be back to herself, she seemed stronger now, and Mustang Creek offered a high level of assisted living. Different assisted-living centers offer different levels of care, and, unfortunately, The Conservatory couldn't provide the level she needed.

"They don't have bridge there. They do have tattoos, though," I retorted, being a little irrational.

"I think things will be different with Candice," Mary offered in an effort to reassure me as I followed her back in the kitchen. Candice was the lead assistant in the house Lucille would stay in at Mustang. Each house there had different levels of care for its residents. The house with the highest level of care was full, and Lucille was on the waiting list, but Candice's house was the next-best thing. Plus, Mustang assured us they could offer Lucille extra help until she moved to the higher level.

"You're right. Today, I'm turning over a new leaf," I said as I stood up tall. "I am going to withhold judgment about tattoos and be a better person. I promise." Little did I know how profound that statement would prove to be.

After we took another tour, Lindsay, the intake coordinator who was about thirty, with long brown hair and a sweet smile, came by from Mustang Creek so Lucille could sign the paperwork. She was dressed very professionally and had a folder full of papers. She sat next to Lucille's bed and assured us that Lucille would make friends and that Candice was a terrific helper. "She's one of the best we have," she said with a sweet assuring smile.

"And we can be sure that Lucille will have extra help until we can move her to the other house?" I asked.

"Oh yes, and that probably won't be too long," she commented, looking at Lucille and then back at the two of us.

Lucille's expressionless face said it all: she didn't want to go. I knew it, Mary knew it, and Lindsay knew it. "Well, it's nothing like this," Lindsay allowed, sweeping her arm across the great room, "but it's a good place, and you'll be safe."

There was still no expression from Lucille.

"And it's not a nursing home. It's assisted living," I pointed out, making sure she knew I was keeping my promise.

"And I'll be there every day. Maybe even more than once a day. Anything you need, I'm right here, close by," Mary added.

Lucille sighed, rolled her eyes, took the pen, and signed her name to the paperwork.

The next day, I went back to the storage facility. My dear friend, Tony, whom I lovingly refer to as "Tony the Mover," probably because that's how he's listed in my phone, met me there. Tony has done a lot of work for me over the years, and he was the one who helped me move Lucille's things out of The Conservatory. "Where to this time, Mrs. Judy?"

"Not far. Oh, and that white chair needs to go to my place," I said.

Lucille saw Tony walk into the house and past her bed in the great room carrying the white chair. Tony is Hispanic, short like me, and one solid muscle. He could've probably lifted that chair with one hand if he had tried. "Oh good, the Judy chair! Put that in your sitting area," she said, pointing toward my room. "I told you that it was yours, and I'm glad I get to see it here." The chair was going to look great in there, especially since I had redecorated the room to mimic the room at the Peabody. The walls were now Tiffany blue and the floor-to-ceiling drapes were blue and brown silk. As a matter of fact, it looked better than the Peabody, and Lucille had agreed when she'd seen it months back.

I worked all through the afternoon getting Lucille's new room set up—pictures hung, her blue flowering plant in the window, shower curtain up, and her clothes put away in the closet, all perfectly organized. I wanted it to look as close to her old place as possible.

I knew Mustang Creek was a far cry from The Conservatory. It wasn't even a close second. Nothing was fancy at all. If The Conservatory was like a five-star hotel—the Ritz Carlton of assisted living—then Mustang Creek was more like a La Quinta. If only The Conservatory had more "assisted" to their "assisted living" policy.

Once we got Lucille moved in, her television hooked up, and her first meal down, I felt the hardest part was over. Time was running out, and I had a plane to catch. I couldn't believe I was doing all of this just hours before boarding.

"Lucille, I need you to get comfortable and settled in here," I told her as I wheeled her back to her room. "Wish me luck; I have a big task ahead. Helping Katheryn pack up and driving back to Texas from Utah is going to be quite the undertaking."

"I'll be fine," she said in a grumpy voice. "Don't worry about me." She was still not happy about leaving my house. I wish I could have worked it out, but I couldn't have hired around the clock help for weeks on end. Besides, Mary was right, Lucille needed to make some friends and have a space of her own.

If she only knew. I was going to worry about her every moment of every day. I even made sure to train the staff before I left, teaching them how to help her without hurting her almost fully healed arm. I instructed them on what she liked, what she disliked, the best time for her to take her meds, and so on. I'm sure they thought I was rather high maintenance, but I didn't care. It needed to be done and done right.

While I was away, Mary was great. She and her boyfriend, Mark, even went to see Lucille on the weekends. They even surprised me with a video of Lucille walking a few steps, which was encouraging. I was glad Lucille seemed to be doing so much better. Mary, being the fashion diva she is, even outfitted Lucille in designer clothes and shoes, adding pictures of her to her fashion blog and social media accounts. Lucille was becoming quite the talk of the fashion world and loving every minute of it.

"Kat," I said as we were loading boxes, "it looks like I made a good decision. She's getting stronger, and she seems pretty happy."

That honeymoon period didn't last long, though. It ended as soon as Lucille couldn't get the Rangers game on her television. She called me in a panic: "I've hit this emergency button three times. I told them to get the maintenance guy right away."

"Lucille, this is not an emergency," I pointed out, laughing.

"Oh yes, it is!" She demanded.

I was hundreds of miles away and all she wanted to do was argue. It was something I couldn't do anything about until I got back. I could hear myself sighing throughout our conversation. It was the first time I had ever felt irritated with her. Then I felt irritated with myself for being irritated, so I did the logical thing and called Mary. "Am I being unreasonable?" I asked, trying not to let the irritation creep into my voice.

"No, not at all," Mary said emphatically. "I felt frustrated today, too. I was headed to class, and she called demanding Longhorn cheese. She has been ravenous lately and very picky about what she's craving."

"What? Longhorn cheese?" I laughed in disbelief.

"'She said, 'Don't come back with anything else.' I was almost late for class," Mary said in a frustrated tone. She was charging full speed ahead in a doctoral program in psychology and couldn't afford to be late or to miss class.

Later that evening, I called Walter to tell him about my day. "Oh, it's the steroids talking," he explained when I told him about Lucille's behavior. "They're making her stronger, but it looks like they're also making her—"

"Mean? Well, not mean, just demanding," I said.

"I'll call down there and cut her dose. That way she won't be so ravenous, either."

The two weeks flew by, and suddenly I was back in Texas. The first thing I did was stop in to see Lucille. She was cuddled up in her favorite chair, covered in the white blanket I had gotten her for Christmas. "Well, you're all cozy," I said.

"Yes, but the food here isn't very good," she said with a sour face. I could always count on Lucille to give a full culinary report.

I had to laugh; she was clearly back to her old self. I wanted so badly to scoop her up and take her out for a five-star meal. I missed our Friday lunch adventures. I missed solving the world's problems, laughing over a brownie with ice cream on top. I missed dressing up and picking a new place each week, and the people we'd meet along the way. I missed it all. "As soon as you're better, we'll go back to the Four Seasons."

"Wouldn't that be great? Sure beats this place."

"Oh, it can't be that bad," I said, expecting her to have nothing good to say in response.

She just rolled her eyes, and we spent the rest of my visit talking about my trip. She wanted to hear every detail. Then she told me all the gossip about her new place. She informed me that there's a lady with Alzheimer's that came into her room every night and tried to steal things. "I just shooed her out of here," Lucille said dismissively. She stuck her nose in the air a bit and added in a snobby tone, "Once I had to have the nurse go get my things back."

"That poor lady. I feel so bad for her," I said quietly as I shook my head back and forth.

Lucille just looked at me like I had sympathy for the wrong person. I kissed her forehead and said, "See you tomorrow. I'm pooped and need some rest." I hated to leave her and missed having her at the house, but I decided to give it a week or two. I had promised her that if she really couldn't acclimate, we'd move her back to my place.

It couldn't have been more than a day or two later that I got a call from Candice who was all business. "Mrs. Judy, Lucille hurt her arm."

"What do you mean she hurt her arm?" I questioned, a bit disturbed by the expression. *How could Lucille hurt her own arm?*

"She was on the bedside commode and complained that her arm was hurting." She stopped, not offering any further explanation.

"Her bad arm? Who lifted her?" I asked, a bit annoyed and angry.

"No, not her bad arm," she replied, never answering the question.

"Okay, I'll be there in a minute to check it out." I hung up feeling mad and frustrated. *Why can't things just move in the right direction? Why do we have to have another issue?* I thought.

Mary was with me, so we both went down to see Lucille. When we got to her room, Lucille was lying in bed crookedly with her feet hanging off one side. "Here, let me help you," I said as I reached over to adjust her.

"No!" she cried as she flinched. "Don't touch me. I'm in too much pain."

"What happened?" I asked all confused and very concerned. "I heard you were on the toilet and your arm started hurting."

"No, that's *not* what happened," she replied angrily as she shook her head. She had a big scowl on her face. "That's not at *all* what happened."

I glanced at Mary. Both our eyes were big. "What happened?" Mary asked.

"I was on the floor, and she pulled my arms, both of them," she cried. "I can't move my arms."

"Go get those girls right now," I demanded, looking at Mary.

She returned with a new girl that I had never seen before. The whites of her wide eyes were in stark contrast to her dark skin. She looked young and frightened.

"That's her," Lucille said accusingly through her pain.

"Lucille said that she was on the floor and you jerked her arms. Is that true?" I asked sternly. I'm sure my face was red, because I could feel my blood boil beneath my skin. "Did you know she had a broken arm?"

"No. Nobody told me that," she stammered.

"Are you kidding me? Go get Candice right now." I sounded like a drill sergeant.

Soon enough, both Candice and the new girl stood there in front of me. I sat on the bed next to Lucille in disbelief. "Candice, this girl claims that nobody told her that Lucille has a broken arm."

Candice looked at the new girl and, in a very unconvincing tone replied, "That's not true. I told you that."

As if I were an attorney questioning the defendant, I demanded, "Were you properly trained on how to handle Lucille? How to transport her?"

"No, I wasn't," the girl snapped back in self-defense. She seemed to be more afraid of me than she was of Candice.

I could tell that Candice was about to argue with that statement, so I sent them out of the room. I felt like I was about to lose it on both of them, and I needed to focus on Lucille.

I carefully pulled back her top to take a look at her arm. Sure enough, both arms looked bad. She didn't look symmetrical, and it looked like things were out of place. "She pulled me hard. I was standing next to the bed, and I told her I needed to sit, so she lowered me to the floor. Then she said, 'It's time to get up,' as she pulled me by both my arms."

I was glad that Mary was there to rein me in, because I wanted to kill someone. My face was red, my fists were clenched and my legs were shaking from all the adrenaline. I was in shock and felt like a wild animal that wanted to protect its young.

I called Walter to get his advice. "Well, she's on hospice, so sending her to the ER isn't a good idea. Besides, they can't operate on either of those arms; not at her age and with her blood-pressure issues. Let me order an x-ray. They can do it there. We can't make any decisions until we know what we're dealing with."

Mary and I made Lucille as comfortable as possible and stayed as long as we could, but I couldn't stay all night. "Lucille, I have to get to Little Walter's band banquet." I told her gently. "Walter is sending someone over to x-ray your arms. We'll stop by after the banquet, and we should have answers by then."

Lucille just looked at me with big puppy dog eyes. I knew she didn't want me to leave. I was torn, and it took everything I had to walk out of that building without making a huge scene. I didn't want to leave without taking Lucille with me. It was one of those moments when your heart tugs you in two different directions.

As requested, we had silenced our phones during the banquet. The kids were having a great time, and all the parents were really into it—all except us. We couldn't stop thinking about Lucille. I was still shaking from all the adrenaline of my earlier tirade. At one point, Walter felt his phone buzz in his pocket, and he sneaked a peak under the table. He looked up at me and said, "Grab your purse. It's Lucille."

He was on the phone with Mary the moment we made it to the hall. "What do you mean, 'care flight'? You're kidding me!"

"What? What?" I asked. Walter motioned for me to be quiet, so he could get all the details.

"The radiologist said it's broken and about to puncture an artery."

Tears suddenly filled my eyes, and hatred filled my heart. I'm not sure which one filled faster. I felt hot all over, especially my face. I'm sure it must have been beet red. I could feel my heart pumping out of my chest and even my eyes were burning as the tears started to fall, streaming down my face.

We rushed to the hospital where things seemed to have calmed down. They ended up taking her by ambulance, rather than care flight, and the hospital radiologist didn't agree with the first radiologist's diagnosis. One thing was certain, though: she couldn't stay at the hospital since she was on hospice. Hospice means only palliative care; no life-saving treatment measures, only comfort. I was fine with that. I had promised her that she wouldn't die in a hospital, and I was as eager to get her out of there as they were to see her go.

Before I could even ask, Walter pointed out, "We can't take her home, honey. I know you want to, but this is a full-time, multi-person job at this point. Besides, you're exhausted."

I knew he was right. I didn't like it, but sometimes the truth hurts. I wanted to take her home so badly. I wanted all the kids from church to come to my house and sing to her again. I wanted to tell her that she was going to get better and have it be true. I wanted something that I knew wasn't going to happen.

The hospice nurse helped us find a private care home, a place that was staffed twenty-four hours a day and where the ratio was one caregiver to three or four residents. It was a bit far from our house, but seemed perfect. It was a regular house, and the best part was that Lucille would have the master bedroom. Walter and I spent our Saturday taking a tour, and we immediately knew it was the right place. It was warm and homelike, and she would have a soaring ceiling in her bedroom and a view of the pool. We signed the papers, paid the deposit, and went back to the hospital to tell her about it.

The next day, Tony the Mover, Mary, Kat, and I went to Mustang. We loaded up her things to head to the new place. It took everything I had to keep it together. Just the smell of the Mustang made me sick, and my mind wandered back over everything that had led us to that very moment.

The place was spotless and there was the scent of lemon in the air, as if it had been recently cleaned. A plate of freshly baked cookies sat on the counter facing the dining room. Out of the corner of my eye, I noticed Candice standing there, all dressed up, and asked Mary, "Do you notice anything different about this place?"

She looked around and replied with a puzzled look, "Yeah, I don't remember any of them wearing uniforms before."

"I know, right?" I said, rolling my eyes and shaking my head.

Kat added, "And some lady is walking around with a badge and a clipboard asking questions."

"Oh, I bet they are," I said sarcastically, looking at Mary and Kat. I wasn't surprised because the hospital said they were reporting the incident.

The ambulance transported Lucille to the new place. I was a little nervous she wouldn't like it, but luckily it met her approval. "I love it," She said with a smile as she turned her head from side to side looking into the living room, then the kitchen and eventually the bedroom as they carted her in. "It's so pretty here," Lucille said. "So much better than that awful place I was at before."

"Yes, this is much better. I'm so sorry, Lucille. I made a big mistake. I never should have put you at Mustang," I said tearfully. I shook my head, trying to drive away my thoughts of self-recrimination and instead tried to focus on being cheerful for her sake. "Mary stocked your fridge with bananas, yogurt, and Longhorn cheese. "Look, isn't that a nice view of the pool?" I asked as I pointed out the window. Her bed was angled so that it faced directly towards the pool. I had paid Tony the mover to bring her furniture and art over so the room would be more like home. "You should be all set." I said with a smile. Then I gave her a kiss and sat beside her bed for a short chat. She drifted off to sleep in no time.

I stopped by to see her every day after work and called her each morning and each night right before bed. Pat, her aide, was so pleasant and didn't mind holding the phone to Lucille's ear. She was a tall, thin lady with wrinkles from years of smoking, and a head of short gray hair. She was older and experienced, and aside from the occasional sneak to the alley for a cigarette, she seemed perfect.

There was even a cat that came in to visit Lucille now and again, though I knew she didn't really like cats. Once, while she was staying with us, she woke up one night with George, my orange twenty-pound Maine Coon tabby, standing on her chest and staring into her eyes. She told me that was enough cat for one lifetime.

Lucille's life wasn't ideal, but she tried to make the best of it. I felt confident that she was comfortable, which gave me some small relief. She really wanted to get to her 104th birthday and I knew that this place was her best chance of making it. A small part of me still hoped and prayed for a full recovery, although my mind argued with my heart over what would really be in her best interest at this point.

Chapter Thirty-Four

Revival of the Ruby-Red Slippers

When I came into her room, she was lying in the bed with her head slightly elevated, so she could see out the window. She was covered with the top sheet and the white furry blanket I had bought for her last Christmas. She had been resting with her eyes closed until she heard me enter the room.

"Judy, I'm tired," she said in a quiet, soft voice. "This is no way to live. This is no life," she said as I approached her, carrying a vibrant blue orchid. "I love you. You need to understand that if it's my time to go to Heaven, I can." I noticed that Lucille's face had lost its glow. Her eyes seemed sad and heavy.

It was June 3, one day before my forty-fifth birthday. On the twenty-sixth, she would be 104. This pronouncement of hers was anything but festive in a month when we should have been celebrating. It meant that our plans for the year, our to-do list, were going to become a never-gonna-happen list. I had to face the fact that the end was coming, that our time had finally run out. There was no more sand in the bottle; there would be no

more Friday outings. This year, I might be the only one celebrating a birthday. I felt sad and although I understood, I didn't
want her to go. I couldn't imagine Fridays without her—or
Mondays or Tuesdays for that matter. My heart sank in my chest
because I felt as though she was asking for my permission. Who
was I to deny her what she wanted, much less what she probably
needed?

"Have you ever seen anyone this bad off bounce back?" she
inquired in a doubtful tone.

I looked over her body, as if I were scanning it before I could
give an answer. Her arms were still bruised; her once-strong body
was weak and lifeless. Her extremities were retaining fluid due to
inactivity, making her appear waterlogged. I mustered the biggest
lie I had ever told and said, with the fakest smile I had ever given,
"Yes. As a matter of fact, I have seen people way worse than this
get better."

She looked at me and tilted her head sideways ever so slightly,
as if to say, "Really? You can't be serious." Her eyes said it all: she
wasn't buying it. She knew it wasn't true.

She looked up at the ceiling and cried out in anguish, "God,
where are you? Why have you left me? Why aren't you here?" A
single tear ran down her cheek.

I replied, as if I actually had the authority to do so, "He is
here! He never left you. We just have to endure 'til the end. All
of us. He's proud of you. He's here, I promise." I said it, and I
believed it. Not a word of it was a lie.

"Okay," she replied softly, turning her head toward me with a
faint smile. "I love you, Judy." She knew I meant what I said and
that I was telling the truth this time. I could see it in her tired,
half-mast eyes.

"I love you, too," I said, managing to push past the lump in
my throat.

We made small talk for the rest of the visit, perhaps the most superficial conversation we'd ever had. As I stood up to leave, she asked me, "What should I do now?"

"Rest. Just rest," I said quietly and lovingly as I placed one hand on her face and looked into her tired eyes.

"Okay," she whispered as she closed her eyes.

"Tomorrow is my birthday, so I'll see you on Sunday." I reached over to kiss her cheek and noticed that it felt different. The texture of her skin was tough and cold; it felt foreign against mine. It made me feel as though I was no longer in charge of her destiny—God was.

The next day, I felt almost guilty for being out and about, enjoying myself. Walter spent a great deal of time making a special gourmet breakfast of crème brulée French toast. I knew he was trying to take my mind off the inevitable. Breakfast was extremely tasty, but super sweet. It was like having dessert at eight a.m.

Katheryn and I had lunch later, but I was in such a fog that I was barely present and engaged, no matter how hard she tried to gain my attention. To this day I couldn't tell you where we went or what we ate. I just couldn't stop worrying about Lucille. Katheryn knew I was struggling. "Mom, go have fun the rest of the day." She said, reaching for my hand and giving it a squeeze. "I'll go see Lucille. Don't worry, everything will be fine."

Later, at a couples' massage with Walter, I had a hard time relaxing. He took me to the Gaylord Texan Resort's Relache Spa, which is a perfect spot for couple's massages. It's modern with light wood, earth tones, and minimal art. They even have a quiet room where you can lay on chaise lounges in the near dark and listen to nature sounds as you curl up under a soft blanket. I had turned my phone off but couldn't stop thinking that I needed to stay connected, just in case Lucille needed me. It was like being covered in a blanket of guilt: guilt for thinking about anything other than this moment that Walter was trying so hard to create, and guilt for pampering myself and not being with my dear friend. I was emotionally torn.

"That was great," I said to Walter as I slipped my robe back on when the massage was over. "I'll meet you in the lobby."

I had promised myself I would stay unplugged until our date was over, giving Walter my full attention, but the anticipation was getting to me. I turned my phone on in the locker room and smiled as I peeked at a video of Lucille that Katheryn had sent over. "Judy, I hope you're having a wonderful time. I'm doing *great*! Happy twenty-ninth birthday," she said with a forced wink and a smile. She looked tired and I could tell that it was all she could do to make that video. "See you tomorrow." I didn't notice it then, but later when I replayed that video, she was slurring her words a bit.

Just like that, I could breathe again. The feeling of impending doom had been lifted, and I could actually try to enjoy my birthday now, guilt-free and worry-free. I even thought that perhaps she was turning a corner and getting better. Maybe the next birthday we celebrated would be hers.

Later that night, as we were getting into bed, Walter looked at me, concerned, and said as he pulled back the sheets on his side of the bed, "Let's go see Lucille first thing in the morning, before church."

"Okay, that sounds like a good idea," I replied in relief. Then we cuddled up tight in the middle of our queen bed as if we were one person lying there, not two. He knew I had been worried about her all day, and I think he was just as worried as I was. We had both tried to block out our fear and concern for the day, but as we were snuggled up tight together in bed, the reality of it all hit us once again. I don't even remember breaking our grip or moving to our own sides of the bed, but at some point, we did.

In the morning, I jumped out of the shower quickly, remembering that my phone was still on silent from the night before. I had missed a call—several calls, actually. They were all from the same number, the number to Lucille's place. My heart sank. I didn't even listen to the messages, I just called back immediately.

"Hey Pat, it's Judy," I said, my voice quivering.

"You need to come over now. This morning, I came in to check on her, and she's unresponsive. She's just staring straight forward." Pat seemed shaken, and I could tell that she didn't want to deliver such bad news, especially over the phone.

As we started the twenty-minute drive, I felt an intense pain overtake my whole body, radiating from my heart. My head felt hot, and I scrubbed my hands up and down, back and forth over my face, like I was trying to wash away the thoughts in my head. Tears flooded my face and dripped down through my cleavage as if it were a creek bed housing a river of despair.

We entered Lucille's room, and I went straight over to her. Pat was right. Lucille was lying down, staring straight ahead, and she seemed completely unresponsive. Her breaths were quick and shallow. I recognized the sight: it was time. This was the point of no return. Walter switched into doctor mode, checking her pulse and respirations. He checked her pupils, and they were unresponsive to the light.

"She must have had a stroke," he said with a frown. I could tell he was struggling with his own emotions as he choked back tears and became very solemn. Being a doctor is hard, but when the patient is family or someone who feels like family, it's even harder. This is the role they never teach you about in medical school. Even with forty years of private practice behind him, nothing had prepared Walter for this moment. He was watching his patient, his friend, die, and there was nothing he could do to stop it.

So many people over the years had said insensitive things to me like, "She can't live forever" or "You know the day is coming." Of course, they were right, but that didn't make this moment any easier. If anything, it made me even angrier at all those well-meaning, self-proclaimed advisors.

I walked toward the bed and climbed in, cuddling up next to Lucille in that small, twin-sized bed. She looked peaceful. The smell of Chanel No. 5 was still lingering on her blanket, and I started stroking her hair. My tears made puddles on the peach-colored pillow we shared. This would be our final moment together.

I looked her over and couldn't help but notice that she was wrapped in love. She was wearing her special green-and-white flannel nightgown that had been made by one of my friends from church; it had been reconfigured so she could get both her broken arms into the sleeves. Draped over her was the incredibly soft, off-white, faux-fur blanket that I bought her for Christmas. At least Lucille was going to leave us in style. She looked incredibly comfortable for someone who was actively dying.

I bent over to talk to her.

"She can't hear you," Walter said in a disappointed, but loving tone.

"She'll hear me," I replied, so sure of myself. I remembered how when she didn't know anyone, she knew me. I remembered all the times we'd shared together, and that nobody knew each other's fears and dreams better than we did. We were the best of friends. Besides all of that, I knew in my heart that God would grant me closure and give me one last moment with her.

"Are you in pain?" I asked, my hands softly brushing back her white hair.

"No," she replied softly but unmistakably.

I looked back at Walter, and his eyes were huge. I thought he was going to fall over in shock. I wasn't shocked; I knew she would hear me. I was as sure of it as I had ever been of anything.

Mary arrived at this point, looking as if she just dropped everything and ran out the door. She was wearing ripped jeans, a pink cashmere sweater and old Nike tennis shoes. I could tell that she was a bit shaken by the way she looked at me with glossy eyes. I had never seen her cry before, but I knew today would be the day. When I had called her from the car, I didn't even have to ask her to come. She just said, "I'm leaving now." I knew that Mary had never seen a dead body before; we had discussed that in the past. I felt bad that the first dead body she would see would be that of someone she loved.

"Grab a silk flower from the drawer," I said, pointing toward the dresser. "Find one that matches her gown."

Mary and I both knew that we were preparing Lucille for her departure. She picked the perfect one, blue-green with rhinestones in the center.

"Can you call the boys and let them know?" I asked Walter. He started dialing before I even finished my sentence. I could hear his voice crack as he broke the news that Lucille would be passing soon. I'm sure it brought back memories of his own mother's passing; he had been on the receiving end of such a call. Regardless of how old you are, losing a parent is a life-changing event.

As requested, Walter held the phone up to Lucille's ear so Joe could tell his mother how much he loved and adored her one last time.

"Did you hear Joe?" I asked. Her pupils were still fixed and staring forward.

"Yes," she replied faintly, but audibly. The fact that she could say something more than just, "No," was proof that she was actually hearing and understanding me. There was no medical explanation for how this could be possible. I like to think of it as God's grace.

Moments later, the hospice nurse entered the room. I was trying to keep my focus on Lucille and these precious final moments, but I heard her mumble something about giving pain meds. I looked up, my eyes swollen and my face soaked with tears. I was shocked that she could make such an assessment of the situation in under thirty seconds and from across the room. "She doesn't need pain meds," I said sharply.

She stood in the doorway, completely disengaged and with a near monotone voice she said, "She looks anxious or like she's in pain. We should give her something."

I glanced over at Walter. He knew exactly what I was trying to say. He stood up and walked over to the nurse, quietly explaining, "She doesn't need pain medication. She's not in any pain."

"How do you know?"

"She said so," he replied.

The nurse looked at Walter like he was out of his mind. How could a completely non-responsive patient say anything? I know she thought we were crazy, but I didn't care.

"Well, I suppose there's nothing for me to do here, then," she said as she left the room. I was relieved; I didn't want anything about this moment to feel like a hospital—sterile or cold.

"Are you afraid?" I asked Lucille.

She quietly replied, "No."

Mary and I looked at each other, and then looked back at Lucille. I was so glad that Mary was there, sitting on the other side of the bed, stroking her hand and comforting her. I pointed at the orchid I had just brought over two days earlier. "Mary, look at that: all the petals have fallen except one, and it's gotten droopier and droopier since I arrived."

"Wow, that's weird," she said, slowly shaking her head back and forth in disbelief.

It was as if the plant were crying tears of petals.

We sat quietly, Walter, Mary, and me. We were all sharing in this moment. Bonding. We were together with one purpose, but with our own sets of thoughts and memories playing through our minds.

Mary had moved down the bed a bit so Walter could be close by Lucille's head. I draped my right arm around the top of her head and intertwined the fingers of my left hand and her right as we lay there together. I found myself thinking how strong her hands had been, thinking back to that shoulder massage in Memphis when she was taking care of me.

"Are you ready to go?" I said sweetly into her ear. I don't know why I asked. Maybe I just needed to know that she knew this was it.

"Yes," she replied, perhaps a little more audibly than her past responses had been.

I climbed out of the bed, my body stiff from lying on my side for so long. I reached into the bathroom closet and pulled out her ruby-red slippers. I'm not sure what prompted me to get them, but it was as if I had rehearsed this moment and now everything was going according to plan. In truth, I had never let the thought of her dying go this far. Every time I imagined her actually leaving, I would quickly change the channel in my mind to something else, anything else.

No, there was no rehearsal, no plan. It was just happening, happening for the first and final time. Perhaps it was divinely orchestrated. All I know is that each moment felt right.

I peeled back the blanket to expose her feet and noticed they were a new color, a color I had never seen before, at least not on her. This reddish-purplish tint was proof that her circulation was slowly shutting down. I placed the slippers on her feet, and they glistened in the sun that shone through the big window. I replaced the covers and said, as if on cue, "It's time to go home, my dear friend. It's time to go home." Tears continued to fall from my eyes until my shirt was completely soaked.

I climbed back into bed with her and held her tight. I felt my emotions welling up; I knew this was it. It was the deepest sorrow I had ever felt. "I love you," I said loudly, forcing it out through the pain and the tears. "You're my best friend, and I hope to be half the woman you are." I held onto her and wanted so badly to turn back time, but I knew it was useless. There was no going back; the only way out of this pain was to go through it.

Suddenly, I felt calm. The lump in my throat started to dissolve. I felt as though it was over. I looked at her chest, and she was still breathing. I looked back at the last petal, the one right at the top of the orchid, and it was moving ever so slightly, as if it was about to fall. I had felt her soul depart, even though she was still breathing. "It's time to take this off," I said as I lifted the oxygen tube.

Moments later, I saw the last breath she would ever take. Before climbing out of that bed for the final time, I kissed her head. "Goodbye," I whispered, only this time, I knew there was no one there to hear me.

I stepped quietly over to the plant by the window; the last petal fell into my hand. Walking back over to Lucille, I placed that single blue orchid petal over her heart. I had kept my promise. She didn't die alone, and she didn't die in a hospital or a nursing home. She died surrounded by love, and true to form, she died in style.

Chapter Thirty-Five

※

The Other Side of Peace

The days that followed were in sharp contrast to the peaceful moments of Lucille's passing. I often found myself deep in thought, reflecting on our friendship, the time we spent together, and the multitude of memories, but each time I focused on a happy thought, it was immediately overshadowed by the dark events that led to her death. My heart was full of anger at the people who had failed to watch over her, who had allowed her to fall, or who had actively harmed her through their own negligence. The only thing worse than that anger was the guilt I carried for not doing more. Why didn't I keep her at my house? Why didn't I just hire someone I could personally supervise? I could have done it. I could have run a tight ship, just like my mother used to. I had watched her do it for so many years, so why didn't I?

The pain from all that anger and guilt was slowly eating away at my heart, and I could feel myself becoming hard and bitter on the inside. I didn't like my new self. I didn't know how to cope with the reality that Lucille was no longer there, sharing old memories and making new ones. She wasn't by my side to help me keep swimming through this trial.

I did the only thing I knew how to do: I went to the office. The distractions there were welcome, because they seemed to be the only way to pause the negative reel of thoughts that played in my mind's eye day and night. I quickly fell into a cycle: work, get up and shut my office door, cry, get over it, open the door, and work again. I didn't even bother greeting anyone when I came in, not even Judy 2. The one thing I was grateful for was having my own private office again. There was nobody to tell me to cheer up, to ask me how I was doing, or anything else. It was just me in my own little space.

I was so thankful for Joe and Sue, who kept in touch by phone. Since Lucille was cremated, we had to find a way to remember her, to put together some sort of memorial. The planning process helped, because it made me feel like I was still helping her, still showing her how much I cared about her.

"I have to do her legacy justice, Walter. This is such a tall order," I said.

A few days after her passing, I headed over to Lucille's old room to pack up her things. "Thanks for helping," I said tearfully to Katheryn, who had come along. She was dressed for the task at hand in shorts, a t-shirt, and tennis shoes. Her curly hair was unruly, the way it always gets when she doesn't take time to straighten it.

"Oh, Momma," she said as she reached over and touched my hand. The rest of the ride was very quiet. I couldn't help but think of all the other times I had made this trip and how this one felt so different. There was a sense of duty and finality. It was one of those things you don't want to do, but you push through the pain and go through the motions, trying to distance yourself from the emotion of it all.

Once again, there was Tony with his muscles and his moving

truck. His smiling yet reverent face was a welcome sight. We embraced for a moment. "Thank you for coming," I said, pulling back and wiping away a small tear. "I can't cry, Tony, or everything will take ten times longer." I said, laughing through the tears.

We literally rolled up our sleeves, and Tony, his assistant, Katheryn, and I all got to work. The room felt empty, so completely different from the last time I was there. It was just a room now, and the things inside were just things.

The sun peeked through the window and landed on the orchid, bare of all its blooms. Below it, the fallen blue flowers lay shriveled up, yet still vibrant with color. I stared at them for a moment before scooping them into a little white trinket bowl lined with cherubs. These flowers, just like Lucille, were dead and lifeless, but the beautiful blue reminded me of her spirit: so colorful and vibrant, never fading.

"Let's make a stack for the sheets, towels, and medical supplies so we can donate them. We also need a stack to toss and one to keep," I instructed Katheryn, pushing away my melancholy thoughts. "Oh, and that wig looks like it's seen better days. Toss that one, but keep the newest one. Someone may need it."

"What about all this?" Katheryn asked as she opened a small refrigerator. There were the snacks that Mary and I tried to keep Lucille stocked up with: Longhorn cheese, blueberries, and yogurt. It was weird to look at the food and think that she had expired, but the food hadn't. Before I could answer, Katheryn took it out and donated it to the other residents.

There was one banana sitting on top of the small mini-fridge. It was bruised and squishy to the touch. Seeing it reminded me of the first time I saw a bunch of green bananas on her counter. Lucille always bought green bananas—the greenest, hardest ones she could find. She had no doubt that she would be around to see them ripen. Those green bananas always gave me a weird sense of comfort. I was thinking about the first time we met, how I noticed green bananas on her counter. As long as she was still buying green bananas, it was a good sign. I picked up the banana, looked at it thoughtfully for a moment, and then tossed it in the trash.

"Look at this, Mom," Katheryn said as she opened the bed-side table drawer. It was filled with old photos, cards from family members, notes from me, and everything else Lucille had wanted to keep close by. "Let's empty all the drawers into boxes so we can wrap and protect the furniture. We can go through all that later with Joe, Sue, and anyone else who wants to."

After packing away the last of Lucille's folded clothes, I came across the drawer with her flowers. There were so many colors, shapes, and sizes—one for every outfit. A smile drifted across my face as I picked them up one at a time, remembering each Friday lunch she wore them to. I could almost label them individually with the memories they represented and the outfits she wore with them. I slowly placed them in a box, careful not to crush their delicate petals.

When I opened the last drawer, I could smell her perfume faintly as if she were right there in the room with us. It was her drawer of ribbons, the ones that had adorned her neck for so many years. There seemed to be hundreds of them: solid colors, polka dots, stripes, and patterns. Each one was about twelve inches long, and many had frayed edges. I stuck my head in the drawer to get one last whiff of her. "Nobody's going to want these. I know I need to throw them out, but it's just . . ." I paused, a tear in my eye. "It's just that they still smell like her." I stoically scooped them up and carried them to the trash. A tear fell, and I wiped it away with my sleeve, hoping Katheryn didn't see it.

"Mrs. Judy, is this it?" Tony asked reverently, as he carried out the last piece of furniture.

"That's it, Tony. We did it," I replied with a bit of relief in my voice. Then we shared a smile, a real smile, the kind that has dimples.

Later, I poured myself into bed, exhausted both physically and mentally. Walter woke me at three o'clock in the morning as he tossed and turned. I was awake just long enough to remember that it was all reality and not a dream; Lucille really was gone. A single tear hit my pillow as I drifted back off to sleep.

Tap, tap. Katheryn was at the door knocking quietly. The taps got louder, drawing me out of my slumber, and when I finally opened my eyes, Katheryn was standing over me. She was still in her clothes from the day and she looked exhausted, with heavy eyes and dark circles around them. I hadn't seen her since we got home; we were both grieving, and neither of us felt like talking after we got back.

Katheryn handed me a bag with what appeared to be a present. Slightly panicked, I thought, *Did I miss a holiday? A birthday? What is this?* "Kat, it's four in the morning!" I exclaimed, a little irritated that nobody would let me sleep through the night, escape the pain, and reset my emotions.

"I know, Mom," she said quietly with a smile, "but I had to give this to you while it still smelled like her."

I opened the bag and pulled out a white quilt that was covered on one side with all of Lucille's neck ribbons. Each one had been carefully sewn in and attached to the next. She had arranged them so artistically that their colors seemed to tell a story: the story of her style, her life, and all our memorable outings. "I stayed up all night sewing it for you. I knew you didn't really want to throw her ribbons away, so I snuck them out of the trash when you weren't looking. Do you like it?" She asked, leaning closer to me, earnestly seeking my reply.

"Like it?" I asked, with tears of joy streaming down my face. "I *love* it. Thank you, Katheryn. Oh, my gosh! I love it so much. You're amazing. What a gift." I held it close to my heart, rocking back and forth in bed as all the emotions of the previous days suddenly came to a head. She was right: it still smelled like Lucille.

"Good night, Mom," Katheryn said lovingly as she tucked me in and draped the beautiful ribbon quilt over me. What a role reversal after all the years I had tucked this dear child of mine into bed at night. I drifted into a deep sleep, covered in my own blanket of love, and woke up the next morning finally feeling rested.

Tasks are great because they keep you occupied. It's hard to be angry, sad, or feeling guilty when you're busy. I wished I had a whole mansion to pack and move; the distraction would have been worth the hard labor. But I didn't. I just had the kind of work that requires your mind rather than your body. So there I sat at my computer the next day, working. Work, tears, anger, more tears, and more work. Maybe this was why my parents liked work so much—it was their therapy.

A few days later, I was in the car for longer than my usual five-minute commute. It was a drive I had been dreading because it's too easy to get lost in your thoughts when you drive. Thoughts were something I preferred to avoid at that point. But, as expected, my body went on autopilot and my mind took over, playing that movie again and again.

I could feel my hands go numb from gripping the steering wheel too tightly. It was as if I were choking someone with that grip. Choking the people who let her fall, choking the untrained aide who broke her other arm, choking myself for letting her leave my home. My grip became tighter and tighter, and the tears started to fall, not one at a time, but like a flash flood. I didn't care, didn't even bother to wipe my red, hot face. I was like a volcano of anger exploding from the inside out.

Then it happened: it felt like she was right there in the car with me. I felt her strong hands cover mine, rubbing them lovingly. I heard her say, "It's okay. Shhh . . ." It was her, no doubt about it. "Let it go," she said softly in my ear. "It all happened for a reason, so stop being angry. I told you the secret to life the first day we met, and this isn't it." Even through my anger and pain, I knew she was giving me the key to unlock my fear, anger, and guilt. "You know what you have to do," she said knowingly, as wise in death as she ever was in life. Finally, when the voice stopped and my hands loosened their grip on the steering wheel, I knew exactly what I had to do.

Chapter Thirty-Six

Doing Her Justice

About ten days later, I was curled up in the Judy chair in my room, covered with the same faux-fur blanket that gave Lucille comfort in her final hours. I had gone several days without tears, and things seemed to be normalizing. Nobody was home, and I found myself talking out loud to Lucille as if she were right there with me: "I sure miss you," I sighed. "It's time to plan your memorial, and I just need to know what you want. How can I ever do you justice, my dear, sweet, best friend?" My words rang out in the empty room without an answer.

My mind went back to those final moments with Lucille, the moment when I left the room, looking back at her for the last time ever. Suddenly, blood rushed to my head and my voice grew louder. "I don't like cremation! It really creeps me out. How do I know you're okay? How do I know what they did to you or what they did with your ashes? I know this was your wish, but I'm having a really hard time with it." I almost felt guilty for putting my feelings out there. After all, who was I to question her decision?

Just then, my phone dinged. Normally, I would jump up and read it immediately, but not this time; I couldn't have cared less about it. Instead, I sat there talking, crying, reminiscing, and working through everything I had suppressed over the last week and a half.

"I can still feel your hand in mine. I remember your fingers," I said aloud. I pictured her hands. Without even realizing it, I had apparently memorized the dark spots on the back of her hands as if they were landmarks on a map. For some reason, I was fixated on her hands. I closed my eyes and drifted off to sleep.

When I woke up and stumbled to the bathroom, I reached for my phone. Rubbing my swollen eyes, I looked down at the text message I had ignored earlier. "We will arrive on Wednesday . . . Thursday morning we will pick up the urn at eight thirty . . ."

It was a long text from Sue, proof that our thoughts and prayers are heard and often answered. How could she possibly know I was wondering what had happened to those ashes? It gave me a warm feeling inside, a sense of comfort.

Wednesday rolled around, and Joe and Sue arrived at our house with luggage in tow. They looked a bit tired from the trip—and the emotion that went along with a trip like this. Joe was in shorts and a golf shirt and Sue was in a button up blouse, cropped brown pants, and sandals. I felt a sense of relief as I hugged each of them. I felt so close to them, like they were my own siblings. I guess they are, in a way. We will always be bonded by the love we had for and the love we received from Lucille.

"It's weird coming to Texas and not seeing Mom," Joe said, his face a picture of sadness and loss. We all knew the coming days would be a rollercoaster of feeling, healing, and closure, and now I was climbing onto the ride with them. I could even hear the ride attendant in my mind say, "Please remain seated until the ride comes to a complete stop."

Joe and Sue had arranged for a Catholic mass at St. Anne's,

the church Lucille had attended for many years. Katheryn, Mary, and I, all dressed in plain, dark colors, decided to ride together, since none of us had ever been to St. Anne's before. As we approached it, Mary called out, "There it is," pointing to a large building with domes on top.

"That can't be it," I replied, almost refusing to turn in. "That's a mosque."

"Judy, mosques don't have crosses on top." Mary and Kat both started to giggle.

Feeling a little foolish, I turned in. I swear the Catholic churches I remember looked very different.

The service was held in the small St. Mary's Chapel within the larger cathedral campus. It was the first and last time I saw the little black box that held Lucille's ashes. It sat on a small table at the front of the chapel beside a photo of her smiling that infectious smile that could brighten any situation. A solid white candle next to it burned a single flame in her honor. It was so unsettling to think that her colorful, lively life was reduced to some gray ashes inside a black box.

Being in the chapel reminded me of my own religious past. I grew up Episcopalian, and the wooden benches, the decorative altar, and the walls lined with art representing Stations of the Cross were very familiar.

The cold breeze blowing from the vents was a stark contrast to the hot Texas air outside. Beside me, Katheryn's legs were covered with goose bumps, and she wrapped her arms tightly around herself, as though she were giving herself a hug.

She had never been in a Catholic church before, and she kept looking around, as if she were trying to make sense of all the symbolism. "It feels so heavy in here," she said to Mary.

Mary nodded. She had grown up Catholic, and her experience with the church had been less than positive. She once told me about the emotional pain she had experienced in her old parish, so I was shocked that not only had she agreed to go to the mass, but that she was actually the one to suggest it in the first place. We never discussed how she felt about reopening her childhood wound, but I could tell she had a bit of a nervous energy as she fidgeted in the pew. Nonetheless, her love for Lucille far outweighed her frustration with any religion.

A few old friends, some members of the church, and the family were scattered throughout the pews. I couldn't help but reflect that the older you get, the fewer friends you have that are still alive to attend your own funeral.

The cold, hard room was quickly warmed by memories of Lucille as her grandchildren told their favorite stories about her. Sue read the prepared speeches of those who couldn't make it, each one personal and heartfelt.

One of my favorites was the story of Lucille getting her exercise, walking laps around the backyard when she came to visit the grandchildren. "High heels and all, regardless of any mud, she walked every day. We were allowed to join her so long as we could keep up."

Making apple pie, playing practical jokes . . . the stories went on and on. Sitting there and listening to their memories completed the circle. For years, I had heard about each and every one of the grandchildren, listening as Lucille rejoiced in their accomplishments. I knew just how much they had meant to her. Strangely, I felt like her family was also my family. I loved each and every one of them, some of whom I had never even met. Now, I had the pleasure of hearing their side of the story, and I cherished every one of their carefully prepared words.

When Joe spoke, I could feel a lump form in my throat. Something about seeing a grown man cry always gets to me. He was dressed up in slacks and a dress shirt. Even with his gray hair and gray mustache, he looked young and full of life, much like his mother always did. I felt his pain and could see the sorrow in his eyes. His speech was brilliantly written and reflected his amazing control of the English language. It was like listening to the work of a famous writer. Lucille would be proud, as would her own mother, the schoolteacher. But it was when he started talking about Lucille's hands that chills ran down my spine. There they were again—those hands. I sat there, connecting those age spots in my mind.

The next afternoon was the Celebration of Life at my church. It was held in the Relief Society room, where the women of the church gather each week. Appropriately, the padded seats were in one of Lucille's favorite colors: turquoise.

As I helped set up the chairs, I heard Lucille ask, "Where's my chair? Hey, it's my birthday, and I need a chair!" She was right. It was her birthday. I chose that day because I knew how much she was looking forward to her birthday. She wanted all her friends and family to be with her. I pulled one chair up alongside the tabletop lectern, then I grabbed her pink cane and leaned it against the seat. I pinned a flower with white feathers and sparkling rhinestones, fitting for the birthday girl, on the cushioned seat back. I knew she loved it. I could feel it. There was a sense of happiness that filled the air, much like the way Lucille always changed the energy of a room with her very presence.

The rest of the room was decorated with as much color as possible. "A girl's gotta have color," Lucille used to say. It didn't feel like a funeral; it was more like the celebration it was intended to be.

Church members scurried around, helping out, and friends were filling helium balloons and attaching them to white strings and blank note cards. When they finished, all the balloons lined the front of the room behind the lectern.

Just outside the entrance sat a table with her things. When I packed up Lucille's room, I had filled a suitcase with various items that I felt would be important to her. You can always tell what's important to people because those are the things that follow them: the things they keep over the years, the things you find in their bedside table after they leave this earth.

As people entered, they admired the display. There were photos of Lucille in her nursing uniform just after graduation. Her diploma from Cambridge Mount Auburn, still in its original leather folder, stood proudly. A large oval photo of her, her sisters, and her parents in front of the old farm sat upon the table, leaning against the wall. Her two favorite skirts were laid across each corner. Mixed in with all the artifacts were the flowers from her drawer. I knew that people coming to the party would recognize them; perhaps the flowers would bring back their own memories of times spent with Lucille.

Mom arrived in a colorful dress to honor Lucille and her sense of style. "This is so nice," said Mom with a smile as she held the program. "And all those things out there? It's like she's right here."

"Thanks. I really wanted the focus to be on her legacy and what she taught us: persisting, forgiving, and enduring until the end. Oh, can you hand these out?" I asked as I handed her a long white box full of freshly pinned flowers.

"Of course I can." She replied with a big smile, seemingly happy to be included and to have a job to do.

As I looked out at all the people, each with their own little flower pinned to their shirt, I was amazed at the size of the crowd. So often, friends die off, family is scattered, and people have little left when their time comes. Not Lucille, though. She never stopped making friends or making a difference. The proof was all the people in those seats.

DarLynn, a good friend of mine who visited Lucille many times, offered the opening prayer, and a member of our church delivered a sweet message, and then I was up. The bishop himself would have come, but his flight was delayed. I wasn't sure I could make it through my speech without a flood of tears. I was happy to pay tribute to Lucille, but it was the final step, the last stop on the bus to acceptance.

"Go ahead; this should be good," I heard Lucille say.

I stood still for a moment at the lectern, looking out at everyone gathered there: Mom, Dad, my kids, Joe and Sue, people from work, friends from church, Karen and a few others from The Conservatory, Atu, Vel, and so many others. Even Dr. Anderson was there with his wife. I knew then that I wasn't swimming alone. I was among a pool of others who cared, who loved, and who supported each other. I also knew that, in her own way, Lucille had impacted each and every one of them.

I don't remember much about the beginning of my talk, but I ended it with, "And that's what she felt was the secret to life. I promise that if you follow this advice, it will change your life, now and forevermore."

I sat back down next to Walter, and he patted my leg as if to say, "Good job."

Little Walter picked up his trumpet and played one of my favorite tunes, "Memories" from *Cats*. It was so incredibly moving as the notes filled the room, bouncing off the walls and back to the front.

When Little Walter was done, I smiled at Joe, and up he went. "I've been asked to speak about perseverance and self-reliance, both of which Mom believed in and taught us." He went on to deliver another incredible speech, filled with beautiful usage of the English language and, more importantly, filled with heart.

Mary was next, and she surprised us all. Young, thin, and dressed in a black skirt to match her black Christian Louboutin shoes and a vintage top covered in black, gold, and silver sequins, she made a fashion statement that would have made Lucille proud. She was so well-prepared, holding everyone's attention as she spoke about the lessons she had learned from Lucille and how this experience had changed her life and helped her grow. "Enduring to the end is something that Lucille definitely knew how to do. One time, I was nervous, and she gave me the best advice: 'Don't be afraid to be wonderful.'"

Each message seemed to be divinely inspired. Judging by the heads nodding in agreement, the smiles, and, of course, a few falling tears, it was clear that these were all words people needed to hear. It wasn't just a celebration of life; it was motivation to live.

After the service, we all grabbed balloons to symbolically send a message to Lucille in Heaven. Mine read: "I hope I did you justice, my dear friend. I sure miss you. Happy birthday!" As the balloons faded into the distance far above, I began to smile again. It was the first time in a while. I imagined Lucille up in Heaven, smiling down. I also remembered our conversation about God, and I knew that someday she would be there to greet me with a big wave, a smile, and a hug, just like she'd promised.

Chapter Thirty-Seven

❧

Blueberry Cobbler

That night I slept soundly. It was the best I had slept in months. When I woke the next morning, I felt happy, like things were right in the universe again. I was smiling in the kitchen as I rustled around making a good hearty breakfast for everyone. I was talking to Dad and thinking about how well the celebration went, wondering what people thought when they found those balloons with the notes.

Joe, Sue, and I needed to go to the storage unit that day and start sorting through Lucille's things. Before, I had felt that going there was weird or intrusive, so I tried to avoid it. Now, something inside me had come to peace with the idea. This was the final task. The rollercoaster ride was about to come to a stop.

"Dad, do you think you can go with us? Some of the stuff we have to move is really heavy, and we could use your muscles," I asked after breakfast, already knowing he would say yes. He's the type of guy that always says yes.

He agreed without any hesitation, just pausing to add, "Let me get my shoes on."

"Prepare to sweat," I warned him. "Even though it's air

conditioned, it's hard to keep a place cool when the heat gets like this." It was an especially hot day and I wanted to prepare everyone ahead of time. I was the only Texan in the group, and I know how quickly you can overheat, especially in a storage unit. "I'll bring lots of water."

We arrived in two cars, knowing that we would need the room to bring things back. Joe and Sue were planning to take some items home in their suitcases, but the furniture would remain in storage and eventually go to Katheryn. When Lucille didn't need most of it anymore, I had bought it from her to help cover her health expenses. She disliked taking handouts, so this arrangement allowed her to maintain her dignity, something she seemed extremely grateful for.

The storage unit was full of hard surfaces. Concrete floors led to metal garage door after metal garage door. The lights were on motion-detecting sensors, so the place lit up sequentially as we walked toward the door of Lucille's unit. I removed the lock and rolled the door up. Everyone's eyes grew wide as we realized just how big a task we had ahead of us.

"At least we're on a corner unit. This way we can spread stuff out," Dad pointed out.

"Well, let's make a plan," Sue said extending her arms out, palms up, and then returning them to her hips. I was so thankful for her decisive personality in that moment. I didn't want to be in charge, so I was glad she was taking the lead. The teacher in her came to life as she started giving us directions. "Let's put everything we're going to donate down this hall, and everything we're going to keep or need to go through, down this one."

"Sounds like a plan," Dad and Joe replied in unison, as if on cue.

We started sorting and moving things out rapidly, almost like we were well-versed in this activity.

"Keep?"

"Yes."

"Donate?"

"No, keep. But you can donate that."

Exchanges like this went on and on, back and forth. Joe and Dad moved all the heavy things, while Sue and I focused on opening boxes and sorting. It was hot, but we were on a mission. It helped that Joe and Dad got along so well. It was like they had known each other for years. They would talk and move, move and talk.

"My dad has been through this sort of thing before," I said to Joe at one point when we stopped to take a break.

"Sure have," he confirmed, looking at Joe with an understanding expression. "It's never easy. It also seems like it's never really done. I still have some boxes of my dad's to go through. I did as much as I could, but the rest is in the barn."

Sue was careful to prepare a box of items for each grandchild. "They may not think they want anything, but *someday* they'll thank me," she said in a motherly tone as she bent over a box marked "Elizabeth."

My dad and stepmom had thoughtfully presented each of us kids with things that had belonged to my grandparents when they passed, and they mean more to me with each passing year. Through these keepsakes, their memory lives on and on.

"Here's all her purses," Sue said. "We should probably go through them."

She was right. Some had a few hidden dollar bills, all had tissues, and there was the occasional cookie Lucille must have forgotten about. When I pulled out the last purse I'd seen her carrying, it contained a small, signed picture of her and Suzanne Somers together. She must have shown that picture to everyone. She always had it with her everywhere she went. I held it for a moment, smiled, and, with Sue's permission, placed it in my purse.

After several trips to the donation station, we loaded up the cars one final time with the items that Sue and Joe were going to take home and the boxes intended for the grandchildren who lived in Texas.

"Where should we put these?" Joe asked as he carried the boxes through the front door. "They're for Erin and Colter." They were the only two grandchildren who lived close by.

"Leave them right there in the entry," I replied.

"I don't want them to be in your way," Sue piped up.

"Why don't we see if Colter's and Erin's families want to come over for dinner tomorrow night and pick 'em up?" I suggested.

Sue tilted her head as if to say, "Why not?" She picked up her phone and started dialing. A few minutes later, she found me again and said, "They'll be here."

"Perfect. We can all have one final toast to Lucille. With apple cider, of course."

"Of course," she replied with a grin.

The next night, we all sat around the long wooden dining table that seats ten, but usually only on holidays and special occasions. White placemats, white napkins, and fine crystal glasses adorned the setting, just like Lucille would have liked it.

"Let's make a toast to Lucille," Walter proposed cheerfully as he raised his glass. All of our glasses were filled with the sparkling apple cider that Colter had so graciously arrived with.

"Not yet!" I yelled as I flung myself from my chair to grab the blueberry cobbler and place it on the table. "As you know, blueberries were her favorite."

The table erupted with chatter of agreement as we scooped pieces for everyone. "Don't eat it just yet," I said, fumbling with my phone. Then I reached my arm to the center of the table, making sure everyone could see it. "Are you ready?" I asked, not waiting for an answer.

My phone contained an image of Lucille, sitting at this very table, with the same white placemats. She wore a beautiful red dress, a red ribbon in her hair, and another one around her neck. A white flower was on her lapel. She was sitting up very straight in her chair.

I hit play, and she proclaimed, "In my hundred and three and a half years, this is the best blueberry cobbler I've ever eaten. Hey, chef, you're doing great!"

Everyone cheered, a few with a tear or two in their eye. "To Lucille," Walter said, holding up his glass. "She taught us all so many lessons. What a great woman. We were so lucky to have her in our lives."

"To Lucille!" we all cried.

As the glass touched my lips, I thought back to the moment a few months earlier, when Lucille and I were sitting in this very spot. She was right: being together and eating blueberries certainly did make for a great last chapter. But just like before, it wasn't really the last chapter.

Chapter Thirty-Eight

The Final Chapter

In the days that followed, it was as if the skies had parted and light began to enter my world again. One day, I sat down and began to write once more. I wrote, and I wrote, and I wrote. No other book I had ever written flowed like this one did. When I was writing, it felt like she was right there with me, her fingers pressing down on mine against the keyboard. With each word, I relived our times together. I found myself laughing and sometimes crying through the memories.

Most of my writing took place in the Judy chair, but on Fridays, I made a point of venturing out to that same quaint little tea shop by the Carlyle where I'd bought Lucille's waffle a la mode. I was still having my Friday lunch with Lucille. It may have looked like I was sitting at a table for one, but in my heart, I knew it was really a table for two.

The feelings were so intense that people would come and go, hours would pass, and yet I was completely oblivious to the world around me. My sole focus was on my writing, on the story that was flowing out of me. Being able to focus was such a gift and something I will never take for granted again. I felt free, like

I had been bound by the chains of Lyme disease, anger, and loss and those heavy shackles had finally been removed.

Then, one Friday, while sitting in my usual spot at the café, my keystrokes stopped. I was done. I sat there sipping my green tea, quite satisfied that I had finally completed the manuscript. I closed my computer, wrapped up the cord, and stored both away in their case. With a smile on my face and a huge sense of accomplishment in my heart, I headed out the door.

That night, an uneasy feeling came over me. "You're not done," I heard Lucille's voice say. "Remember what I told you." Her voice was so clear, it was like she was sitting right there on the edge of my bed. Her tone was that of someone giving a direct order, but in a loving way. "Don't do it until you're ready," she continued. "You have to mean it."

I immediately knew what she was talking about, and this was the first time I ever truly wanted to reject her advice. A cold sweat broke out over my whole body. *Why is she tormenting me like this?* I thought. It was easier to imagine that it was all a dream, so that's what I did. At least for a few days.

"Is the book done?" Mary asked with a smile as she organized a stack of magazines on the kitchen island. "How far have you gotten?" She was wearing the most ridiculous shoes; they looked like furry slippers, but they were designer and I'm sure they'd cost a fortune. Her hair was perched atop her head in her signature unicorn style, and she was full of energy as she bustled around the kitchen, straightening things.

"I thought it was done, but it turns out I can't write the final chapter until it happens." The words came out of my mouth, and I couldn't believe it. I had just confirmed what I knew to be true but didn't want to accept. Lucille had said it, and I had heard it loud and clear. I thought losing Lucille was hard, but what she was asking me to do was ten times harder.

I explained the whole thing to Mary. The conversation started like many others we had shared over the past two years: "I promise I'm not crazy, but . . ." I went on to tell her everything: how Lucille had come to me with clear instructions, and how I wanted so badly to ignore it all and pretend it was just a wild dream.

By this time, I had her undivided attention, and we were both sitting on the bar stools on either side of a small round wooden table that sat off to one side in my kitchen. "Yes, you have to do it," she said as her hand hit the table. "She's right, and you know it," Mary said with unwavering certainty.

"I know," I grumbled, looking down. I couldn't bear the thought of doing it, and I couldn't bear the thought of not doing it. I was faced with an insurmountable task.

Weeks went by, and the more I procrastinated, the more convinced I felt about what I had to do. I thought about it constantly, day in and day out. I thought about it when I woke up, all throughout the day, and when I laid my head down to sleep.

Then, one day, I finally did it.

The whole way there, I gripped the steering wheel, desperately wanting to turn around. It was as if Lucille's strong hands were right on top of mine, steering me in the right direction. My heart began to pound as I pulled up to Mustang Creek. As much as I didn't want to be there, God gave me grace. I thought about my first job and how for years I had carried around the guilt of having dropped that poor old lady in the nursing home. At that, I felt compassion, not anger, for the first time.

As anxious as I had been in the car, I felt relief as soon as I stepped out. My heart was no longer pounding, and my steps became purposeful. I suddenly felt that this task was not just doable, it was necessary. Lucille was right, and I was not going to fight it any longer.

"Candice, I'm glad to see you," I said, actually meaning it, as I strode toward the front desk. Her blonde hair was a bit messy like she had been busy working all morning. Her clothes were tightly fitted across her curvy body. I looked at her tattoos, suddenly remembering something I had once read about how people often get them to cover up or deal with their pain. I thought about how much she must have endured over the years. Perhaps she was never heard, so she used her body as a billboard. Tattoos are something I will never understand, but this time, I didn't find them disgusting, just interesting.

She looked at me, and I could see fear in her eyes. "Can I talk to you for a moment?" I asked. "Also, is the other girl here today? I'm sorry, but I can't remember her name."

"She doesn't work here anymore," she said under her breath.

I wondered why. Was it because of what happened? I didn't ask, just simply said, "Okay." I motioned toward Candice's office door. "Can we talk privately?"

She walked in quietly, and I followed. I couldn't believe that I was actually there and that I was actually going to do this. I think my heart was pounding as much as hers. I felt sorry for her. Her steps were sheepish, as if she were being led to the slaughter. Given the state of mind I had been in when she last saw me, I could understand her angst. She stayed close to her desk; she probably wanted something familiar to lean on.

"Lucille passed away. I'm not sure if you heard."

"No, I hadn't," she said as her eyes began to water. I could tell she was very nervous. She seemed uneasy, with tons of nervous energy. She didn't seem to know where to put her hands or how to stand.

"Here, sit down. This will only take a moment, and then I

promise you can get back to work." With these words, I felt a bit more in control, something I hadn't felt in a long time.

She was hesitant, but she sat. I sat down right beside her, probably too close for her comfort. "I've harbored a lot of bad feelings toward you, Mustang Creek, and the girl that broke Lucille's arms."

Candice nodded as she reached for a tissue. "I know," she said, as a single tear made its way to the corner of her mouth.

"I want you to know that I forgive you." As I said these words tearfully and with a faint smile, I realized that I meant them. I knew it was the right thing to do and the right time to do it.

I also knew I wasn't alone. I could see Lucille there with me, not with my eyes, but with my heart. She gave me a high five and was clapping and bouncing up and down. "'Atta girl, Judy girl. We did it!" she said jovially.

Candice looked up, and relief was written all over her face as it slowly transformed from an expression of stress and uncertainty to a look of relief. She smiled and reached out for a hug. I hugged her back. It was a real hug, the tight kind you give someone you love. My own eyes started to tear up, but the tears never fell from the well.

I pulled away, looked her in the eye, and said, "Now get back to work."

We both chuckled as she wiped away her tears. As I left her office, I smiled at the other residents in the living room and made my way out the front door. My step had a spring in it, something that had been missing for quite a while.

As I drove home, I thought back to that vision of Lucille. She had said, "We did it." Why "We"? Why not "You did it"? Then it hit me: this last chapter was for both of us. We had done many things in our almost four years together, but true friendship meant loving and supporting each other through the good, the bad, the hardest things one could ever face, including forgiveness.

I suddenly jerked awake. I sat straight up in bed and looked around with one hand holding me up and the other wiping my nose. *How could this have been a dream?* I thought. It felt so real, like I was right there. Perhaps it was God's way of preparing me for the moment when I actually would take action. I don't know. What I do know is that my heart was changed. Even if I had not physically completed the act of forgiving Candice face to face, my heart had already done the internal work.

Weeks went by, and I knew I needed to go. For one reason or another, the timing was never right. Then, one Thursday night, I made up my mind. For sure, without fail, I knew I was going to go over there the very next day.

"What time did Lucille finish eating lunch at Mustang Creek?" I asked Mary the next morning as she was pulling a load out of the dryer and placing it on the kitchen island to fold.

She gave me a knowing look and replied, "They were usually done by one."

"Well, I'm going to take a short nap then," I said.

I lay down on the bed and covered myself with both Lucille blankets, the soft cream one and the ribbon one. As soon as my head hit the pillow, raindrops that sounded like marbles started to hit the roof, each one making a deep thud. The drops that hit the flue inside my bedroom fireplace were high-pitched, like the tapping of a cymbal. Together, the raindrops formed a symphony that soothed my soul. When I was a child, my mom told me that rain comes from angels in Heaven crying. Sometimes they cry tears of sadness, but sometimes, especially when the sun comes out right after, they cry tears of joy.

"Mom, it's time to get up," Katheryn said softly as she tapped on the door and peeked her head in.

I was in a deep slumber, completely relaxed, but I sprang out of bed at her command, as if I were a soldier on a mission and met her at the door with a "thanks."

Mary was in the kitchen working on her laptop. I looked over and smiled and winked at her as I grabbed my purse. I opened the front door to a bright sunny sky, proof that the angels were crying tears of joy. Katheryn walked me to the door, and I gave her a big hug as I walked out. "Bye, Katheryn. Love you. See you in a bit," I called over my shoulder as I hurried to the car.

Since fall was upon us, the air outside had changed. Just two hours earlier, it was sunny and hot, but the rain had cooled things off considerably, so I ran back in for a sweater. That's Texas for you, and as they say: If you don't like the weather, just wait a few hours, it'll change.

I was incredibly calm, much calmer that I had anticipated. I was experiencing something pastors and priests talk about— peace that surpasses all understanding. It was eerie, and as I drove toward Mustang Creek, I kept waiting for the anxiety to come, but it didn't. Perhaps the dream had helped me; perhaps it gave me the confidence to follow through on this.

Before I knew it, I was there, pulling into that familiar parking space. As I climbed out of the car, I realized that I was wearing the exact same thing I had the first time I went to take a tour of Mustang. *Out of all the sweaters in my bureau, why did I grab this one?* Maybe I was subconsciously wishing I could turn back time and make a different decision. Maybe it was just a coincidence.

I walked briskly up the sidewalk to the wooden front door and turned the handle. As I pushed the door in, it created a vacuum, and the air from inside blew across my body. It was filled with a scent that was all too familiar. Suddenly, my mind was flooded with images, particularly all the bad ones. For a split second I froze and found myself choking back tears and emotions I didn't want to relive.

Sitting in the living room were two familiar faces, ladies that Lucille sat with many times at dinner. I smiled and nodded as I walked toward Candice's office. It was dark and locked.

"Is Candice here today?" I asked the first lady I came to. She was sitting in a wheelchair, with a patchwork quilt over her legs. Her hair was solid silver, combed straight and tucked behind her ears.

"Candice?" she replied, looking confused.

"The blonde with the tattoos."

"Blonde?" she parroted, looking at the lady next to her. "I'm afraid you're looking at the two most non-observant women you have ever met. I know there was a lady here, but I have no idea what color her hair was."

Hopeless, I thought. Maybe Lucille had been right. She used to tell me that most people in this home had Alzheimer's, but until this conversation, I had never noticed. I thought for a moment about how lonely Lucille must have been. She was so social and had nobody to really talk to. Perhaps that's why she chose to eat breakfast in her room the last couple weeks she was there.

I went to the house next door, but nobody was in that office, either. I went on to the next house, and that office was also dark. I was starting to feel as if I were losing my mind.

As I entered the home with the main business office, I was greeted with a big smile from Elizabeth, the person who had taken me on the original tours of Mustang Creek. She was neatly put together in black pants and a colorful flowing blouse. She was obviously the face of the operation, as she always appeared so professional and proper. As I got closer though, she must have recognized me because her face changed. I could see that she was wondering why I was there. "Can I help you?" she asked, her big smile having rapidly faded to a more concerned expression.

"I'm looking for Candice, but nobody seems to be in any of the three houses I checked," I replied.

Elizabeth was giving some older lady the sales pitch, and she probably wanted me out of there as quickly as possible. "Everyone is in the house across from here for an all-staff meeting," she said, returning to that big, fake smile. "Go on over there. You'll find her in that one." She pointed at the house directly across from hers. Then, whether she realized it or not, she waved her hand as if to shoo me out the door.

The sun had come out, and I could feel the temperature rising again. The humidity became suffocating, so off came the sweater.

I approached the house where the meeting was and could tell that it was filled with employees, lots of employees. I couldn't hear what was being said inside, but I recognized the tone of voice that was being used by the speaker, and it wasn't pleasant. They were clearly in the part of the staff meeting where the boss tells everyone what they could do better. I sat down on a wicker chair just outside the door.

I felt sick to my stomach and had to ignore the fight or flight response that welled up in me as the hair on my head stood up and my palms grew sweaty. I tried to pray, but I couldn't focus. The only thing between Candice and me was the brick wall behind me. Then it hit me: *What if the other girl, the one who broke Lucille's arms, still works here? What if I see her?* I hadn't prepared myself for that.

As I sat there in a pool of dread, I heard one lone blue jay in the distance. Every few minutes, he would let out a screech. Then the screeches started to get louder and closer together, each one piercing the thick humid air. I realized he was screeching about sixty times a minute, about half my heart rate. I guess that's the way medical people measure things: in heart rates.

The anticipation was mounting. Part of me wanted to get up and leave, but I knew I needed to stay. Then the blue jay stopped. There wasn't a sound. The air was thick and heavy, and growing heavier by the moment. I wanted the blue jay to screech again. I needed something to focus on, something to count, some sort of distraction.

One employee came out, then another, then another. Nobody made eye contact with me, and there was not a smile in sight. *Must have been a bad meeting*, I thought. Each time the door opened, the chatter of employees inside slipped out, temporarily giving life to the quiet front porch.

Suddenly, chills ran down my spine and a flood of blood rushed into my head. The door opened, and two girls came out together. *That's her. That's her. The one that broke Lucille's arms*, I thought. *Wait, I don't even remember her name. Maybe that's not her.*

That's her, that's her, I heard in the back of my mind once again. I wondered if it was my own thoughts, or if Lucille was right there, prompting me.

The girl's outfit was anything but professional. Her black shirt exposed most of her back and looked as if a wild animal had shredded it. Behind the shreds, I could see a large tattoo. *Is a tattoo a prerequisite for getting a job here?* I mused.

As they walked away, they talked and cursed like two mad sailors. There was no doubt that they hated their jobs and hated whatever they had heard in that meeting even more.

I wanted to say something to her, but I couldn't. I wasn't positive that it was actually her. Besides, she frightened me with her F-bombs and body art. The two girls turned the corner, still complaining, and disappeared from sight. I felt myself let out a sigh of relief.

More people came out. One lady finally turned to me and smiled. She was holding two big red cupcakes. I couldn't help

370

but wonder if they were both for her. I felt bad for wondering that instead of focusing on the fact that she had actually smiled at me.

One more came out, then another, and another. All had cupcakes. It looked like the others should have stayed a minute longer; they had clearly missed the best part. It served them right for leaving with such a bad attitude.

Finally, a very large, friendly lady, dressed more appropriate for a staff meeting came out to the porch holding a plate with several cupcakes. "Hello," she said pleasantly.

"Hello," I replied with a smile. "Any chance that Candice is in there?"

"Candice? No, I don't think so, but you can check."

I couldn't believe it. Where had she gone? Did they tip her off that I was looking for her?

"I'm looking for Candice," I said to a group of ladies as I walked into the house.

"She's at corporate," said one lady from behind the kitchen counter.

"Well then, I wish I hadn't just sat out there for an hour. I was told she was at this meeting," I said, a bit frustrated and disappointed.

"Who told you that?"

"Elizabeth."

"Sorry, she probably thought Candice was here. Should I have her call you?"

"Yes, thank you," I said as I stepped back toward the door. "Wait, do I need to give you my number?"

"Candice has your number," she replied with almost no expression.

I belatedly realized that I was talking to Lindsay, the one who had come to our house to get Lucille's intake signature. Lindsay definitely remembered me. I hadn't even said my name. I found it a bit creepy that Candice still had my number.

My heart was calm as I walked back to my car. The air didn't seem so heavy and thick anymore. In the distance, I heard the blue jay with his occasional cry again, but its tone had softened.

I drove away from Mustang Creek, wondering if Candice would ever call.

I didn't have to wonder long. Candice called and texted that very evening. I didn't reply immediately, so she called and texted again the next day.

I can't explain why, but the idea of going back again seemed daunting and had lost its appeal. I had to force myself to text Candice back, but I did, simply requesting a quick meeting with her.

As I once again drove down that familiar road, I knew this was it. Finally, I could accomplish this task, a task that no longer seemed insurmountable. As I pulled in, I decided to park in a different parking space, one right in front of the building. I'm a creature of habit, but this little break from routine seemed to give me power. I felt as though I was ready for a new beginning and an ending to a painful chapter in my life.

As I placed my hand on the front door, I braced myself for the scent that I knew was coming. But this time, it only smelled like waffles. Lucille's favorite. That scent gave me peace and comfort. It also gave me courage because I knew it meant the start of a good day. Lucille used to say, "Any day that starts with waffles is going to be a good one."

I observed Candice as she made her way around the residents at the tables. She was helping them with their meals, but I caught her looking at me a few times. She seemed a bit disheveled, a bit nervous as she moved back and forth between the residents and then back to the kitchen again. I thought *she's not being very efficient, she could do that in so many less trips back and forth. Is she stalling?*

I didn't quite know where to stand and found myself moving around a bit as I looked on. Eventually, I broke the tension and simply walked up to her. "Candice, got a minute?"

"Yes, ma'am," she said politely.

I walked over to the couches in the living room, surprising myself, since I had always envisioned this happening in her office. The living room was open to the dining tables, but, as if on cue, most of the residents headed to their rooms.

Candice and I sat face to face on the couch. I was only inches away from the person I had felt so much resentment for, but I felt calm. As tears welled in my eyes, I asked, "Do you know why I'm here?"

"Well, I initially thought you were coming to tell me that Lucille had died, but I searched for an obituary and saw that she had died a while back."

"She did. It wasn't too long after leaving here. She died from complications from her broken arms."

Candice gasped, and tears filled her eyes. "You have no idea how much I've cried over that. I just keep thinking, 'What if?' 'What if I had been in that room?' 'What if—'"

I stopped her and gently and kindly said, "We all can play the 'what if' game, but it won't bring her back."

"I wondered if I should even be doing this type of work. You can ask anyone around here; this whole thing is almost more than I can handle."

"You should keep doing this work. I watched you with these residents, and you really do care."

"I do," she said, holding back tears.

I shared my own dark moment, the moment when I dropped

that lady and my own mom had to report me. I told her of the shame and sadness that I had carried with me for years.

I reached over and placed my hand on her forearm. I was touching her tattoos, but I wasn't afraid of them, of her, or of seeing past her tattoos into her heart. I looked her right in the eye and, with tears streaming down my face and a bit of snot dripping from my nose, I said, "Lucille taught me a lot of things, lessons that I will carry with me my entire life."

Candice nodded her head in agreement. I could tell that she was listening, really listening, as she looked back at me.

"She taught me the secret to life. I'm going to tell you what it is, because I wish so badly that I had learned it long ago. When Lucille and I first met, she told me that the single most important lesson in life is *forgiveness*. I forgive you, Candice. And someday I want you to use this lesson to heal your own life."

Candice stood up, and we embraced in a tight hug, the kind you give your family. As sure as I am that the sun will rise tomorrow, I know that hug was not two people embracing, but three.

For almost four years, I was fortunate enough to have a best friend. A real best friend, the kind most people never get to experience. We laughed together, cried together, and grew wiser together and we met the most amazing people along the way.

Lucille's sense of style, not only in clothes but in life itself, is what made her so incredibly memorable. Together we solved the world's problems and even made a dent in our own issues. She taught me how to love unconditionally, and most importantly, she taught me the most important lesson on how to grow old, happy, healthy and wise—she taught me how to forgive.

Epilogue

It's been three years since Lucille passed away. Not a day goes by that I don't think of her and remember our journey. A picture of the two of us together sits on my bedside table and another framed photo rests on the mantle in the great room, where she stayed. When life gets overwhelming or I need to contemplate what seems to be a big problem, I usually find myself meditating in the Judy chair in my sitting area. Somehow that quiet time helps me feel especially close to Lucille, as I reflect on all the things she taught me. It magically helps me keep things in perspective.

My mother is still alive and doing remarkably well. I talk to my dad quite frequently and both of my parents have read the book and shed a tear or two. Reading it has opened up new conversations and a deeper understanding of who we all are. My goal is to spend as much time with them as possible.

Walter and I both set aside time to spend with our children and grandchildren, as well as with each other. As for family vacations, we took nineteen of our family members to Hawaii, so that we might make memories together against the backdrop of the rolling turquoise ocean, beautiful flowers, and great food. Walter and I recently took a romantic getaway to Florence, Italy for our twentieth wedding anniversary, where we actually unplugged from phones, computers, and television for eight straight days.

From time to time I still struggle with workaholism, but my Lyme disease helps keep that in check. Most days are great, and I am symptom free, but if I work too hard, get overwhelmed, or fail to get enough sleep, the disease rears its ugly head, giving me no choice but to slow down.

Many members of Lucille's family still keep in touch, and I feel as though they are also my family. In a surprising twist of fate, they probably are. While working on my genealogy about a year after Lucille died, I found that I had relatives from my dad's side with the last name Fleming. As you can imagine, this sent chills down my spine and a smile to my face.

To this day I have no doubt that Lucille was sent into my life as a gift from God. I believe she still looks out for me from Heaven above and I know that she will always be the best friend I have ever made. Someday, when I am old and filled with both wisdom and style, I hope and pray that I can influence someone in the incredible way she influenced me. Then, when all is said and done, she and I will once again see each other on the other side, picking up right where we left off.

Acknowledgments

This book would not be possible without the love and support I have received not only from my own family, but also from Lucille's family who so graciously shared their mother and grandmother with me. Writing a book of this nature takes time, patience, emotional support, and cooperation, all of which you have given me.

A special thank you to Jennifer Banash, my editor, who believed in this project and poured her heart and soul into the editing process. She encouraged me on more than one occasion to keep pushing forward.

To Brooke Warner and all of those at She Writes Press, thank you for the courage you have to publish women like me who have a story to tell. You give such credibility to women writers and I know I'm not alone in my gratitude for you and for this imprint.

Kat Wendling, my daughter, illustrated the cover, capturing the spirit of my lunches with Lucille. She even got it right when it came to ice in my glass, but none in Lucille's. Kat, not only were you part of the story, you're also now part of sharing this story with others. Thank you.

I have great gratitude to Suzanne Somers for writing this foreword. I know that Lucille was smiling from Heaven the day you, Suzanne, someone Lucille adored, took the time to make such a kind and thoughtful gesture.

The number of people along the way who supported this

project through proofing and chapter feedback is humbling. Each and every one of you helped make the final version what it is. Thank you Dana Grieve for reading and re-reading, highlighting, suggesting, and offering such emotional support. Melissah Moore, you are such a great friend. I still owe you for the vast number of tissues we went through on your couch as we worked through some of the most emotional chapters. Your feedback was so valuable. Emily Allen, if it weren't for you finding Lucille, this book would never have existed. The cheeseball edits we made at the beginning of this journey are still a favorite memory of mine. Of course, Mary Bennett Herndon, how could I ever thank you enough for being part of this story on so many levels. You are my friend, my confidante, and we will forever share the days of Lucille.

Last, but certainly not least, Walter, words could not do justice to the rare breed of husband you are. You offer support, love, encouragement, and always go above and beyond to show that you believe in me. Thank you for being part of this journey and for the support and encouragement to share my Lucille story with the world. The best decision I ever made was to marry you. I love you.

About the Author

Judy Gaman is an award-wining author, speaker, and the CEO of Executive Medicine of Texas. She spent almost ten years on the air as she hosted the nationally syndicated *Staying Young Show*. You can now catch her on podcast with the *Stay Young America!* health and wellness podcast. Judy is also a Fox News Radio healthy living contributor and writes for several publications.

She received both her undergraduate and graduate degrees from the George Washington University and is currently enrolled in a graduate certificate program in Strategic Management through Harvard Extension School. She lives in Texas with her husband Walter and together they have ten children and five grandchildren.

Can't Get Enough of Lucille?

During the time Judy and Lucille spent together they spent lots of time on television and radio. These interviews capture not just the essence of their friendship, but valuable advice on how to stay young and healthy.

> **Visit www.LoveLifeLucille.com to see Lucille throw out the first pitch, Lucille giving advice on longevity, and much more!**

Want to Read More from Judy Gaman?

As an award-winning author, speaker, and healthy living expert, you can find other books by Judy Gaman. Here are some non-fiction titles to look for:

Age to Perfection: How to Thrive to 100, Happy, Healthy, and Wise
ISBN-13: 978-0984073122

Stay Young: 10 Proven Steps to Ultimate Health
ISBN-13: 978-0984073108

Visit www.JudyGaman.com to learn more about Judy, book her to speak, or invite her to visit your book club.

Judy's podcast *Stay Young America!* can be downloaded from most podcast directories. Judy Gaman, along with doctors Mark Anderson and Walter Gaman, fills each episode with great information on how to get and stay healthy.

SELECTED TITLES FROM SHE WRITES PRESS

She Writes Press is an independent publishing company
founded to serve women writers everywhere.
Visit us at www.shewritespress.com.

Motherlines: Letters of Love, Longing, and Liberation by Patricia
Reis. $16.95, 978-1-63152-121-8. In her midlife search for meaning,
and longing for maternal connection, Patricia Reis encounters
uncommon women who inspire her journey and discovers an
unlikely confidante in her aunt, a free-spirited Franciscan nun.

Don't Leave Yet: How My Mother's Alzheimer's Opened My Heart
by Constance Hanstedt. $16.95, 978-1-63152-952-8. The chronicle
of Hanstedt's journey toward independence, self-assurance, and
connectedness as she cares for her mother, who is rapidly losing
her own identity to the early stage of Alzheimer's.

Green Nails and Other Acts of Rebellion: Life After Loss by Elaine
Soloway. $16.95, 978-1-63152-919-1. An honest, often humorous
account of the joys and pains of caregiving for a loved one with a
debilitating illness.

Filling Her Shoes: Memoir of an Inherited Family by Betsy Graziani
Fasbinder. $16.95, 978-1-63152-198-0. A "sweet-bitter" story of
how, with tenderness as their guide, a family formed in the wake
of loss and learned that joy and grief can be entwined cohabitants
in our lives.

Edna's Gift: How My Broken Sister Taught Me to Be Whole by
Susan Rudnick. $16.95, 978-1-63152-515-5. When they were young,
Susan and Edna, children of Holocaust refugee parents, were
inseparable. But as they grew up and Edna's physical and mental challenges altered the ways she could develop, a gulf formed
between them. Here, Rudnick shares how her maddening—yet
endearing—sister became her greatest life teacher.